HIGH JINKS ON THE KLONDIKE

Also by Richard O'Connor
SHERIDAN THE INEVITABLE

HIGH JINKS ON THE
KLONDIKE

By Richard O'Connor

THE BOBBS-MERRILL COMPANY, INC.
INDIANAPOLIS   Publishers   **NEW YORK**

First Edition

ACKNOWLEDGMENTS

THE AUTHOR wishes to express his gratitude for permission to quote passages from the following works:

A. A. Allan, *Gold, Men and Dogs,* published by G. P. Putnam's Sons, copyright 1931.

Rex Beach, *Personal Exposure,* published by Harper & Brothers, 1940.

Thomas Beer, *The Mauve Decade,* published by Alfred A. Knopf, Inc., 1926.

William Ross Collier and Edwin Victor Westrate, *The Reign of Soapy Smith,* published by Doubleday & Company, Inc., 1935.

Merrill Denison, *Klondike Mike,* published by William Morrow & Company, Inc., 1943.

Jack Hines, *Minstrel of the Yukon,* published by Greenberg Publishers, 1948.

Edward Morgan with Henry F. Woods, *God's Loaded Dice,* published by The Caxton Printers, Ltd., Caldwell, Idaho, 1935.

Murray Morgan, *Skid Road,* published by The Viking Press, Inc., 1951.

Robert W. Service, *Ploughman of the Moon,* published by Dodd, Mead & Company, Inc., 1945.

Arthur T. Walden, *A Dog Puncher on the Yukon,* published by the Houghton Mifflin Company, 1928.

CONTENTS

PAGE

1   "A Horde of Fools" 11

2   The Great Stampede 19

3   Wax Museum: *Soapy Smith, As Ever Was* 37

4   Slammerkins in Long Underwear 70

5   Squaw Men and Siwash Maidens 91

6   Wax Museum: *The Knight of the Golden Omelette* . 104

7   Literary Pay Dirt 116

8   Thespis in Deep Freeze 140

9   Three Kinds of Law 158

10   The All-Inclusive Saloon 176

11   Ladies Fair but Frail 188

12   Wax Museum: *The Arctic Saga of Wilson Mizner* . . 207

13   Friendship on Ice 224

14   The Big Sports 241

15   The Hundred-Percenters 258

Epilogue by a Fireside 271

Bibliography 275

Index 281

HIGH JINKS ON THE KLONDIKE

"A Horde of Fools"

THE KLONDIKE gold rush was in many ways the most fascinating, as well as the last, outburst of the mass spirit of adventure on the American continent. Many of the gold-rushers are still alive and not at all reluctant to discuss their experiences, and millions of words have been written on the subject. But an obscure memoir long out of print in one brief paragraph tells something of the attitude and motives of the Klondikers that cannot be effaced by the torrents of romantic prose and poetry that have been written about the "Golconda of the Arctic." The Honorable Stratford Tollemache, a British traveler, wrote with well-bred amazement about the gold-rushers, mostly American, in Dawson during the first winter of the stampede. That mining camp was literally cut off from the world; there was no telegraph, no wagon road, no railway, and the warm-weather line of communications, the Yukon, was frozen. Only an occasional dog team made the 600-mile journey to the Alaskan coast. One might have expected that Dawson would be one aching mass of homesickness, with men weeping over tintypes, lockets and locks of hair representing loved ones far away at home.

Alas for piety and wholesome sentiment! And alas for the loved ones who may have believed that their menfolk were languishing in some lonely cabin!

The Honorable Tollemache's reminiscences, which, fortunately for home-coming Klondikers, were not widely read, made it lamentably apparent that they were overcome by an overwhelming sense of freedom and that instead of pining for home and wife or mother they headed for the saloons and dance halls, where "the combined effects of dance girls and bad whisky soon obliterated any feelings of regret for their wives and families on the outside." Back home they might be singing, "There'll Be a Hot Time in the Old Town Tonight," but the Klondikers knew what a pallid falsehood that was; the "hot time" was to be found right where they were, far removed from Victorian restraints and the lavender delicacies of their womenfolk. Never before or since have so many American men had such a hell of a good time, without the perils of war, provided they stayed fairly healthy and had a fair amount of luck.

It would be far too drastic a generalization to allege that their womenfolk drove American men into the mass adventure in the Yukon; other reasons besides a growing female tyranny at home and the desire for gold impelled them to join the stampede. Still, there was no doubt that many men were chafing and restive under the growing domination of women, the increasing power of what Thomas Beer has called The Titaness. As Beer wrote in *The Mauve Decade,* "It is not alleged against the women of the Mauve Decade that they invented cheap cruelty and low social pressures, but they erected these basenesses into virtues by some defensive sense of rectitude, and a generation of sons was reared in the shadow of the Titaness, aware of her power, protected by nothing from her shrill admonitions. Is it matter for such wonder among critics that only satire can describe this American of our time who drifts toward middle age without valour, charm or honour?" It is undeniable that at times the migration to the Klondike assumed the character of a flight from home, wife and mother.

Agitation for women's suffrage and abolition of the double standard was reaching its crescendo, and the moral superiority of women was dinned into men's ears with merciless reiteration. When men's voices joined in this controversy, they added only confusion— as might be expected when a man ventures to tread on such ground—to the women's single-minded theme of their greater moral purity. Senator George F. Hoar of Massachusetts appealed to men to allow women to purify politics by giving them the vote— and the Reverend John Buckley warned that female morality must not be endangered by letting them become involved in the filth of politics. The ladies themselves argued from such a lofty pedestal that, as one woman wrote, "They raised enemies for themselves in the clubs and whisky distilleries with every breath."

The American male of the nineties, it can be argued, had not yet accustomed himself to thinking of women as vessels of all that was pure and noble in humanity, nor to the corollary implication that he was an uncouth animal who would be saved in spite of himself by his mother, wife, sisters and aunts.

The perceptive Mr. Beer made an exhaustive survey of magazine fiction during this period, probably on the grounds that it is an excellent reflection of how people thought about themselves, or at least how editors assumed they thought. In the popular fiction, particularly that produced by women writers, the heroine was a creature of such exasperating nobility and impossible rectitude that it seems incredible that she could have been accepted by readers as a human being. The males in these stories—one could not call them heroes— were simply echo chambers to amplify the protestations of feminine virtue. Invariably the heroine, confronted by the sexual beast in a man, brought him to heel simply by a stare of wonder. That new figure of knighthood, the football player, was inspired to bone-crushing epics on the field by a violet sent to the dressing room between halves. The ancestor of today's soap-opera Cassandra, Aunt Hattie, the embodiment of rural wisdom, straightened out sophisticates from the city by dispensing fried chicken and advice in equal portions. If women really believed themselves to be what popular writers maintained they were, it is starkly apparent that their menfolk must have been ready for any sort of adventure that would carry them out of the range of their invincible sanctimony.

The new comic weeklies, Mr. Beer wrote, showed this reverse side of the medal. ''Women, it seemed, were bullying husbands and fathers for money to be spent on frocks, French tenors, flowers for actresses and actors. Women were listening to Oriental philosophers and reformers, sitting to expensive painters, running abroad to hunt down titled Europeans, gouging men's eyes out with hatpins, hiding his view of the stage with vast hats, adorning his house with costly gewgaws, making him damned miserable in all ways.''

The All-American Girl had been invented by such popular illustrators as Howard Chandler Christy and Charles Dana Gibson— a slender, ethereal goddess whom one would be permitted to worship but not to expect of her anything more intimate or mundane.

But it was not alone the American woman, and whatever frustrations and resentments she may have been arousing in her menfolk, aware of her newly exalted position, that impelled the mass movement to the gold fields. There were thousands of women in the stampede, too; some of them intent on profit, others on sharing the risks of their men, still others gallantly determined to prove themselves men's equals; few of these were eager to be placed on any sort of pedestal. Many Americans were looking for a new frontier, now that the West had been civilized. The North was the last great uncrossed frontier. And the fact that gold was first discovered in large quantities on Canadian soil, rather than Alaskan, was a geographic quibble that did not inhibit our fathers and grandfathers, who were often cavalier in their attitude toward the now respected boundaries of the Dominion.

It is difficult to imagine that if gold were discovered today in such an inaccessible place—with the dangers and the adverse odds the same as they were in 1897 to 1900—that tens of thousands of Americans would drop everything and take off.

The diverse backgrounds of the gold-rushers were significant in themselves as an indication of how widely this itch for getting away from it all affected the American people. There were figures of the Old West like Calamity Jane, Wyatt Earp, Lucky Baldwin and Joaquin Miller, the sweet singer of the Sierra. There were two such opposite characters as Soapy Smith, the biggest sinner north of Seattle, and Father Judge, the saintly Jesuit who saved hundreds of Klondikers' lives. There were such prospectors as Swiftwater Bill Gates, who made a couple of fortunes and lost them in matrimonial ventures and antic spending; Robert Henderson, the unlucky Sutter of the Klondike, and George Carmack and his uninhibited Siwash bride. There were worthy widows and the hardworking future Countess Carboneau, along with the more colorful sisterhood of Diamond Lil, Nellie the Pig, Diamond-Tooth Gertie, Big Annie, the Oregon Mare, the Grizzly Bear and the lesser-known women of Lousetown and Paradise Alley. There were such diverse types as "Susie Bluenose," who conducted a one-woman crusade against drinking, and the dance-hall girl in Dawson who auctioned herself off for the winter to the highest bidder. There were men to whom the gold fields were a proving ground for their talents and who became famous in later years—Tex Rickard, Jack London, Alexander Pantages, Rex Beach, Robert W. Service, Wilson and Addison Mizner, Jack Kearns and others.

Another indication of how widely this escapism affected Americans was to be found in capsule form at a certain claim along Bonanza Creek. A Salvation Army man was observed wielding a shovel at the bottom of the mine, an ex-missionary cranked the windlass, an archdeacon of the Church of England worked the rocker and a former faro dealer did the cooking.

The more formal historians have assigned a variety of intricate

motivations for the migration to the Klondike, but the letters of
the gold-rushers and the recollections of those still alive indicate
that they were impelled by a dissatisfaction with the drabness and
lack of opportunity in the United States of 1897—so it appeared
to them—and a parallel restlessness, a yearning for new fields of
opportunity (all the better if sprinkled with gold dust). The
Klondike had an irresistible promise for Americans of that time; it
seemed like the fabled end of the rainbow. A lady travel writer
with more perception than most of her sisters wrote: "A man may
sell his potato patch in town lots and become a millionaire without
attracting attention; but let him 'strike pay on bedrock'—and
instantly he walks in a golden mist of glory and romance before
his fellow men. It may be because the farmer deposits his money
in the bank, while the miner 'sets up' the champagne to his less
fortunate friends."

The thousands who seized the dubious but glamorous opportunity offered by the gold rush, and the other thousands who
envied them but stayed at home, included many who believed there
was no high place for them in the unadventurous economy that
seemed to be shaping up. The year 1893 was a bitter memory.
There had been a financial panic which consequently paralyzed
industry and threw millions out of work. And in succeeding years
there had been Coxey's Army and its march on Washington (whose
leaders were arrested for walking on the grass near the Capitol);
riots in the Chicago railroad yards; the Molly Maguires of the
Pennsylvania coal fields; the symbol of "the cross of gold" raised by
William Jennings Bryan, a political hero in the West, a "wicked, rat-
tlepated boy" in the East; the movement to free Cuba and other possessions of the Spanish Empire in the Western Hemisphere, which
was to culminate in a brisk little war while most gold-rushers were
tucked away in one of the more inaccessible corners of the continent. The "Gay Nineties" may have fizzed, but not always with
elation, and along with the mustache cups, bicycles built for two,

volunteer fire companies and cuckoo clocks, there waited across the threshold of the new century the automobile and the airplane.

The gold rush, however, was not such a solemn and despairing affair as may be indicated above. The nation was ready for a fight or a frolic, and it got both as the new century wheeled majestically into place. The fighters went off to the Philippines and Cuba, the frolickers, for the most part, had already capered off to the mining camps of the Yukon, from which arose heady noises. The razzma-tazz of the mechanical piano and the frenetic beat of the ragtime bands. The tinkle of bottles and glasses. The pop of champagne corks. The rattle of dice and the whirring of roulette wheels. The silken rustle of the light-o'-love.

There was actually a gold rush within *the* gold rush, the thieves, whores, pimps, swindlers, gamblers, confidence men, divekeepers, bandits and other rascals of many devious trades, who proposed to do their prospecting the easy way; not in the creeks and gullies of the Klondike country, where a man could get calluses on his hands and frostbite on his face and scurvy in his flesh, but in the pokes and pockets of the miners themselves. It was so much smarter to wait comfortably in the saloons, gambling joints and music halls, than to dig in the frozen creeks and risk cabin fever in the winter solitudes of the tundra. Gold was not where you found it, in their opinion, but where it found you.

It is this aspect of the Klondike gold rush—this smoky, whisky-fumed, patchouli-scented atmosphere, this indoor view of what was an outdoor adventure for most gold-rushers—that will be ex-amined for the most part in this revisitation of the Klondike. The interior gold rush, as it might be called, had been highly profitable before, in the mining camps of California, Colorado and Nevada, where the real wealth had rarely been grasped and retained by the prospectors who took the risks and found the gold or silver. Some of these soft-handed stampeders were unalloyed criminals who stole or swindled; others operated with a slight show of respectability in their saloons, dance halls and gambling houses, and equally if less noticeably villainous were the blood-sucking merchants who made their fortunes charging outrageous prices for all the necessities of life.

The first ships bearing the news of a big strike in the Klondike had hardly discharged their boisterous passengers before knavery was afoot and heading North. In San Francisco, the hardiest of the prostitutes and drunk-rollers, the most ambitious of the pimps, crimps and gamblers, the nimblest of the blackleg lawyers took passage immediately for the Alaskan ports. Underworlds from there to New York were almost as quickly emptied of their least desirable elements. Not more than a few weeks behind were the thugs and sharpers and early-day spivs of England, South Africa and Australia, eager to join their American cousins in the great sport. Thanks to the telegraph and the transoceanic cables, the news spread fast enough to allow a fairly even start for all. Consequently, by the time the first great wave of prospectors, amateur and professional, reached the northern ports, a highly expert reception committee was waiting for them, with painted faces, knockout drops, blackjacks, crooked dice, marked cards, poker tables with "accommodator" slits through which one's luck might be improved, rotgut whisky, barrel-house music and all the other paraphernalia.

"A horde of fools" was the opinion John Muir, the great naturalist who knew something of the hardships of the North Country, expressed of the men and women stampeding to the gold fields.

No one agreed with Muir more devoutly and fondly than the knaves and bawds who formed their own cynical little gold rush.

2

The Great Stampede

Gold! We leaped from our benches. Gold!
    We sprang from our stools.
Gold! We whirled in the furrow, fired with the faith of fools.
Fearless, unfound, unfitted, far from the night and cold,
Heard we the clarion summons, followed the master lure—Gold.
                    —Robert W. Service

IN THE TENDERLOINS of San Francisco, Denver, Seattle and other western cities, the first intimations that an Arctic bonanza had been located were welcomed with the utmost gladness. The underworld, unorganized and unbusinesslike as it then was, had fallen on hard times. Recent depressions and the harassing activities of the reformers contributed to a feeling that a hard-working crook and his ever-loving doxy no longer had a secure and recognized place in life. In later years the underworld, learning the flexibility of more respectable forms of commerce, would turn from one project to another under economic and moral pressure (from bootlegging to bookmaking, union racketeering and kidnaping after the repeal of the Prohibition laws, for instance), but in the nineties the criminal classes clung to orthodox pursuits: prostitution, robbery, the confidence games and other time-tested practices.

The dives of the Barbary Coast, the "boxhouses" of Seattle, the gambling dens and bagnios of Denver were mostly padlocked or operating under such sorry restraints that the business of fleecing, debauching and outwitting one's fellow citizens was hardly worth while. One kept a hand in for just such contingencies as the Klondike gold rush, but it was a lean nervous claw indeed.

No one watched the arrival of the first gold-bearing ships from Alaska with more vulturine interest than the underworld of the Pacific-coast ports, unless it was the water-front merchant who hoped to profit immensely by outfitting the northbound prospectors soon to be funneled through these ports from six continents.

For many years there had been whispers of great gold fields in the Klondike, but the Western states were fairly immune to such rumors until the actual gold, in sizable quantities, had been run through the assaying process. There were too many stampedes in living memory that had fizzed out, too many family exchequers depleted by rumors of gold in the hills, too many walls plastered with worthless mining stocks.

But cynicism vanished in an instant when the steamer *Excelsior* docked at San Francisco on July 15, 1897, and two days later the *Portland* at Seattle. There was $750,000 in gold aboard the *Excelsior,* approximately a million aboard the *Portland.*

A TON OF GOLD, trumpeted the Western newspapers with a better sense of drama than talent for mathematics. Even more impressive were photographs of successful miners staggering ashore under small but weighty burdens. A Bull Durham sack of gold was as heavy as a sash weight. A moose-hide bag of dust or nuggets bent a strong man's back.

And the miners themselves, ordinary as any set of men to be found loafing around a street corner, were equally impressive in their unprepossessing way. Crude, uneducated with one or two exceptions, frowsy with the long unwashed years of northern wandering, they looked more like candidates for night court than royal suites and expensive restaurants. Yet they had made their fortunes in remarkably short time, discounting, in many cases, the fruitless years they had spent in pursuing the golden mirage, and they inspired in the most doltish minds the thought that "If an ordinary, bowlegged, squinty, runty, broken-down little squirt like that can make himself a fortune overnight, why can't I?"

Most people knew little about Alaska and the Yukon Territory except a few hazy legends and the fact Alaska had been bought from Russia for a half-cent an acre and was referred to as the back yard of the United States. Few even knew that the Klondike and its tributaries were located in Yukon Territory and that gold-rushers would be governed by the laws of Canada, a fact driven home with considerable emphasis by the red-coated, superbly disciplined and incorruptible Mounted Police waiting at the Canadian boundary

All eyes were caught by the headline:

GOLD! GOLD! GOLD! GOLD!
Sixty-eight Rich Men
on the *Portland*
STACKS OF THE YELLOW METAL

And they conveniently ignored such warnings as:

WINTER WILL SOON SET IN
SUFFERING SEEMS INEVITABLE

What gold seekers must endure—
Their chief food in winter is
bear fat, and a bath or a
change of clothing is
death

The mass imagination was inflamed by the stories of the returning Klondikers. Gray-haired William Stanley and his partner

Gage Worden returned with $112,000, leaving partners behind to look after their still productive claims. Stanley, valuing his claims at $2,000,000, proclaimed that "there is no doubt that the Klondike is the best place in the world to make money." Other Klondikers' tales were equally fabulous. H. Dore of Montana had only $17,000 in gold dust but was more enthusiastic than his luckier colleagues: "El Dorado Creek is the greatest placer proposition in the world. There has never been anything discovered on the face of the globe like it." John Wilkerson displayed $50,000 in dust and nuggets and admitted, "Without practically a stroke of work me and my partner are coming out with $25,000 apiece." Frank Phiscator brought out $96,000 and announced with majestic simplicity, "We've got millions." Professor T. S. Lippy, former secretary of the Seattle Y.M.C.A., admitted holding $85,000. A Fresno fruit farmer reported that he had made $130,000 in a winter's digging. A Southern Negro—surely a reincarnation of Uncle Tom—said he was going home with $30,000 to pay off the mortgage on his aged former owner's plantation.

From all over the United States, and soon from Europe, South Africa and Australia, thousands of men and women began the great stampede from the Pacific ports to Alaska and the Yukon. A spawn of hucksters established themselves along the water fronts to accommodate the gullibility of northbound traffic. These outfitters and legitimate water-front merchants who succumbed to the temptation of leeching on innocents with only the vaguest idea of what they would need in the Yukon made millions out of selling useless or flawed equipment to the stampeders.

A typical item was the "Yukon stove," a contraption sold by the thousands in Alaska-outfitting stores along Seattle's First Avenue. It was a burner advertised as consuming coal, oil or gas. An unhappy purchaser later described the disaster that befell him when he tried to use the stove along the trail:

The sample burner kept going by the solicitors seemed to work all right. A lady who had been testing its oven qualities assured me it would "bake potatoes beautifully." As proof she held up a good-sized tuber that had been partially cremated. I bought the burner for $18. We set that coal-oil-gas burner up in our tent. It roared like a small Vesuvius in full eruption. Flames shot from every crack and opening in that stove. I worked the pump with frantic haste—it was no use, the whole thing was going to blow up. I started for the door of the tent, but a lad who had seen the burners work before said, "There's no danger." He coolly took out his pocket knife, cut the lead connecting pipe, took the burner on a stick, and threw it outdoors. There were a good many suckers in Seattle in those days.

Another fast-selling and equally useless item was a still the size of a fifty-pound lard can which was supposed to filter water for drinking. Maggoty meat, wormy hardtack, shoddy mackinaws all were in plentiful supply. Other profiteers took advantage of the housing shortage and rented sleeping space in barns and stables, advertising, "Flop in the hay. Six bits."

Even without being distracted by such lures for the unwary, the Klondiker could use up his life savings buying the entirely necessary equipment. Every scrap of food, every piece of hardware, clothing and bedding, as well as such solaces as books, tobacco and alcoholic beverages, had to be bought in the States or purchased at a much higher price in the Alaskan ports of entry.

The "Klondike fever" struck all classes and types of people, above all the congenital optimist to whom the gold fields were literally the end of the rainbow.

Such a Micawber was one miner described by the newspaper correspondent Frederick Palmer in the Klondike early in 1898. He had panned out $900 in gold dust but wrote his wife that it amounted to $10,000. Gently cynical, his wife replied in a letter: "God bless you, Charlie, but we've made too many ten thousands without ever getting them for me to count my chickens before they're hatched. I'm being as economical as I can, and telling the neighbors that I hope you'll make a good year's wages, but that it's too early to tell yet for certain." There were many such Charlies in the northbound exodus.

The want ads of newspapers from coast to coast reflected this feverish determination to reach the Klondike at any cost. In the San Francisco press: "Will deed my ranch for a stake in Alaska. Make me an offer." . . . "For sale. $400 buys sewing-machine store. Leaving city. Good chance for smart party." . . . "Fine saloon in lively neighborhood. Place worth fully $1,500 but offered cheap as owner will leave city soon." In the New York *Times:* "Student has scheme to take party of ten to the Klondike. Many local businessmen are behind the project. $500 required." In Seattle: "Wanted. Twenty ladies to organize a company to send eight men to Alaska. $200 required." In Chicago: "Wanted. A victim of the cigarette habit would like some philanthropist to grubstake him in the Klondike. Has had considerable experience digging wells and other work suiting him for mining." Kentucky forgot its preoccupation with fast horses, fine bourbon and beautiful women; the editorial staffs of the Richmond *Register* and the Lexington *Herald* each collected enough money to send a reporter apiece to the Klondike to dig for gold.

Many of these "grubstake combines" were formed among employees, families and union members to send their most venturesome or capable candidate to the gold fields to make a fortune for them all. More elaborate financial structures were erected to prospect on the grand scale; among the subscribers to stock in the Klondike Exploration Company, Ltd., was the Duke of Fife, son-in-law of the future Edward VII of Great Britain. The Boston newspapers reported a unique little exodus: "Fourteen Hebrew working men of this city out of employment are determined to walk to Alaska or lose their lives in the attempt." This group was headed by Charles L. Wise, who was an unsuccessful candidate for mayor of Hartford on the Socialist ticket in 1891; even the followers of Marx and Engels were not immune to the gold-rush fever.

Prospectuses headed ALASKA HO! were widely circulated to attract armchair adventurers to the possibilities of sharing the financial, if not the physical, risks of prospecting in the Arctic: "Who has not heard of Jack Crawford, poet, author, scout, loved and honored by Army Men for his uprightness and integrity, high in the regard and trust of the newspaper profession! . . . Experienced, vigorous and shrewd, he will lead and direct under this Corporation an expedition of practical and expert miners in the new Alaska Gold Fields. Mother Lode claims will be taken up for this Company to be sold at enormous profits. . . . Write for prospectus."

Optimism flourished in many strange and wonderful ways. Inventors concentrated on making travel in the Arctic easier and swifter, if not safer. Jacob S. Coxey, his ragamuffin army disbanded, had sufficiently recovered his enthusiasm for the untried to announce the invention of a "Klondike Bicycle" designed to carry freight or an extra passenger. His folding cycle had attachments on the handle bars and rear wheel to carry 500 pounds of freight and an extra set of wheels. As Coxey's prospectus explained, "The plan is to load it with a part of the miner's equipment, drag the vehicle on four wheels for ten miles or so. Then the rider will fold up the side wheels and ride it back as a bicycle to bring on the rest of the load." General Coxey, not always the clearest of thinkers, had forgotten to take into consideration the lack of roads and the general impracticability of the rugged North for cyclists, whether on two wheels or four.

Imaginations that soared even higher than Coxey's suggested the development of the balloon as a mode of transportation over the coastal range between the Alaskan ports and the Klondike.

Undeterred by the disappearance of Professor Salomon Andrée and two companions, who ascended for a flight over the North Pole in July 1897, the balloonists believed they could carry both passengers and freight over the mountains to the gold fields. Frank Corey was building an airship in Kalamazoo and announced that he would soon open a fortnightly air-travel service to Dawson from the Alaska coast. He was flooded with applications for his passenger list. Another balloonist secured $150,000 from the Jacobs Transportation Company of Seattle to organize a similar service. His plan was to carry passengers from Tiskle Bay, near Juneau, to Dawson. This ebullient pioneer of air transportation, Don Charles Stevens, announced that he would hang out his sign, ALL ABOARD FOR THE KLONDIKE, and "when I've got my passengers, I'll cut the rope and away we'll go." Neither of the balloons ever ascended, for all the hot air expended on them.

So desperate were people, men and women alike, to reach the gold-bearing creeks that they were willing to agree to almost anything to get the journey under way. "Klondike Mike" Mahoney, a youthful veteran of the Yukon trails, where he drove dog teams several years before the gold rush, came outside at the height of the "Klondike fever" and found himself amazingly popular, especially with young ladies who possessed more determination than moral scruples. At least a score, he said, proposed various means by which they would accompany him to the Klondike; only a few insisted on marriage.

A dance-hall girl named Blondie, whom he described as a "big, handsome jolly wench," was unblushingly direct in her proposals. "How much do you want to take me with you when you go back in?" she asked. "I've over a thousand saved and I could get a little more. You can have that, and me, and a fair percentage on anything I make if you'll take me back with you. . . . Oh, I'm not hard to get along with! I can cook, sew, mend, sing and do everything else any reasonable man could ask. The nights must get awful cold and lonely on that trail."

Mike inquired whether Blondie was proposing that he marry her.

"I don't see why you should," she said. "It might complicate things later—but I might even be willing to go that far."

"Do you mean to tell me you'd be willing to hand over all your money and trust yourself to a man you never saw before, just to get to Dawson? It strikes me that it's one hell of a price to pay."

"I don't think so," Blondie replied, with all the seriousness of a banker considering a transaction in all its ramifications. "You said yourself there's so darn few skirts in Dawson that any good-looking, halfway agreeable dame ought to be able to grab herself off a millionaire the minute the cleanup starts. It's an opportunity that comes to a girl once in a lifetime. I'm willing to toss in everything to grab it while I've got the chance. I'll cook for you, I'll sleep with you, I'd even run hitched with your dogs if you asked me to, so long as I get to Dawson."

Mahoney in later years affirmed that he rejected the girl's proposal.

The matter of choosing a partner for the journey was not to be taken lightly, as Frederick Palmer, the well-known newspaper correspondent, warned in a book published in 1898.*

Partnerships formed so gaily in Seattle by men who thought that being a partner was being a playfellow could not be expected to last long at pulling sleds through the slush and going to bed in a robe or sleeping bag that was cheap and inefficient, with a supper of sandwiches made of sticky flapjacks and cold bacon. As he grew more angry with his partner he grew fonder of his dog. Jim might beat his poor Newfoundland who was too nervous to pull even if he had ever been taught how; but if Tom, who was cooking, kicked the Newfoundland for stealing the bacon off the plate or sticking

---

* *In the Klondike,* New York: Charles Scribner's Sons, 1898.

his nose in the butter, it was the last straw. He demanded a division of goods on the spot.

Palmer, who had investigated the problems facing the inexperienced prospector with a commendable thoroughness, said that the man from the Eastern cities was laboring under a considerable handicap in joining the great stampede. "The Easterner learned that the Westerner knew better than he how to take care of himself. The Westerner always cooked a warm supper, and dried his footwear before going to work in the morning; while the self-neglect of the Easterner made hundreds of doctors at Dyea and Skagway the busiest in the world. Spinal meningitis was often the penalty of sitting down to rest when dripping with perspiration without throwing a coat over the shoulders."

In the half-worlds of San Francisco and Seattle, the dive operators, their shills, floosies, bartenders and dealers were undergoing the delightful agony of not knowing which way to turn for the biggest share of the profits spilling out of the mass movement to the gold country.

There were three areas to be worked over by the diligent purveyor of pleasure. One was at the exit ports, where the tenderfeet arrived with wallets full of folding money to buy their outfits and arrange for their passage. The second was at the entry ports of Alaska, where the traveler was inclined to be in a considerable hurry, with his eyes fixed on the horizon to the north shimmering with a golden aura. The third was in the roistering towns of the gold fields; Dawson, Lousetown (more politely but rarely called Klondike City), Eagle, Fort Cudahy and Forty Mile. The greediest and most mettlesome entrepreneurs headed for the mining towns, of course, most of them ignorant of the fact they would have to accommodate themselves to the Canadian laws. With considerable satisfaction, they soon noted that the Mounted Police were anything but puritannical in their attitude toward the various vices, drawing the line only at violent crime.

Many a prospector-errant of the frailer sort was separated from his cash and possessions before he could embark from the Pacific port cities, and returned home shamefaced or joined the legion of missing men rather than face his neighbors' jeering inquiries.

The keepers of the brothels, saloons and dance halls along Seattle's Skid Row were especially adept at tapping the cash reserves of the thousands of men with time to kill and money to spend while they waited for transportation to Alaska. Two years after the Klondike strikes, Seattle had become one of the three principal centers of the white-slave traffic in North America, a main supply depot for the northern commerce in flesh. In the business district, there were more saloons than restaurants and stores. It was along the tough Seattle water front that Soapy Smith recruited many of his journeyman thugs for the invasion and occupation of Skagway. "Little Egypt," who acquired much valuable notoriety when she was tried in New York on a charge of having danced in the nude for a party at Sherry's (and was acquitted), was the star attraction along Seattle's Rialto.

But it was the "boxhouse," an amusement center that had been padlocked several years before by a reform administration but later opened up for the outlanders whose morals apparently were not so precious as the local citizenry's, where Seattle's grimier impresarios cleaned up, chief among them John Considine, whose takings provided the foundation of a theatrical fortune. Most gold-rushers who passed through Seattle, the main exit for Alaska, remembered the boxhouses and their dubious methods of entertainment. A magazine writer described the typical scene:

A nervous opium-eating individual was hammering away at a piano. In a hall-like space before the stage were a hundred or more boys and men. Not a woman was to be seen in the rows of seats—only men smoking and chewing tobacco and boys eating

peanuts. Around the sides of the room and at the end opposite
the stage were built out of thin pine boards small apartments with
an opening toward the platform and a barn-like door leading into
the narrow passageway along the wall. In each room was an
electric torch button which communicated with a bar set up behind
the stage. The boxes were unlit save as a stray beam might enter
at the window. In these boxes were women, one in some, more in
others.

Women with dresses reaching nearly to the point above their
knees, with stained and sweaty tights, with bare arms and necks
uncovered over halfway to their waists, with blondined hair and
some with powdered wigs, with faces rouged and powdered, eye-
brows with winkers smutted up and blackened, there stood the
female contingent at the doors and in the boxes.

Most of the boxhouses had cribs attached or near-by rooming
houses where the regulations dispensed with baggage, registration
or any proof of a legal relationship between the persons engaging
rooms. The less inhibited patrons found the curtained boxes
sufficiently discreet for their purposes.

Once clear of the water-front stews, deadfalls and merchants,
the traveler was still confronted with danger, unless he was fortunate enough to obtain passage on a regular ocean-going steamer.
Most were not. The armada bearing gold-rushers north was the
weirdest assembled since Napoleon prepared to invade England.
Every vessel barely capable of floating was pressed into service
on the Alaska run, a flotilla out of a sailor's nightmare, old tramps
rusting in the mud flats of Pacific harbors, side-wheelers, tugs,
river boats, yachts, whalers, cutters, ketches and schooners. Within
weeks the Inside Passage, the route protected by 50,000 islands
off southeastern Alaska, was strewn with the wreckage of this vast,
leaky and poorly manned fleet. And still thousands of men and
women fought their way aboard any vessel brazenly promising to
land off Alaska.

There was the voyage of the fittingly named *Rustler,* "a wretched little cockboat" only forty-five feet long, which crammed seventy passengers aboard although it was licensed to carry only twenty-five. The captain formerly drove a milk wagon in San Francisco. The passengers promptly soaked themselves in whisky to numb themselves to the perils and vexations of the voyage. Once when the passengers rushed to the port side to watch a passing Indian craft the *Rustler* heeled over as if she had been struck by heavy seas.

The enterprising owners of the tug *Sea Lion* loaded two scows, the *A-jax* and the *B-jax,* with passengers and hauled them to Alaska in twenty-six noisome days during the first feverish weeks of the stampede.

Even less fortunate were 200 gold-rushers who trustingly allowed a captain to place them aboard rafts hitched to his ship. A herd of cattle was driven aboard other rafts. In the Gulf of Alaska a storm blew up, and the captain had to be restrained from cutting the rafts adrift and sending his passengers to certain death. No doubt he would have mourned the cattle, for when they reached Dutch Harbor the captain sold them at twenty times the purchase price in Seattle.

When the cheechako landed on the beach at Skagway, the danger to his person and his morals only increased tenfold. The town was under the domination of Soapy Smith and his versatile crew. A newcomer was confronted with a choice of temptations: the painted woman, the crooked gambler, the bartender and his ready hand at dosing drinks with benumbing chloral hydrate. If the traveler was so priggish as to reject temptation, he was followed all the way to the summit of Chilkoot Pass and the Canadian boundary by Smith and his shell-game artists, and stood an excellent chance of being bludgeoned and robbed on the trail if he still insisted on hanging onto his money and possessions. Colonel Steele of the Mounted Police was shocked at conditions in Skagway and reported after a visit there: "In the dance hall the girl with the straw-coloured hair tripped the light fantastic at a dollar a set, and in the White Pass above the town the shell-game expert plied his trade, and occasionally some poor fellow was found lying lifeless on his sled where he had sat down to rest, the powder marks on his back and his pockets turned inside out." Travelers literally had to flee the soil of their own country to the protection of the Canadian law. Colonel Steele told of being awakened one Sunday morning by a pistol fight between two gangs in the street outside. "Bullets came through the thin boards, but the circumstance was such a common event that we did not even rise from our beds," Steele recalled.

The thoroughness of the Smith organization's tactics was attested by Keeler's pawnshop, whose proprietor's slogan was "I'll give a hundred dollars to any man I can't trade with, if he wants to trade." The advantages, of course, were all on Mr. Keeler's side. He had a large tray of exquisite old cameos, obviously heirlooms passed along by fond mothers, which he had acquired from stampeders depleted by Skagway's night life and its busy parasites.

The hardships of negotiating Chilkoot and White passes were greatly exaggerated by Klondikers, who made that trek a mighty and undying legend of striving and suffering. It has almost become a national Golgotha in the mythology of the American frontier. To the detached observer, such as a young Eastern physician who was caught up in the stampede, Skagway and its diversions were more likely to turn back a gold-rusher than the fabled passes. "The passage of the Chilkoot tested a man's guts rather than his legs," he said bluntly. Hundreds of stampeders who returned home from Skagway in dejection attributed their defeat to the rigors of the journey when actually they had been laid low by whisky, women and dice.

For hundreds of miles, from Seattle northward, on the sea, up the mountains, over the portages, along the waterways leading to the Yukon, a vast procession of fortune hunters was laboring on its way to the Arctic Golconda, as the headline writers phrased it.

Once emerged from the bottlenecks at the beaches of Dyea and Skagway, where the weak and dissolute were readily excused from further trials, they washed up and over the barriers which a geologic caprice had erected, and elbowed, scrambled and jostled for leading positions in the foot race for polar treasure.

Perverse, charitable, greedy, quixotic, callous, sentimental even under the prod of ambition, people still had time to be human, and being human they seemed to be wearing the pantaloon of comedy a little more often than the mantle of the statelier emotions. And beside the comic there were touches of the bizarre liberally in evidence. A muralist painting on a gigantic canvas would probably include such scenes and circumstances as these:

Along the trail from Chilkoot Summit to Lake Bennett, an elderly woman with determined leathery features, clad in a man's mackinaw, breeches and moccasins, cracked her whip over the only team of animals she was able to obtain to haul her sled—four goats. She had lost her husband and all her children, and was hauling the equipment for a laundry which she intended to set up in Dawson and start a new life for herself.

A bride and groom who joined the gold rush for their honeymoon sent their baggage ahead of them by pack train over White Pass, keeping only a small valise and neglecting to retain a change of clothing. They fell through the ice of a creek near a Mounted Police post, where the bride was provided with the only change of clothing available. So she rode into the nearest settlement wearing the scarlet coat and yellow-striped breeches of a Mountie.

Whatever their feelings about the women they left behind them, the stampeders had to acknowledge that the women of the gold rush showed a rare gallantry of spirit. A stout-hearted young woman who had started a laundry in Skagway with a wash tub and a few bars of soap rushed out to the camps along the Chilkoot trail when she heard that a meningitis epidemic was raging and there were few nurses to care for its victims. She worked so heroically that she was called "The Belle of Skagway" by a police official grateful for her assistance. Even to this inspiring episode there was a comic curtain line. A newcomer innocently called her "Skagway Belle"—which inferred a calling much less honorable than her own—and she vigorously boxed his ears.

A physician who kept a careful record of his adventures in the Yukon wrote of "fancy ladies in Parisian folderols, dressed loudly enough to beat the band, and being carried into Dawson by their owners as so much invoice of superprecious freight destined for the market," as well as uncomplaining wives, "the gay and wholesome life of any gathering, at times when their men were often bitter, tired and spiritually grim." One woman who especially caught his eye was a "plump little partridge" from St. Paul who just naturally assumed leadership of a party of twenty-five by virtue of her unquenchable spirits. One of her laws was that everyone "wash and boil out every other Sunday—that is, when we can keep track of the Sundays!"

In contrast to the "plump partridge" who led the expedition was a big Irishman glum as she was cheerful. "What did I ever do to be served with a life like this?" he groaned. In addition to being a chronic malcontent, he suffered from hypochondria. The party's medicine chest was badly shaken up along the trail and the drugs it contained were hopelessly mixed together. Complaining of a stomach-ache, the downhearted Celt scooped up a handful of pills compounded for a variety of disorders and swallowed them. The next day his stomach-ache was anything but imaginary.

The gentler nature of women was also occasionally in evidence. At Sheep Camp two men were caught looting a food cache and promptly sentenced to death by a vigilante court. The wife of one of the members of the vigilance committee stood up and pleaded for the men's lives with the eloquence of a Portia. It was doubtful whether the thieves had cause to be grateful in the end. They were stripped to the waist, horsewhipped, then tied together and "blue-ticketed" to the coast; probably they died of exposure along the way.

There was a certain giddiness in the atmosphere, deriving in part from the fevers of the quest and possibly from the high altitudes. The physician quoted above believed it brought out "all manner of social nastiness, including greed and sudden and unreasoning anger, with falling out of lifelong friends. . . . It also brought out great charity—in unexpected places, sometimes from men whose talons never knew the ministrations of a manicurist, or sleeky men whose freight was a roulette wheel or a bundle of theatrical blondes."

The "lacquered politeness" of the Japanese trail mates was gratefully observed, and—this must have caused many travelers to doubt their eyesight or their sanity—the wattle huts of Maori tribesmen who came from Australia to join the stampede popped up along the trail. More curious than Maori huts was the aluminum shelter a Bostonian had designed for himself; it proved highly impractical, since it heated up like an oven in warm weather and when the temperature dropped its interior was caked with ice, which "dripped like a sprinkler system" when a fire was lighted.

Giddiness affected even the sled dogs, who should have been thoroughly acclimated. Colonel Steele noted that when their owners joined the dogs in helping haul the sleds over rough terrain "their tails wagged with the enjoyment of being in the same team as their masters."

Honor among thieves evaporated on the heights. A bespectacled bandit on his way to Dyea with $900 he had robbed from stampeders was ambushed by another gunman, who snarled, "Cough up your pile, or I'll blow your specs off!"

The gold craze tightened its grip on men with every step they took toward the Klondike. One of the more amusing symptoms of this seizure was reported at Lake Bennett. A rumor spread around the settlement of stampeders building boats on its shores that gold dust was being found even on the trails in the vicinity.

Investigation by cooler and wiser heads showed that what the inexperienced took for gold dust was actually scrapings from the brassbound runners of sleds. Real gold, they would find, hid itself away much more securely.

3

Wax Museum:
Soapy Smith, As Ever Was

IF ONE MANAGED to survive the experience without being murdered, robbed, drugged, sandbagged, maimed or swindled, it must have been a delight and a pleasure to meet Jefferson Randolph Smith. He had the fine manners of a Southern gentleman, the charm of a Cagliostro, the persuasive powers of the devil himself. He was exceedingly chivalrous toward those weaker—if not at the same time richer—than their fellows. Women and children and stray dogs could turn to him confident of gentle treatment, especially if they did so in public. There was no doubt of his villainy, but he had certain saving graces, the wit inherent in most great swindlers, a sense of humor and a sardonic appreciation for the weaknesses of humanity. As he gracefully put it, "The way of the transgressor is hard—to quit."

The uncounted thousands of men and women who participated in the gold rush to the Yukon tributaries in 1897 and 1898 were subjected to countless obstacles before they could even dip out their first pan of gravel or stake their first claim. There were the con men, thieves and sharpers waiting at the ports of exit—San Francisco, Seattle, Portland and Vancouver—to trim the gold-rusher before he could leave civilization. There was the strenuous competition for space aboard the ships bound for Alaskan ports. There were the steep mountain passes, the long portages, the voracious insects, the diseases common to such a narrow funneling of humanity and the winter-locked trails. But none of these was more likely to send a man back to the States in defeat than Jefferson Randolph Smith and the men and women of his sharp-toothed command.

This many-sided rascal—who became a sort of folk hero as Soapy Smith of Skagway, brigand and philanthropist, a Robin Hood to the sentimental, a black scoundrel to many others and a puzzle to all—was beyond comparison the most artful grifter who frequented the mining camps of the last century. It is a pity that Mark Twain's days as a wanderer in the West had ended before he could make the acquaintance of Soapy, his methods of separating suckers and their money and his curious yearning to be acclaimed by his fellow citizens as a patriot and public benefactor. It would have taken a Mark Twain, perhaps, to explain Soapy and his glittering contradictions, or at least make them more credible.

Soapy, unfortunately, never took the trouble to hint at the sources of his behavior. We know that he was regarded as the leader of a murderous gang which ruled Skagway, the port of entry for most Yukon-bound prospectors, without interference from any constituted authority; that his gang caused the deaths of countless men shortly after they arrived on Alaskan soil; that he himself was merciless in trimming his clientele. We also know that he was indeed the benefactor of widows, orphans and stray dogs, as well as many victims of his own rackets, when they had no one else to help them amid the gold-fevered mobs on the beaches of Skagway and Dyea. And we know that he was subject to a desire for respectability which took such turns that he died broke and

intestate, although he and his cutthroat band had taken hundreds
of thousands of dollars from the gold-rushers. But how to reconcile Don Quixote and Long John Silver existing uneasily but side
by side in the same human being?

When Soapy and a carefully selected group of assistants set out
from Denver for Skagway, that shanty town on a shelf of Alaskan
beach under the towering coastal mountains which barred the way
to the gold-bearing creeks inland was in the first stages of its ex-
plosive growth. On July 26, 1897, there was one log building on
the beach which was its future townsite. A month later there were
2,000 inhabitants and thousands more landing every week and
pushing inland as rapidly as possible. From Skagway the trail led
to the foot of White Pass. Six miles along the barren coast was
the Indian village of Dyea, which was the jumping-off-place for the
shorter but steeper and more perilous route over Chilkoot Pass, of
terrible memory. Skagway, however, was the favorite landing place
because of its tidewater harbor, its newly established freight transport service over White Pass and its greater facilities for equipment and entertainment.

It was only fitting in view of Skagway's development into the
most larcenous town in Alaska that it was founded on stolen property. A Captain William Moore and his son owned the beach land,
but, shortly after the first flood of immigrants washed up there,
a "citizens' committee"—straight-faced withal—passed a law de-
claring that no man could own more than one lot. Captain Moore
was not even allowed tenancy of that one lot. He died in bitterness after fighting this usurpation through the courts long after
the Skagway boom had ended and his real estate was again of little
value; it was finally decided that Moore had been robbed, all right,
but the recompense was only a fraction of the damages suffered.

By the time Soapy and the first contingent of his gang arrived,
Skagway was a settlement of raw-frame stores, log bunkhouses,
tents, a few jerry-built hotels. The town had become so over-

crowded that appeals were sent to the States to warn other gold-seekers to stay away until spring. Wide circulation was given to William B. Haskell's bitter-coated capsule of advice to all who thought that an easy fortune could be scraped off the topsoil of the Klondike:

Go along and find a creek. Everything is taken up for 50 miles around but you may get something farther away. "What shall you do when you find it?" First, pay the government location tax. Then just move a hundred tons of ice to one side. Below that you will find something like 20 feet of frozen mud. Just thaw it and toss it out. Near bed-rock you will see gravel. Perhaps there will be gold in it and perhaps not. That's a chance you take. Just pile the gravel up and in the spring you can wash it out. You can't do so before because all the water will be ice. "What if there is no gold in it or not enough to pay?" Oh, then you won't be any worse off than hundreds of others. . . . These are the frozen facts, young man, about gold-hunting here. If they are not sufficiently frozen, you will be if you disregard them when the mercury gets well on the downward path to sixty degrees below.

The advice did not succeed in discouraging any appreciable number of those whose understanding of the hardships of an Alaskan winter was dimmed by the tales of fortunes being made in a few weeks of digging. They crowded into Skagway that autumn, restless, bored, eager to proceed on their journey, ripe for the plucking by Soapy and his lads.

Although he once lorded it over the Denver underworld and had been the virtual dictator of the mining camp of Creede, Smith arrived in Skagway with little more than his ready wits, his suitcase filled with iron knuckles, walnut shells and rubber peas, a few sets of crooked dice and a change of clothes, and his determination to establish himself as the politico-criminal boss of the town. With him were Slim Jim Foster, Red Gibbs, Syd Dixon, the "Reverend"

Bowers and George Wilder, the latter two especially adept in the allied bunco arts of steering and shilling.

Charles Bowers, with his pious, bless-you-my-good-man airs, was renowned as the best bunco steerer in the profession. First of all, his manner was so disarming that the most suspicious of intended victims was ready to trust him. Secondly, Bowers was reputed to know the grips, passwords and distress signals of every lodge, fraternal order and secret society in existence in the Western World. Once he spotted an emblem in a man's lapel, he approached with a glad cry and identified himself as brother and comrade, eager to give advice and share in good fortune, all in the spirit of brotherhood.

George Wilder was the gang's banker. He was the only member of the organization who ever saved money. Although he was able to stand on his merits as a thief, Wilder was taken along with the first contingent to Skagway principally because of his bank roll.

Syd Dixon was also an oddity among his colleagues—he was a gentleman fallen on bad times. Not an unusual role for a man to assume in that meretricious trade, but Dixon apparently was the genuine article. He was once a member of Eastern society and a world traveler, but had become addicted to the use of opium and fallen in with Soapy as a steerer, shill and "actor" in Smith's various con games. He apparently had little taste for the roles he was called on to perform, in contrast to the enthusiasm with which his fellows practiced their calling, and worked with them only to obtain the money to keep him in opium and clean linen.

Other members of the Denver-Creede organization followed Soapy and his companions to Skagway as soon as the money could be scrounged for their passage. The most picturesque of the lot, perhaps, was Henry Edwards, notorious as "Yank Hank Fewclothes." Edwards, who claimed direct descent from the celebrated Puritan clergyman Jonathan Edwards and who often parodied the fiery sermons of his antecedent with ribald skill, wrote poetry and peddled honey on the streets of Denver when he was not occupied with more criminal pursuits. When Soapy first accepted Yank Hank into membership—possibly because of his weakness for the company of poets, no matter how untalented, and because he loved to have himself more or less immortalized in verse, no matter how ineptly sentimental—he tossed the recruit a twenty-dollar bill and admonished him, "Three things make a man look disreputable— one old hat and two old shoes. Get yourself some new ones. Just because you're a poet, you don't have to look too much like one." Yank Hank's sobriquet was derived from the fact that he never wore a coat, vest or overcoat, even in the coldest weather—at least not until he met Soapy and was forced to dress up to his new vocation.

Other members of the gang included Jimmy Bruce, known to his associates as "the great gobblefish" because as a side line he practiced usury and accordingly was looked on with contempt; Big Ed Burns, a huge fellow prized for his strong-arm talents rather than any intellectual qualities, which were plainly lacking, one of whose chores was to follow Soapy and ward off beggars, thereby preserving his chief's reputation for openhanded generosity; Joe Palmer, a hard-faced specimen who was the most accomplished gunman of the crew; Frisco Red Harris, a punch-drunk prize fighter also employed mainly in the physical aspect of the gang's operations; "Judge" Van Horn, a large-bellied lawyer who drank himself out of his practice and acted as Soapy's legal consultant; and Doc Baggs, who, next to Soapy himself, was the most accomplished manipulator of confidence games and who was reputed to be the originator of the gold-brick swindle.

Among the tinhorns and cutthroats who joined Soapy's gang in Skagway without previous service in Colorado were such fellows as King of Terrors, Jay Bird Slim, Fatty Green and Kid Jimmy Fresh. Green, also known as "Shoot Your Eyes Out," was a cold-eyed citizen utterly lacking in the fat man's supposed joviality. He dealt with customers who objected to being bilked and called for legal retribution, usually by murdering them. All that is known of the rest is that they probably earned their nicknames.

With the help of these choice subordinates, Soapy Smith established himself as the absolute ruler of Skagway. He not only raised himself above the law, he *was* the law, and he attained that position in a few months of the winter of 1897-1898.

Before examining the methods by which he laid hands on the power that gave him life-or-death control over the lives of thousands who participated in the Klondike rush, poured hundreds of thousands of dollars into his pockets and those of his followers, and seemingly made him the prototype of the modern gangster, it would be instructive to look into the history of his operations in Colorado. They were the proving grounds for almost every step in taking over Skagway as his personal domain.

Soapy arrived on the Denver scene in 1883, at the age of twenty-three. His origins, like those of most semilegendary figures, were clouded over by the conflict between his own romantic hints and the deducible facts. He was born in Georgia in 1860; beyond that, no one can guarantee the truth of any tales regarding his early life. Soapy himself indicated that he came of an aristocratic family whose fortunes were wrecked by the War between the States and the subsequent Reconstruction—but what Southerner in those days, heading West and leaving poor prospects behind him, did not romanticize about the white-columned manse, the spreading cotton fields and the departed glory of his family? The theory that Jefferson Randolph Smith was of gentle birth—and was converted to crime by hard times—was belied by the character and conduct of his brother, Bascom Smith. Granted that Soapy himself had acquired a fine set of manners somewhere between Georgia and Alaska, his brother Bascom, according to all who knew him, was a crude, brawling bumpkin who could not possibly pass as the son of ruined gentry.

In his teens, Smith set out along with thousands of young men of his generation for the Western frontier, became a wandering cow hand and was employed in the great cattle drives up the trails from Texas to Abilene and Dodge City.

It was the romanticists' theory that Smith turned from honest labor because of his bitterness over the Reconstruction and the carpetbaggers' mistreatment of his family. It seems more likely, however, that Soapy struck out along the primrose path one day in San Antonio when he attended a circus. The principal attraction for the youth was a fascinating game in which a fast-talking entrepreneur pitted his skill and wits against all comers through the medium of three walnut shells and a pea. If you chose the shell under which the pea rested, you picked up the stakes—simple as that, all you needed was a sharp eye. Soapy quickly lost all his assets, his pay from several months on the trail to Abilene. And that was the turning point in his life. If money could be acquired that easily, why spend one's energy nursing herds of cattle over the dusty plains? The youth joined the circus, hung around the grifters until he was accepted by the fraternity and began manipulating the shells himself.

Another lucrative skill he picked up along the road to Denver was the soap game. It was in Leadville, the scene of a Colorado gold and silver strike, that he came under the tutelage of a man named Taylor as one of his assistants, known in the trade as a "shill," "booster" or "capper." Taylor would set up his suitcase and tripod—keister and tripe to the trade—and gather a crowd around him on a street corner. Then he would begin wrapping cubes of soap, ostentatiously inserting fifty, twenty, ten, five or one-dollar bills in some of them. He offered the soap for sale at one dollar a bar. To encourage buyers, or speculators, Taylor's shill would buy a cake, find a ten-dollar bill wrapped around it, whoop with joy and disappear. Later, of course, the shill would return the ten dollars.

Soapy traveled with Taylor for a few years until his mentor retired, and in 1893 he made his Denver appearance, keister and tripe
in hand, like a crooked young Dick Whittington. He established
himself on Seventeenth Street, which then led from the Union
Station to the center of the city.

By his personality, his intuitive ability to command other men
and his skill at maneuvering in the twilight where politicians, law-
enforcement officers and the underworld meet, Smith soon rose to
a position of influence. Despite his youth, he was an impressive
figure. He had a black beard, recently grown, which contrasted
oddly with his light gray eyes, a slim but vigorous physique, a
quiet deferential manner, an air of authority. He never threw his
weight around until it was absolutely necessary, but was ready
enough with his fists or guns in a showdown. Usually he was able
to settle matters by compromise. Thus, to the gratification of the
police, he never trimmed a local citizen, always out-of-towners
venturing out of the railroad station and into the persuasive company of the Reverend Bowers, Doc Baggs or Judge Van Horn. If
the victim became too insistent on recovering his losses, Smith
would not allow him to embarrass the police with his complaints—
either he would return part of the loot or detail one of his strong-
arm men to close the customer's mouth forcibly. Actually there
were not many such embarrassments, for most victims were too
ashamed of their own greed and gullibility to expose themselves.

Safe as we are from Soapy's depredations, we find something
almost amusing about the ingenuity with which he attained pre-em-
inence in the confidence games of Denver, the center of the Rocky
Mountain mining booms and the Western wellspring of easy money.
Among the enterprises he superintended were two gambling
houses, both identical in furnishings and equipment. One was the
Arcade, a second-floor, "square" house where gamblers gathered
from all over the country with assurance of scrupulous honesty at
the tables. It was famous throughout the West. Soapy, however,

established an identical house, also on the second floor of a building near by. There nonprofessionals would be steered in the belief they were being taken to the Arcade, and there they were ruthlessly shorn with the aid of loaded dice, rigged wheels and crooked dealers.

The "bandit barbers of Seventeenth Street" were responsible for many coups by Soapy's bunco gang. Whenever a promising sucker fell into their hands, they nicked his hair just above the collar; this immediately identified him as a prospect for Soapy's steerers, who prowled the streets night and day.

Another of the establishments waiting to shear such woolly sheep was the Up and Down, as it was known among the *cognoscenti*. It was a fake stock exchange furnished with clattering telegraph keys, a ticker and a blackboard on which quotations were listed. The "brokerage" wires led to a near-by hotel room where prices on the nonexistent stocks fluctuated in accordance with a turn of the cards. It was a great success in trimming outlanders who were innocent enough to believe they were being admitted to the realm of high finance.

Other methods were devised for rooking those who could not be lured by soap and shell games, gambling houses and plunging in ghost stocks. There were "friendly" poker games to which the Reverend Bowers steered his many lodge brothers, fake mining enterprises, shares in lotteries, partnerships in nonexistent businesses and salted mines.

Friction was inevitable in all these operations; sometimes Soapy's success would arouse jealousy in the underworld, and an interloper would have to be cut down. When it came time for gunplay, Soapy's methods of outwitting the law and cheating justice were, as usual, highly original. He and all his confederates were armed with pistols of the same make and caliber, and when they had their victim cornered they all fired at once. No judge or jury could possibly determine who fired the fatal shot, and, if that were im-

portant, it distributed the burden of guilt on the assassins' con-
sciences.

In a few years Soapy was the undisputed leader of the confidence men of Denver and, if not the ruler of the entire underworld, he was its most influential member. Police found it a delight
to deal with him, not only because of his generosity but his tact in
passing along the share of the swag they expected. Politicians
noted benignly that he well understood that it was the underworld's function at campaign time to contribute to the political
machinery which took such good care not to interfere with it,
providing the local voters were left alone.

Soapy showed his delicate comprehension of the official mind
when a poorly informed policeman arrested him for the old soap
swindle. (Until the end of his days, no matter how grand his
position in the underworld, Soapy kept his hand in by occasionally
going out on the streets and setting up his soap and shell games;
perhaps he regarded them as a private form of social security.)

The police judge before whom he was arraigned demanded that
Soapy demonstrate how his game was worked. Smith took care to
wrap one of his cakes of soap with a fifty-dollar bill and saw to it
that the judge selected that one. The judge unwrapped his soap,
tucked the fifty-dollar bill in his vest pocket and roared at the
arresting officer, "You have been hounding an honest businessman
for pursuing his lawful calling. His merchandising methods are
fair and honorable. Case dismissed!"

Soapy and most of his colleagues joined the rush to Creede when
silver was discovered there in 1891. The mining camp swelled
from its original population of one N. C. Creede, who first tapped
the thick veins of silver, to approximately 10,000 within a few
weeks. There was no local government, no police, no one to demand a share of the takings. Creede was just about the right size
and age to swallow up, Soapy believed.

Within a few weeks Soapy was able to accomplish this grandiose plan. It was not so incredible as it seems, when one considers that he and his henchmen knew exactly what they wanted and how to go about it while no one else in Creede thought of anything but the silver to be gouged out of the earth. He simply let it be known that he was the law in Creede, and settled back to see if there were any challengers. Merchants and miners were perturbed but had no organization to dispute his claims. Smith proceeded to appoint his own police chief, Captain John Light, a Texan whose ability as a gunfighter was widely respected. He also appointed other city officials. Herman Straus of the famous mercantile family visited the town and was offered the mayor's office by Soapy, who announced that he wanted the best possible men in public office, as long as they were not unreasonable from his viewpoint. Straus found Soapy charming but declined the offer.

The only opposition to Soapy's proclamation came not from the righteous but from Bob Ford, the proprietor of Ford's Exchange, a combination barroom-dance-hall-gambling house.

Ford was better known as "the dirty little coward who shot Mr. Howard and laid Jesse James in his grave," in the words of the cowboy lament. A mean, shifty-eyed fellow of dangerous temper, Ford had shot the famous bank robber in the head to claim the $10,000 reward for James "dead or alive." It was safer to invoke the "dead" clause. He lived in perpetual fear, however, that a member of the James gang or one of his victim's kinfolk would catch up with him. Despite the anxiety that gnawed at him night and day, that made him always sit with his back to the wall and sleep with a gun under his pillow, Ford was arrogant and bullying. When he passed along the word to Soapy that he didn't care to submit to the newcomer's authority, Smith walked over to Ford's Exchange and faced up to him. There were no witnesses to the interview, but Soapy's style of diplomacy—the soft word covering an iron resolution—sufficed to pe   iade Ford that they could get along together. Soapy, it was remarked, had the bland facility of being "benevolent but highhanded."

Ford was finally justified in his fears several months later. A wandering cowpuncher named Ed O'Kelly, whose background and motives have always been a mystery, beat him to the draw at the Exchange and shot him to death. O'Kelly's explanation was cryptic: "I don't burn a man's mother's heels, nor I don't rob pocketbooks, nor I don't pull off women's toenails with pincers, but I can still kill such lowdown critters as Bob Ford." That wasn't a strong enough explanation for the people of Creede. Although they feared and disliked Ford and shared in the general belief that he was indeed "a dirty little coward," they collected in the street outside the Exchange and proceeded to render summary justice, for such cold-blooded killings were regarded as high crimes, no matter how unpopular the victim. Soapy, however, coolly ordered the mob to disperse, thereby setting himself up as a public-spirited believer in law and order. O'Kelly was then removed to jail and later sentenced to prison.

Public opinion was also inclined toward Soapy for his support of an itinerant preacher who appeared in Creede. The evangelist was heckled by hoodlums when he attempted to deliver a soapbox sermon on the main street. He had heard that Soapy was the law in Creede and sent word that he would appreciate protection during his soul-saving crusade. Soapy not only appeared with his toughest henchmen and drove off the hecklers but announced that the evangelist would be given a proper church in which to spread the Word. "The town needs religion," Soapy declared. He and his men collected $600 within a few hours for construction of a frame church. Soapy turned the money over to the preacher. But that night he delegated one of his footpads to sneak into his protégé's room and steal the money. Next morning, after listening to the preacher's lament over the stolen church funds, Soapy returned the money to him with an admonition that he must be more careful in such a sinful place.

It all contributed to the legend Soapy was building around himself as the "Robin Hood of the Frontier."

When the Creede boom died down, largely because Congress repealed the Sherman Silver Act and caused the price of silver to drop from $1.29 to 50 cents an ounce, the town settled down to quiet ways and Soapy decided it was no longer a lucrative field. His gang had profited from its stay there by hundreds of thousands of dollars; the exact figures are unavailable since it was long before tax accountants and bookkeepers became attached to the staffs of all right-thinking underworld chieftains. But whatever Soapy's share of this two-year bonanza, he had given away and squandered most of it. Even the more respectable citizens looked on his departure with a rather wry regret. The town's leading merchant told him, "We'll miss you like we miss the steam calliope at the circus. But things are getting settled here now, and we're going to run Creede on new lines."

"Fair enough," Soapy said. "All of us have a time to work, a time to play and a time to go."

Again Soapy and his men took over control of the Denver underworld. His particular domain was the Tivoli Club, a gambling house in which he took the advice of Gentleman Syd Dixon and posted a sign reading CAVEAT EMPTOR.

Even with that frank warning the Tivoli prospered, but it was becoming difficult to stifle complaints against his "high-handed benevolence." Two Southern Californians dropped $1,500 in the gambling house and complained so loudly and effectively that the Denver Fire and Police Commission felt it necessary to call on Soapy for an explanation.

Soapy obliged with the eloquence and irony which delighted his disciples:

"Gentlemen, I wish to assure you that we are not gamblers. The Tivoli is not a gambling establishment. We are reformers in the true sense of the word! I am running an educational institution. The famous Keeley Institute provides a cure for the drinking habit. At the Tivoli I have a cure for the gambling habit. The man who steps into my place is faced with the sign, CAVEAT EMPTOR. That is the danger beacon, a warning to all to slow up before rounding the curve. The stranger is not compelled to play; he must use his own judgment. But he is not discouraged. Why should we tell him it is useless to buck our tables? Let him learn for himself. He has no chance of winning. In my games, the player cannot win. But when he leaves, he has learned a valuable lesson—an experience of the greatest value.

"Gentlemen, I should be recognized as a public benefactor! I could name many men who have renounced gambling, have been cured of avarice and cupidity and restored to mental health by taking my treatment. At the Tivoli we are engaged in the instruction and reformation of those grasping and selfish souls who can understand only the kind of lessons which we provide. Praise, not censure, should be our portion. The defense rests. I leave my reputation in your hands."

This nimble bit of sophistry resulted in Soapy's being dismissed almost with apologies.

Reform, however, was in the air. Davis H. Waite was elected governor of Colorado on his promise to clean out the rascals and to "fight iniquity until blood runs as deep as the cavalry's bridles." It almost did, though it was the militia, not the United States cavalry, which was called out to begin the blood-letting. When the Fire and Police Commission defied Governor Waite's orders for a cleanup, he surrounded the City Hall with militiamen. Inside that edifice a curious combination of forces prepared for a siege—the police force, the fire department and the stoutest fellows of the local underworld, Soapy Smith commanding. Soapy contributed many cases of rifles, ammunitions and 500 pounds of dynamite to the defense, and it seemed that a bloody battle was inevitable. Soapy was prepared to blow half of the town off the map to retain possession of the City Hall. The general commanding the militia refused to open fire, however, and the Denver City Hall war ended without a casualty, except the injuries done the sovereign pride of Colorado.

But the reform movement could not be halted, and Soapy found it advisable to leave the city for a cooling-off period. He proceeded alone to Mexico City and embarked on the most audacious confidence game of his career. Introducing himself as Colonel Jefferson Randolph Smith, he proposed to President Porfirio Diaz, a genuine "blood to the bridles" man who ruled Mexico as an absolute dictator for thirty-five years, that he organize a Mexican Foreign Legion after a recruiting campaign in the American Southwest, then conduct a no-quarter campaign against the rebellious Yaqui tribes of northern Mexico. Soapy wanted 40,000 pesos to begin recruiting among the badmen and adventurers who were finding the American frontier a bit cramped, but the hard-headed Diaz gave him only 4,000. Shortly after Soapy returned to the United States, Diaz learned that the gringo colonel was a notorious swindler and called off the whole scheme. Just what Soapy's motives were in this proposition is still a little foggy; probably he hoped to bilk Diaz out of larger sums. There is a possibility, however, that he might have intended to organize the Foreign Legion— he always fancied himself as a military leader—and then turn it against Diaz.

In the year or so before gold was discovered in quantity in the Klondike, Soapy's fortunes suffered a distinct comedown. Denver had wearied of reform—again—but the Blonger brothers had established themselves during his absence and were providing so much competition that the profits were severely reduced. It was with relief rather than any nostalgia for his departed influence over the Denver underworld that Soapy left for Skagway and the greatest achievements of his career. . . .

When Soapy set himself the task of taking over Skagway, he was thirty-eight years old and a master of skulduggery, in the prime of his powers as a leader and misleader of men. In Creede he had learned that the time to move in and assume control was before law and order had been formally established, when he could brush aside any attempts to set up the civic machinery and make the simple declaration that henceforth Soapy Smith would dispense justice and punish miscreants, unless they happened to be members of his own gang. In Creede he had proclaimed, "I am the law." In Skagway he announced more forthrightly, "There is no law in Skagway." Anarchy suited him better than the pretense of appointing a mayor, a chief of police and other controllable bureaucrats. Skagway, he decided, could be administered more efficiently without such gestures to tradition. The port's citizenry, a floating population with the exception of a few merchants and traders and his own banditti, would make no passionate appeals for honest government; the prospectors' only interest was to push on to the Klondike or, coming from that direction, to board a ship for the States and spend their earnings.

As in Creede, when he saved the slayer of Bob Ford from lynching, a grand gesture established Soapy in the minds of his new fellow citizens as a leader of men, a crusader for justice, decency and fair play.

The scene of this *coup d'état* was on the muddy mockery of a street called Broadway, the principal thoroughfare of Skagway, in a saloon adjoining the Palace Theater. The bartender, John E. Fay, had quarreled with two customers—Deputy United States Marshal John Rowan and a private citizen named Andy McGrath—and ended the dispute by drawing a revolver and shooting both of them dead. Soapy had been operating his soap game near by when he learned that a lynch mob had gathered at the saloon and was proceeding to string up the bartender.

Soapy flailed his way through the indignant throng and took his stand beside Fay, who already had the rope around his neck.

"Anybody who tries to string him up will get a bullet in the head," Soapy announced. His gray eyes surveyed the crowd with their peculiarly disconcerting effect. "Lynching doesn't go here. You've all lost your heads. How do you know this man deserves hanging?"

Soapy added that if Fay was lynched he would guarantee a "general slaughter" by nightfall. The crowd fell back resentfully. Soapy gathered a band of volunteers, including his own lawless associates, to guard Fay until he could be sent down the Lynn Canal by steamer to Sitka for safekeeping until his trial (at which he was acquitted on grounds that he acted in self-defense).

The gesture might have worked against Soapy this time, since Marshal Rowan's wife gave birth to a baby a few hours after her husband was murdered and public indignation rose again. But the moment he heard of this circumstance Soapy began taking up a collection for Mrs. Rowan and by nightfall he had a total of $700. The next two days he collected another $1,500 and decreed that it be divided between Mrs. Rowan and the widow of Andy McGrath.

This was the time to announce his assumption of rule over Skagway, while the memory of his defiance of the lynch mob and his subsequent compassion for the two widows was fresh in the minds of all. He let it be known, not through publication in what passed for a newspaper in Skagway, but by word of mouth spreading from the barrooms and dance halls to the merchants and more respectable elements, that from now on he would be responsible for the public safety. He declared himself in as partner in John Clancy's saloon and gambling house—apparently in the style of latter-day gangsters taking over a territory—and renamed it Jeff's Place. This was to be his headquarters—a roll-top desk in the back room was to be the brain, nerve and muscle center of Skagway. As the gold-rush historian, Glenn Chesney Quiett, analyzed the sources of his power to dominate a community, Soapy "had such a winning personality, was such a fearless bluffer and clever organizer and good judge of men, that he held the community completely in his grasp. He had the true gangster spirit. It wasn't money alone he wanted; it was to be the big shot." Thus Soapy exuded grace in his back-room headquarters while his merry men were robbing miners on the trails leading to and from the Klondike, cheating newcomers with their crooked card, dice and shell games, robbing and killing when blatant swindling and cheating wouldn't work. The Royal Mounted Police veteran, S. B. Steele, recalled of Skagway in the Soapy Smith era: "At night the crash of bands, shouts of 'Murder!' and cries for help mingled with the cracked voices of the singers in the variety halls."

For the victims—and they numbered in the thousands before Smith's reign ended in a bloody day of recompense—there was practically no recourse to established authority.

Even in the absence of local government, the United States had sent only a feeble detachment of federal marshals to Skagway. They were utterly ineffective in maintaining order or dealing with Soapy Smith. A prospector who complained that one of Soapy's gang had robbed him found that neither the marshal's office nor the United States Commissioner would take action without evidence—obviously impossible to obtain—that Smith was connected with the gang. The federal officers admitted there was no hope of anyone offering such evidence, and the complainant was thwarted in every effort to obtain justice. The strongest force in the vicinity was a few squads of United States Infantry stationed at Dyea, but they had all they could handle on that embattled beach. Mont Hawthorne noted on his way through Skagway that Soapy and his confederates "was holding office and carrying out his rules. Even the fellow running the paper was in cahoots with them. Honest folks was plumb disgusted." The "plumb-disgusted" citizens, with a careful glance over their shoulders, referred to Soapy's gang as "the pallid pimps."

There are no statistics available on the extent of the Smith gang's depredations, but some historians have estimated that several hundred men lost their lives under the guns, knives and bludgeons of the merciless crew and countless others were beaten, wounded and robbed. Wilson Mizner, later celebrated as a wit, playwright and legendary roisterer, paused in Skagway to observe the methods of Soapy Smith with more than academic interest. "Not less than fifty people were killed by the gang," he said later, "and fights were nothing but rough mutilations in which the stranger hadn't a chance. As is usually true, the underlings of Soapy were more vicious than he ever was, but it was his power which made it possible." Mizner also noted that there was an element of terror in Soapy's reign, something like that applied in a modern police state. "It was impossible to be sure who was included in his gang," he recalled, which made every "plumb-disgusted" citizen careful about voicing criticism in public.

James Wickersham, a federal judge and Alaska historian, said that Soapy's dominion of Skagway was unrivaled "since the days of Virginia City." A newspaper dispatch under date of Feb. 25, 1898, testified to this from Seattle:

Officers of the steamer *Noyo* from Skagway today reported conditions of lawlessness at Skagway as beyond description. Soapy Smith and his gang are in full control. Law-abiding people do not dare say a word against them. Holdups, robberies and shootings are a part of the routine. Eight dead bodies were picked up on White Pass on February 15.

In a letter to a friend in the States, Soapy crowed over his hijacking of authority from the federal officials there: "We have got them licked, and we mean to rule absolutely."

After the quick collapse of federal authority, the people of Skagway, the "decent element," made one last attempt to drive out the rascals, vigilante style.

Under the direction of a Major Tanner, a vigilance committee of 101 was formed and a public proclamation posted, which read: "A word to the wise should be sufficient. All confidence sharks, bunco-men, sure-thing men, and all other objectionable characters are notified to leave Skagway and the White Pass. Failure to comply with this warning will be followed by prompt action!"

The formation of committees did not exactly alarm Soapy but the Denver City Hall war had shown him that reform movements were not to be taken lightly. "This town needs a committee," he told his followers, "but not the Committee of 101. We'll give 'em our own kind of committee and it'll be three times as big as theirs." His intelligence system told him that the populace was indeed getting restive, even though his gang seldom picked on permanent residents—well, hardly ever, but occasionally mistakes happened. But there were a number of small merchants who might go either way, who knew that Soapy's methods were disgraceful but who also valued the patronage given them by Soapy and his gangsters. Soapy himself had large charge accounts at a number of stores through which he dispensed charity, often to men who had been picked clean by his own gang. Still, forthright action might definitely line them up on his side.

Soapy's answer to the Committee of 101, therefore, was to announce the formation of the Committee of 303 with a sardonic effrontery. All over Skagway posters announced his move: "The business interests of Skagway propose to put a stop to the lawless acts of many newcomers. We hereby summon all good citizens to a meeting at which these matters will be discussed. Come one, come all! Immediate action will be taken for relief. Let this be a warning to those chechawcos [sic] who are disgracing our city! The meeting will be held at Sylvester Hall at 8 P.M. sharp."

The proclamation was signed by "Jefferson R. Smith, Chairman."

And it was Soapy Smith, chairman, who addressed the meeting he had called in tones ringing with moral indignation. He was quoted as saying:

Fellow citizens, we are here to form a real committee, not a half-baked, irresponsible committee such as we have been hearing about. We have the support of the business element of Skagway. We deplore present conditions, which are caused not by our own people but riffraff from all parts of the world. We will protect ourselves even at the cost of our lives.

There was much more in the same style, for Soapy, once he ascended the platform, became intoxicated by the flow of his own oratory—so intoxicated that he appeared to believe what he was saying. When he finished, his claque of thugs and shills and cappers started an ovation. They frowned on anyone who failed to join it. In a moment the hall was in an uproar, and Soapy smiled down benevolently at his audience. The next day he issued another proclamation headed PUBLIC WARNING which read:

The body of men styling themselves the Committee of 101 are hereby notified that any overt act committed by them will be met promptly by the law-abiding citizens of Skagway and each member and their property will be held responsible for any unlawful act on their part. The Law and Order Committee of 303 will see that justice is dealt out to its fullest extent and no Blackmailers or Vigilantes will be tolerated.

The threat of action against "each member and their property" for any act committed by the Committee of 101 had an immediate effect: the vigilante movement died stillborn.

Soapy was intelligent enough not to take overt advantage of this victory; instead, he expanded his charitable activities and, as in Creede, stepped forward as the champion of religion. Again an itinerant preacher gave him his cue; one begins to suspect that such actors stepped on the stage with more than coincidental good timing. The preacher asked for Soapy's help, and Soapy ostentatiously raised a church-building fund, many of the contributors being saloonkeepers, bawdyhouse madams, dance-hall impresarios and gambling-house keepers. Such support for the clergy not only bathed Soapy in a stained-glass light but inhibited the preacher—a formidable instrument of public opinion in those days—from crying out against saloons, bawdyhouses, dance halls and gambling houses—this side of the New Testament. Later Soapy also solicited funds to buy an organ for the Union Church.

A great deal of Soapy's success was traceable to his sensitivity to public opinion. Even while everyone in Denver, Creede or Skagway knew that he was the leader of the underworld, he was also acknowledged to be a guardian of the law (through an entirely natural distaste for lynchings), a friend of the needy, a pillar of the church (he often attended services with a few of his more presentable associates) and a vociferous patriot. It was the custom to end any discussion of Soapy and his paradoxical character by saying, "Well, you've got to hand it to him, he does a lot of good, too." Soapy's biographers, Edwin V. Westrate and William R. Collier, noted that even "in his hours of supremacy, Soapy Smith was peculiarly sensitive to the development of public opinion." Thus he made a practice of sending out twenty-dollar gold pieces on Christmas to hundreds of people; he provided for widows and orphans stranded at Skagway by the deaths of their breadwinners inland on the Klondike or the passes and trails leading to the golden creeks, and even befriended the hundreds of stray dogs roaming the town. Most of the dogs had been imported by persons who heard rumors back in the States that dogs, to be used in sled teams, were selling for $100 apiece in Skagway. When the dogs proved useless in harness and unsalable, they were abandoned. Soapy himself adopted six of the strays and persuaded scores of other citizens to do likewise. There was no doubt that Soapy had a streak of generosity in his character—nothing proves it so much as the fact he died broke—but he was not above making the most of his philanthropies in winning public opinion. Thirty-odd years later the Chicago gangsters copied his tactics, with Al Capone in the forefront establishing soup kitchens at the beginning of the depression.

A Denver merchant, Joseph T. Cornforth, who visited Skagway in the spring of 1898, wrote to a friend at home:

And whom do you suppose I ran across before I had been in Skagway two hours? None other than our well-known, suave townsman, Soapy Smith. He has reached the height of his career and is ruler of this great camp. He has mobilized a crowd of outlaws, the like of which is not to be found anywhere in the continental United States, nor anywhere else, for that matter.

Anything short of murder goes here and, if it's murder, they call it suicide. Soapy had the nerve to start a church. But he defends all criminals. What his game is, is a mystery to me, but there is bound to be an end to it. His accounts at the merchants' stores for provisions and fuel for the needy people here amount to several hundred dollars a week. He pays for the funerals of friendless persons, and I can assure you that that is no small item. What are you going to make out of a character like that?

Soapy's sense of chivalry, although not an entirely dependable element in his character, was aroused by the case of a Seattle man who came to Skagway seeking his seventeen-year-old daughter. She had run away with what the historians of the place politely called a "tinhorn." "Pimp" would probably have been more accurate. The girl's companion, having an aversion for any sort of personal endeavor, put her to work in a "dance hall." "Dance hall" was often a polite euphemism for "whore house" in Skagway.

The father took his problem to Soapy, who immediately had his men search the "dance halls" for the girl and her lover. They were quickly located and brought to Soapy's office. In a rather bathetic scene, the girl rushed to her father's arms and begged to be taken

home. But the lover, seeing his source of income vanishing, fool-
ishly voiced his opinion that he had some rights in the matter.
"Take this bum out in the yard and give him the works," Soapy
ordered. As he left to escort father and daughter to the wharf
and the steamer which would return them to Seattle, the howls of
her lover and the thud of his assailants' fists made a gratifying sort
of farewell song.

The stories of Soapy's good deeds, however, could not balance
the villainies he himself perpetrated—often with a touch of das-
tardly humor which made it difficult to separate the villainy and
the comedy—and the fouler crimes he countenanced among his
followers. There is considerable evidence that the Skagway underworld got out of hand, expanded in size and violence beyond what
Soapy had planned. Certainly he did not look with favor on the
"12 holdups on an average night" reported in the San Francisco
newspapers; nor the murder and robbery of prospectors on the trail;
nor the killing of a woman as occurred in the spring of '98. It
was bad for business, all around. But if the underworld had become
an uncontrollable monster, he was its Frankenstein.
Rarely has a place been so efficiently organized to deprive a
man of his money. Every weakness, every vice, every blind spot in
a man's character was subjected to pressure from all sides, from
the moment he set foot on the beach until he disappeared over
White Pass. For the woman-starved miner who had spent months
at the Klondike diggings, there were hundreds of whores and
dance-hall girls, many of them recruited from San Francisco's
Barbary Coast and its depraved vocational schools. For the man
who needed more money to get to the Klondike or who had come
back heavy-laden with gold dust and didn't mind risking his poke,
there was every sort of gambling device known. Every kind of
liquor from rotgut to French champagne was available for the incoming and outgoing thirsts. And if a man didn't yield up his
money to these temptations, Soapy Smith had a few score of confi-

dence games and tenderfoot traps in excellent working condition.

One of the least subtle of Soapy's devices was known as "seeing the eagle." In the notorious backyard of his "303," as Jeff's Place later became known, was a huge eagle in a cage. Customers with bulging pokes were invited to have a look at the bird. The high-walled yard had no escape route except through a secret exit. While studying natural history, the customer was sandbagged and robbed, and came to, if he was lucky, in a remote alley.

That notorious back-yard served another purpose at the 303. A Klondiker later recalled the night he drifted into Soapy's gambling layout and watched a drunken man throwing dice under the eyes of a "bull-necked" house man seated on a high platform. The drunken player

begged me to throw for him and change his luck. I refused. Then I threw once for him just to get rid of him. That time he won, so I did it again. The third time the [house man] said, "My gawd, he has won the $10,000 prize!" and he came down from his platform. Soon I was surrounded by a gang. But I refused the money, saying, "It belongs to the other fellow!" The [house man] said that only the one who threw it could get the grand prize, but he added, "Before I pay you, you must show me that you had the money to pay and could have paid if you had lost." I looked them all over and said, "It will be a cold day when I show any of you crooks any money." And I walked out. I found out later that the game was to get the winner of the $10,000 prize to show his money. Then one of the mob would grab it and rush out the back door. If the victim followed, he found only a bare yard surrounded by a high tight board fence. And that was the end of his bank-roll.

The tenderfoot who landed on the tidewater beach of Skagway rarely had the opportunity of getting as far as the 303 before falling victim to one or the other of Soapy's ubiquitous agents. Some of the gang traveled on the ships up from Seattle, posing as agents of nonexistent transportation companies and soliciting orders for delivery of the gold-rushers' property in Skagway. On landing, the victim would be rushed to a saloon, drugged and robbed. When he revived, the newcomer would be presented immediately with a demand for "delivery charges." Being broke, he couldn't comply and would be stripped of his food and supplies as well as his money; and there was nothing to do but beg his way home.

For those who escaped his agents on shipboard, Soapy established a "Bureau of Information," "Telegraph Office" and "United States Army Recruiting Station."

Innocent cheechakos would wander into the Bureau of Information seeking advice on the routes inland. Instead they were pumped for such statistics as how much money and supplies they were bringing in, steered to a hotel room or saloon (if they admitted to being well heeled) and quickly relieved of their possessions. The Telegraph Office was designed to snare the many homesick men who were yearning to get in touch with their families. It advertised "wires to anywhere in the United States for $5." The innocent would send his wire, and a few hours later would receive a collect reply, which also cost $5. Sometimes it would contain a request for money which the Telegraph Office was only too glad to transmit. Few of its clientele ever learned that there were no telegraph facilities out of Skagway. At the Army Recruiting Station, established when patriotic fervor was rising over the coming war with Spain, applicants were ordered to strip for a physical examination in the outer room. While the "Army surgeon" examined them inside, their clothes were looted by the surgeon's confederates. If the victimized patriot was lucky, he might have enough clothes to cover himself when he left the place. If he complained, he stood a good chance of being shot and his body thrown into the sea.

While these various rackets were prospering, Soapy still kept his hand in the shell game which had been the modest beginning of his career. He and his cappers would go out on the White Pass, their packs loaded with feathers or straw, so that fellow travelers wondered how they managed to leap around the rocky slope, nimbly as mountain goats. Soapy would set up his tripe and keister, gather a crowd around and begin the old flimflam. Thus the Klondikers were pursued almost to the crest of the pass before they were finally free of Soapy and his feather merchants.

Scotty Allan, the noted Alaska pioneer, recalled how Soapy and his men robbed a prospector of his savings of $760 one afternoon. The victim was accompanied by his wife, who went crying into the tents of other prospectors making their way over the White Pass. An indignant crowd of sixty or seventy cornered Soapy that night; he magnanimously "forced" his associates to return the husband's money. The next night the woman was back with a new and equally tearful tale. She confessed that she tried the shell game herself, was allowed to win $1,300 and then lost it all. Again a delegation went to Soapy and demanded the return of the money. "He nearly laughed his head off," Allan recalled. "Unlike most crooks, he had a real sense of humor." With a characteristic gesture, Soapy peeled $1,000 off his roll and gave it to the woman.

But that wasn't the end of it. A few days later Allan came across the husband "wandering around all alone."

"Is your wife ill?" Allan asked him.

"No. Gone. Soapy Smith took her."

"So," Allan concluded, "the scoundrel had won after all."

Curiously enough, this is the only recorded mention of Soapy and any sexual entanglement. Like most confidence men, he regarded woman and liquor as indulgences which, indiscreetly used, could turn the tables on him quicker than an unbribable police chief or an indignant grand jury.

In that same spring of 1898, he was forced to deal with a clergyman not at all to his liking. Instead of coming to Soapy for help, the young preacher delivered fire-eating sermons against the Smith regime on the streets of Skagway and began gathering increasingly appreciative audiences.

Soapy, to the surprise of his followers, proposed that funds be collected to build the parson a log tabernacle. Soapy himself pitched in the first $1,000 and personally browbeat the town's merchants for even larger contributions than those which provided for the Union Church and its organ. By nightfall he had collected $36,000 and turned it over to the amazed preacher.

And by midnight one of Soapy's henchman had held him up and robbed him of the entire fund. This time the money was not returned. Soapy had no benevolence for preachers who thundered out against him.

Another fire-eater similarly disposed of was a temperance lecturer from Portland who had the indelicacy to install himself at the swinging doors of saloons and roar profane denunciations of all who drank. His harangues usually began, "You damned dirty sots are all doomed to rot in hell. . . . " and proceeded from that to the unprintable. After the fanatic had caused several riots outside saloons, Soapy ordered that he be placed—as he was, kicking and screeching—on a steamer back to the States.

In May of 1898 all civilian distractions faded away from Soapy's mind. The battleship *Maine* sank in the harbor of Havana, Cuba. With memories of the glorious volunteer regiments of the War between the States, Soapy immediately announced the organization of the Skagway Guards, mounted riflemen on the pattern of Colonel Leonard Wood's and Lieutenant Colonel Theodore Roosevelt's Rough Riders. Colonel Jefferson R. Smith, of course, would be in command. Its ranks were quickly filled, partly from his own gang, partly from other patriots who had lost their money in Alaska and were looking for a free ride back to the States.

Soapy drilled his regiment night and day, and informed the War Department that the Skagway Guards were ready for active duty. Edward F. Cahill, a San Francisco newspaperman, visited Skagway that spring and was impressed by Soapy's patriotism. Cahill wrote:

The famous Soapy Smith is not a dangerous man. He is not a desperado. He is not a scoundrel. He is not a criminal. He will fight to a very good purpose if he must. . . . Cool in the face of danger, absolutely fearless, honorable in the discharge of those obligations he recognizes, generous with his money and ever ready with a helping hand for a man or woman in distress, he bitterly resents the imputation that he is a thief and a vagrant.

Cahill attended a muster of the Guards at which Soapy dramatically warned that they might be called out to defend the coasts of the United States against marauding Spanish fleets (which were actually so decrepit they were hardly capable of leaving their harbors). He quoted Soapy as declaiming:

Spain will send her battleships to seize our ports, and they will try to capture our ships. But, be damned to them and we'll stake our lives against their plots. They will first attack the Eastern coast. We must help there and then double back to the Pacific Coast. Do you realize our country's danger?

Cahill was so carried away that he wrote a poem, "Skagway Guns!" in honor of the occasion. Its last verse read:

An' in the hist'ry books we'll read the Nation's proudest boast
How Skagway men sent Skagway guns to save the Eastern coast;
It bein' the one town where men made sacrifice sublime,
Because their country couldn't build the coast defense in time.

Soapy became so fervent a patriot, in fact, that he ordered the fake "United States Army Recruiting Station" closed at once.

It may be imagined, therefore, how chagrined and outraged was Colonel Jefferson R. Smith when Secretary of War Russell Alger sent word that the Skagway Guards would not be required for service in the field.

But Soapy salvaged something out of the wreckage of his military plans. He ordained that the Fourth of July, 1898, be "the greatest day ever." On that day, the proudest of his life, Soapy and his regiment paraded down Broadway, with its commander mounted on a splendid white horse. He had distributed peanuts, candy and firecrackers to the town's children and decorated the streets with miles of bunting imported from the States. And Governor Brady had accepted his invitation to be the principal speaker of the occasion.

It was just four days after this triumphant hour that Soapy Smith and his dominion were simultaneously destroyed.

On the morning of July 8, a Scottish miner named J. D. Stewart returned from the Klondike with a moosehide poke containing $2,700 in gold dust. The Reverend Bowers took charge of him and steered him to Soapy's 303. Bowers suggested that Stewart come out to the back yard and "see the eagle." After a look at the eagle, Stewart became suspicious of a crowd of jostling, rough-looking characters who had joined them in the yard and gathered around them. He expressed a desire to return to the bar. There was a sudden melee and someone snatched Stewart's poke and ran.

Stewart hurried to the United States Marshal's office to enter his complaint and was given the usual runaround. He then carried his story of the robbery to a number of prominent citizens. Indignation blazed through the town, although such incidents had occurred countless times before. There is no accounting for the fact that all of a sudden Skagway rose up in its long-delayed wrath. The Vigilance Committee of 101, which had so quickly expired the previous autumn, was even more swiftly revived.

The leadership of the committee was assumed by Frank H. Reid, a civil engineer who had laid out the town and long ago had declared, "If Soapy Smith ever happens on my path I'll put a hole plumb through him."

The Committee of 101 first ordered Soapy to return Stewart's poke. Soapy stalled and told the delegation to return at 4:00 P.M. for his answer. Bluff had carried him through more critical situations. At the appointed hour he told the delegation that he would not return the gold dust, that Stewart had lost it at the gaming tables.

Broadway that afternoon was crowded with angry men suddenly determined to rid themselves of Soapy and his gang. Soapy finally realized that he faced a desperate situation. Rifle in hand, he strode out of the 303 and through a muttering crowd, shouting, "If you fellows have anything to say about me or my friends, you can say it now! We're ready for you! Five hundred armed men are behind me!"

Soapy stalked up one side of Broadway and down the other, silently challenging anyone to speak out against him. No one did.

The Committee of 101 announced it would meet at eight o'clock that night on the Juneau wharf to take immediate and presumably violent action against the local underworld. Four men, including Frank Reid, volunteered to guard the approaches to the meeting place.

Meanwhile, at the 303 Soapy brooded over the swift evaporation of his power and influence. In one day, less than twelve hours, the town had risen against him. And his many confederates had scurried for cover; not one of them rallied around Soapy, who had protected them while they prospered. Gambling houses, dance halls and whorehouses closed up and prepared for trouble. Vigilante action was still the most fearsome of prospects on any Western frontier.

Soapy stood alone in that hour, a bitter and raging outcast.

At the bar of the 303, still clutching his rifle, Soapy told his partner John Clancy that he intended to go to the Committee of 101's meeting and face them down alone. Clancy tried to dissuade him but Soapy roughly brushed him aside.

"All right," Clancy snarled, "go ahead and go to hell, then."

Possibly they were prophetic words.

Soapy strode down to the wharf where the vigilantes were meeting.

Reid loomed out of the lingering summer twilight and attempted to bar Soapy from the wharf. At last the two men were face to face in a situation from which neither could retreat.

Soapy swung the butt of his rifle at Reid, who drew his pistol and pulled the trigger. The gun misfired. Soapy then fired his rifle, the bullet striking Reid in the groin. As he fell, Reid pulled the trigger again and shot Soapy through the heart.

Soapy, only four days past his glory as commander of the Skagway Guards and grand marshal of the Fourth of July parade, died then and there. Reid died twelve days later. And that night Soapy's craven thugs and cappers and "pallid pimps," after hearing the cry "Soapy's dead," took to their heels, scrambling up mountainsides, hiding in the woods and fleeing before the frenzied mobs which hunted them down. Scores of them were beaten nearly to death, but miraculously not one of them was lynched. A company of United States infantry came over from Dyea on the double and restored a measure of order. A few days later many of Soapy's henchmen were placed aboard the steamer *Tartar* bound for the States; others were sent to prison, and a few managed to escape but never to return to Skagway.

After twenty years of diligent criminality, Soapy died broke, his takings and winnings given away and squandered to the last dollar. All that remained of him, beside the mellowing memories of the people who met him, for good or evil, from Denver to Skagway, are a few mementoes in the Pullen Museum in Skagway, including a set of iron knuckles and a poker table with its "accommodator" slit through which Soapy improved his luck.

Both Smith, the villain, and Reid, the hero, were buried at the foot of Reid's Falls. Reid's grave is neglected, so quickly is a good deed extinguished in a naughty world. But Soapy's grave is visited by every tourist who comes to Skagway. It is the sort of thing that would have made Soapy's gray eyes light up with sardonic laughter.

4

~~~

Slammerkins in Long Underwear

THE LATE VICTORIAN WOMAN, especially in America, was emerging from centuries of confinement in her male-dominated home. In the United States, she was still twenty years away from the privilege of voting, but she had become emancipated in many other ways, having earned the right of equality by sharing the hardships and dangers of the frontier and having already placed herself on that unique self-elevating pedestal which was to raise her higher and higher through the years. American women of all types, aspirations and social backgrounds simply refused to be shut out of the Klondike stampede. They ranged in moral stature from Diamond-Tooth Gertie to lady missionaries; in social standing from the daughter-in-law of the Secretary of the Treasury to "Diamond Lil" Davenport of the mining camps. In other gold rushes, of course, there had been a secondary wave of prostitutes, dance-hall girls and adventuresses. The Klondike saw, as well, the emancipated woman determined to show the world that she was equal to any man. Many were frankly out to enrich themselves, others to help establish a civilization, find a husband, seek adventure, try for a career that might be denied them in the more stodgy atmosphere Outside.

There was no doubt of their welcome. Many male gold-rushers may have taken off mostly to get away from their womenfolk but the balance found life in the North Country almost unbearably bleak without women of one kind or another. One of the first Klondikers to return to the States with a bulging poke, John J. McKay, made that vividly apparent when he told a newspaper interviewer:

Any woman, innocent or full of guile, can become a bride, with a wedding present of thousands of dollars from the happy groom, within thirty minutes after she lands at the creeks. There is but one lady in town who is not married and she has refused every single man in Dawson City. And they have knelt before her with uplifted hands full of gold. She wears short skirts, carries an umbrella, and wants to vote.

Wilson Mizner, no outstanding respecter of womanhood himself, said that they could expect "a respect that amounted to adulation" and that "any woman of any kind whatever was treated with tolerant friendship. . . . Everything was measured by performance for both men and women. . . ." Spinsters all over the United States thrilled to rumor and report concerning the vulnerability of the Klondikers.

The bitterest woman hater in the stampede could see for himself that emancipation was making terrible inroads on man's estate. On the first return trip of the steamer *Excelsior,* with the vanguard of gold-rushers, a number of women somehow obtained passage and were seen clustered at the rail, clutching bouquets and novels and tear-stained handkerchiefs.

On an Alaska-bound voyage of the steamer *Amur* in 1897, among the 500 passengers crowded into accommodations for 160, were fifty "sporting women," as Edward E. P. Morgan described them, "some of them young and comely, but most of them mature, experienced, hard, bold-faced, strident harpies with morals looser than ashes." Because they were disappointed at not being able to "ply their trade" on the crowded ship, the "fractious and unhappy" bawds railed at the officers and crew and snarled obscenities at their fellow passengers.

One of the loudest complainers was a veteran trull named Big Annie, who was finally calmed down by one of the six clergymen aboard, a kindly old man, who told her: "Indeed it's shameful, the conditions aboard this ship. But try to bear it. We'll all be in Skagway in little more than a week, and once there you'll see that things will be a whole lot better for you and the other girls."

Big Annie was so amazed to hear these words coming from a man of the cloth, who seemed to be saying that a licentious life ashore was preferable to a continent life aboard ship, that her uproarious complaints were finally stilled. Others who heard the clergyman's comforting words were unable to decide whether he "spoke in earnest in a well-meant effort to bring peace and quiet to the harassed ship" or whether he was "perpetrating a bit of sly irony."

On the trails north from Dyea and Skagway the growing number of women showed as much determination and ingenuity as the men in striking for their goal. One stout lady was observed packing her outfit over Chilkoot Pass with a train of six Angora goats. On that wretched route to the Klondike, that first summer of the stampede, men began falling by the way as an epidemic of spinal meningitis spread under frightfully unhygenic conditions. No man in that gold-frenzied horde wanted to halt and care for the ill or even bury the dead; the disease was catching, the best claims were being staked out on the creeks inland, and nobody could afford to be caught on the trail when autumn came. It was the women who risked their lives and their prospects of wealth by staying behind and caring for the meningitis victims in a log hospital.

Despite the suffragette parades and the growing feminist spirit among American women, matrimony was the career that attracted many of them to the Klondike. They marveled at the well-publicized adventures of "the bride of the Klondike," the former Ethel Bush who became the wife of Clarence J. Berry. Berry went to the Yukon in 1894, prospected fruitlessly for a year and returned to the States to marry his fiancée. Ethel furnished a cabin for them at Forty Mile and shared her husband's hardships. When the first discoveries were made near by, Berry staked a claim, Forty Above Discovery, on the Bonanza, where the pay dirt was thin indeed. Then he bought half a claim, Five Above Discovery, on the Eldorado. Here he washed out $130,000 in one season, including a nugget weighing almost one pound and worth $231, one of the largest ever found in the Klondike. What enchanted women back home even more was Ethel's casual description to a reporter in San Francisco, when she and her husband came Outside for a vacation, of how she wandered over the Eldorado claim picking up nuggets as aimlessly as a woman gathering flowers on a hillside and collecting $10,000 worth to take home as souvenirs.

Another enticing set of statistics to the feminine mind, especially to spinsters, was that there were less than 100 women to 5,000 men in Dawson, which was supposed to be teeming with eligible millionaires, at the beginning of the rush. Charlotte Smith, a New England sociologist, proposed to a shipowner that she would gather 4,000 unmarried women in New England towns if he would provide passage to the Klondike for them. "While these women will offer the comforts and affections of home to lonely miners, it will also be a godsend for them. They are living under such wretched conditions in the mill towns," she said. The shipowner declined the opportunity to play Cupid on such a vast scale.

Matrimonial agencies offered their services in a less academic manner. They sold thousands of lists of "wealthy gentlemen," at ten cents a copy, to "poor girls looking for rich husbands." There were also "matrimonial papers" which carried photographs and descriptions of women looking for husbands, and these were read by the Klondikers in larger numbers than any of the more sedate periodicals coming from the States.

"The Heart in Hand" was especially popular among miners at the Sulphur Creek camp, it has been recorded. Two partners agreed that they would send for one wife, who would serve them both as cook and housekeeper but only her husband in the more intimate wifely duties. Together they chose the prospective wife and sent for her. One of them met her in Dawson and immediately married her and brought her to Sulphur Creek. It might have been expected that the other partner, who shared their home, would demand more than his meals and laundry, but he behaved with perfect propriety.

The arrangement worked beautifully until an interloper appeared. He was a husky young man living in the same camp, who, her husband and his partner soon learned, had taken to visiting the wife while they were out working in the diggings. One day the interloper persuaded the wife to elope with him, and they were well on their way to Dawson when the husband learned of the elopement and began following their trail. By the time he caught up with the pair, they had already begun quarreling because the ungallant fellow forced her to haul the sleigh containing their belongings. She was weeping when her husband advanced on them with a bellow of rage. He drew his revolver, told his wife to climb onto the sleigh and forced his rival to haul the whole cargo back to camp, yelling "Mush!" with considerable relish all the way home. A miners' court was convened immediately and handed down its decision: the home wrecker was given an hour to get out of camp.

Other women took more direct means of reaching a suitable husband in the Klondike. A twenty-year-old New York girl wrote the editor of the *Nugget* in Dawson, enclosing her fetching photograph and informing him, "I want to apply for a rich husband through your paper. . . . Have the first man that calls to see the photo pay for this ad." Editor Allen displayed the picture outside his office and was swamped with men eager to pay for the ad and obtain the girl's address.

The same editor noted that there were many opportunities along the trail for unmarried women. A case in point was that of Minnie Berrell, who was on her way to the Klondike in the spring of 1898 with her mother. They were helped over the portages by Abraham Gordon, who had come to the Yukon in '94, staked out several promising claims there and on the American side of the Alaska-Yukon border and had returned home in '97 for a vacation but "escaped all the blandishments of the fair sex." The buxom Minnie's distress found a weak spot in Gordon's defenses, or, as Allen wrote with a flourish, "Cupid is a cunning imp and delights in the roar of a cascade as much as in the perfumed flower gardens of milder climes." When Gordon, Minnie and her mother arrived in Dawson, the young couple was immediately married at the Episcopalian Church.

Other brides had to be content with ceremonies that made up in picturesqueness what they lacked in formality. The *Yukon Press* of Circle City recorded one such marriage involving Frank McGillis, a prospector, and Aggie Dalton, a schoolteacher, who somehow met and decided on matrimony at the mouth of the Dahl River in November 1898. A trapper named French Joe, who apparently established a sort of Gretna Green in the Arctic wilderness, married them in verse as dubious artistically as it was in legality. Aggie's marriage lines were as follows:

> "We have no preacher and we have no ring,
> It makes no difference, it's all the same thing."

And Frank responded:

> "I'll love and protect her—this maiden so frail—
> From those sourdough stiffs on the Koyukuk Trail."

French Joe then proclaimed:

> "For two dollars apiece in cheechako money,
> I unite this couple in matrimony.
> He be a rancher; she be a teacher,
> I do the job up, just as well as a preacher."

Many of the ladies, with feminist pride, headed for the Klondike with sterner ambitions than mere matrimony, however. Phalanxes of maiden ladies bent on professional or business careers were forming all over the United States shortly after the news of the gold strikes. There was a Woman's Klondike Club organized in Chicago in the spring of 1898, with the participants asked to raise $10,000 capital. Its leader, Miss Lillian Lemmon, explained to a Chicago *Tribune* reporter:

"Miss Florence King is a lawyer. Mademoiselle Napier is planning to buy mines. Miss Mattie Hunter is a shrewd businesswoman who will find an ample field for her talents in a commercial way. As for myself, I intend to take along a hectograph and get out a small daily paper. Then I will conduct a sort of mining exchange where transfers of claims may be negotiated. We are now looking for a capable woman physician to join us."

The reporter brashly asked Miss Lemmon, "Aren't you going to look for husbands among the miners who have made the lucky finds?"

"Sir!" she snorted. "We are businesswomen, not adventuresses."

From all the available evidence, however, the Woman's Klondike Club did not manage to set out for the Klondike. Dr. Hannah Gould of New York was more successful, advertising for 150 widows and other women who wanted to make new lives for themselves in the Yukon. Dr. Gould planned to set up a hospital in Dawson, as well as a clubhouse for miners and a brokerage. Among those accompanying Dr. Gould on the steamer *City of Columbia* were a sculptress named Mrs. Keuhne Beveridge and Mrs. A. W. Little of Kentucky who "has money and is going for sightseeing only," according to press accounts. Among the more determined ladies aboard the *City of Columbia* was Miss Nettie Hoven of New York, who worked for her passage to Seattle, then boarded the steamer *Sovereign* at Seattle. The *Nugget,* whose reporters met the ladies on the wharves of Dawson, described Miss Hoven with enthusiasm.

It is doubtful if any other woman had a more varied experience than Miss Hoven has been through since leaving New York on the 16th of December last. She is not a very large woman but she is full of pluck and determination, and her black eyes snap in a way that proves very clearly her ability to take care of herself.

Even pluckier, perhaps, was Mrs. George Black, who became one of the most distinguished women in the Yukon. Her family had appointed her to journey to the Klondike on their behalf to investigate the legality of a claim which was supposed to make them all wealthy. Already the mother of two children and carrying her third child, she was deserted by her husband on the eve of their departure for the Far North. The prospects of danger and hardship may have sent him in full flight from his determined wife, but she continued her journey. Alone and pregnant, she survived the perils of Skagway, the steep assault on Chilkoot Pass and the swirling menace of White Horse Rapids. It was obvious by then that her family knew what it was doing in sending that frail creature into the wilderness rather than one of the outwardly stalwart male relatives. Within six months of her arrival in Dawson, she found that the family's claim was false; saw the death of her own hopes of becoming suddenly and easily rich, and, with the temperature seventy degrees below zero outside her cabin, gave birth to her third child—supposedly the first white child born on the Klondike.

Then she set about mending her fortunes; she established a lumber mill and made a success of it. And her journey to the Klondike turned out happily in another respect, when she married a Dawson lawyer, George Black, who became commissioner of the territory and later speaker of the Canadian House of Commons. During World War I, when he was commanding the Yukon Infantry on the Western Front, she was elected to his seat in Commons.

In her autobiography, *My Seventy Years,* Mrs. Black gave an intimate glimpse of how Victorian fashions tormented the lady Klondikers—"I cursed my hot, high buckram collar, my tight heavily boned corsets, my full bloomers which I had to hitch up with every step." Less fashionable women like Nellie Cashman dressed in mackinaw coats and trousers, but Mrs. Black had been reared in a gentler, if less comfortable, tradition.

Of all the women who ventured into the Klondike, Kate Mulrooney was probably the shrewdest and most successful. No other woman could boast that she came out of the gold fields with a fortune and a hand-kissing French count.

With nothing to help her along the path of Klondike wealth except intense ambition, a persuasive tongue and the fiscal talents of a Levantine trader, she managed to parlay a back-country hostelry into a collection of mining and real-estate properties. It was the humble roadhouse, a cross between an inn and a flophouse, that made Countess Kate's fortune. The roadhouse of pre-Klondike times provided the roaming prospector or trader with a bunk, a few blankets usually teeming with receptive wild life and a meal of bacon, bread and beans. With the gold rush, and under the more fastidious influence of Miss Mulrooney, the roadhouse became a cleaner and more comfortable stopping place for the traveler.

She came to the Klondike in the autumn of 1897, a handsome, healthy young woman with little nonsense about her, except when it served her purpose. The only photograph extant of her in that period shows a resolute face staring challengingly at the camera. To neighboring miners, according to the roving newspaper correspondent, Frederick Palmer, she was a friendly creature with "a bit of an Irish brogue and the tongue of a lawyer." She had been stewardess aboard the *City of Topeka,* but jumped ship in an Alaskan port when news came of the gold discoveries inland.

Miss Mulrooney settled down at Grand Forks, the confluence of Eldorado and Bonanza creeks, surely the richest intersection of waterways in the world.

When she announced that she was building a roadhouse there, most of the miners laughed at her; the kindlier among them tried to talk her out of the idea by pointing out that no one would patronize a roadhouse in that forsaken wilderness. Miss Mulrooney could foresee that Grand Forks would soon be the scene of a stampede, however, and she continued building her hostel with the somewhat pitying help of miners working up the creeks.

She told her sympathizers, with a strong dose of irony, "If any of you were hungry or thirsty, you wouldn't think of buying a drink or a meal up here. You'd walk sixteen miles to Dawson and back for it, wouldn't you? And the boys going over the Divide to Dominion or Sulphur, when they break the journey at the Forks, would hang up in a tree overnight before they'd sleep in a hotel, wouldn't they?"

Miss Mulrooney's roadhouse was both clean and reasonable, and she preserved a fair amount of order in the place. The Dawson restaurants charged $5 for "half a meal," as Palmer observed, but Miss Mulrooney served meat—canned mutton, beef or ham— and "the fixin's" for $3.50. She kept a bowl of applesauce on the table for her patrons to help themselves. The sauce was made from dried apples but was accounted a blessing in that scurvy-ridden country. In the common room a potbellied stove cast its red glow and its blessed heat over the half-frozen miner just in from the trail. Somebody played "After the Ball Is Over" on the mouth organ. Whisky and cigars were available, if the prospector was well-heeled, and there was the prospect of a clean bunk.

The bar and dining room were located on the ground floor of

her log establishment. Upstairs were the tiers of bunks, curtained off to provide an unaccustomed blessing of privacy for the sleepers. There were no sheets, but the bunks were free of insect life.

Andrew, the bartender, wore a white shirt and tie, and his manners were suitable for the quietest club bar in the East. Miss Mulrooney, it was to be observed, had a weakness for soft-spoken gentlemanly types. Andrew, Palmer said, "was as much out of place as the average bartender would be in a chair of moral philosophy."

The amiable Andrew was of little use in maintaining order in the roadhouse, which occasionally was the scene of a heroic drinking bout by a miner celebrating his strike. When some brawny fellow went rampaging through the place, it was always the proprietress who planted herself in his destructive path and blarneyed him out of his uproarious mood. Correspondent Palmer wondered how she managed to maintain order without resort to the bungstarter, and she primly explained, "I always appeal to their better instincts."

It was only a matter of time before she was branching out from the rude hostel at Grand Forks. She built the Fairview House in Dawson, the first hotel in the Yukon to provide sheets on its beds, and she began investing in mining properties. Some of the bigger operators, as a token of their esteem for the capable Irishwoman, included her in their deals for the syndicated development of claims on Eldorado and Bonanza creeks. Alexander MacDonald, the biggest independent in the gold fields, who bought into forty different claims on which other men did the work for a share of the profits, offered a guiding hand in the tricky business of mining investment. It was a relationship that later ended in acrimony, with MacDonald suing Miss Mulrooney for $200,000 and charging "breaches of trust and promise."

One of her better-paying properties was a bench claim on Cheechako Hill just above George Carmack's Discovery Claim on Bonanza Creek. Palmer said her miner friends often gave her "inside information" on the development of new fields before the stampedes began, even after she moved into Dawson and began assuming grander airs than when she was soft-soaping drunks into behaving themselves in her bar.

Prosperity worked a sad transformation in Kate's personality and character, and she was suspected of nurturing social ambitions, now that she was becoming a wealthy woman.

She was no longer the simple unaffected woman who laughed off Frederick Palmer's suggestion that if she went back to the States "the women's clubs would be making a heroine of you as an example of what their sex can do." To this she had replied, "They wouldn't if they heard I sold whisky. Besides, there's nothing new about me. I'm old-fashioned."

Hard-headed as she was, she fell head over heels for the suave and worldly Count Carboneau when he appeared in Dawson as a salesman for Messieurs Legasse et Freres, the French wine merchants. Buxom Kate had resisted the blandishments of the miners at Grand Forks and the businessmen of Dawson, but her heart fluttered every time the Count bent over her hand. To the surprise and chagrin of more than one Klondiker, she married this lily-handed aristocrat, who had little to offer besides his charming self. Even his claim to a title was disputed. According to Mike Mahoney, "the Count was recognized by an old pal who remembered the titled aristocrat as a barber who had often shaved him on Rue St. Denis in Montreal." This, however, may have been a canard circulated by men jealous of the cushy marriage he had arranged for himself. There was no doubt that the Count Carboneau was a "slick article," as the saying went. Acquiring a taste for the local sporting life, the Count tried to buy Mike Mahoney's crack dog team and was irked when Mahoney refused to sell. He tried to avenge this affront to his seignorial rights when Mahoney became celebrated for having made the trip from Dawson to Skagway in the record time of ten days. The Count planted a story in the *Nugget* that a man made the same trip on a bicycle in only eight days. Obviously the Count was a man with a resourceful imagination.

No doubt he needed it in dealing with his energetic wife, once the first sweet bloom faded from marriage. Kate, with the continued growth of her holdings, became a rather hard taskmaster to those she employed. Henry F. Woods recalled working for her as a miner at the Cheechako Hill claim and being paid $1 a day. Even at that insignificant pay scale, Woods was fired by the now imperious Kate because the shovel he was using was too small, in her opinion. The Count Carboneau, Woods said, "has always had my sympathy for I am certain that if, indeed, he was a drone, Kate took it out of his hide."

The advertising columns of the *Nugget* were an excellent indication of the range of careers women were finding for themselves in the center of the gold rush. There were the ads of "Lady Typewriters"—stenographers, as they were to be called a few years later—and the business card of Marie Riedeselle, "leading professional masseuse" who promised "lost vitality restored" and the prevention of scurvy, among other things.

Most of the younger career women, however, found the dance halls more congenial than working in offices or stores, despite a certain amount of social ostracism. Wilson Mizner said the women of the Klondike—unlike the men, with millionaires and barflies slapping one another's backs in the saloons—observed very strict caste rules.

The kept ladies ignored the dance-hall girls, no matter what their ability might be. In the dance halls the entertainers who went to the boxes and did a little light finger-lifting as well as dancing with visitors were a privileged set and were very haughty toward the girls who merely danced without thieving. Dollar-a-dance girls, they were called, receiving a cut in dust of whatever their partners drank. Of course, there were the other girls in town who had no particular ability on any dance floor and were what might be termed "weak." Everybody ignored them in the presence of anyone, but they did a land office business, always. They included some of the plainest fancy women imaginable.

Attempts to trespass on the caste rules usually resulted in violence, according to Mizner, and clawing, eye-scratching, hair-pulling fights between lady gold-rushers were one of the more cherished forms of entertainment in the streets of the boom towns. A lass named Bertha the Adder once became incensed with a hapless associate named Seattle Emily, tore off all her clothing in a brawl on the river front, and then chased Emily through Dawson, pelting her with rocks. Another celebrated encounter involved Nellie the Pig—actually a comely young woman, a dance-hall girl, whose uncouth sobriquet was conferred by Klondikers in honor of her turned-up nose, "retrousse" as magazine fiction writers once delighted in describing it—and "The Petite Sisters Pickering," who specialized in toe dancing and ballads. In passing Nellie, the sisters twitched their skirts aside with such a disdainful flourish that Nellie became enraged.

"Smell something quaint?" Nellie demanded.

"We do not," one of the sisters snapped.

"Then there ain't any smell anywhere, you damned ant-eaters."

The Sisters Pickering advanced to attack Nellie from both flanks but ran into such furious resistance that they were unable to manage a pirouette for a month afterward.

One citizen, hearing he had missed this brawl because he had gone stampeding into the tundra on the rumor passed along by another prospector, sought out his news source and thoroughly trounced him in his exasperation.

Two of the more ferocious dance-hall girls, according to Edward

Morgan, who said that most of the early-comers were "coarse-featured hussies" from mining camps on the Alaskan coast, were the Oregon Mare and the Grizzly Bear. Neither of them was beautiful, and their presence in a dance hall was traceable to the fact that men were afraid to turn them down for a drink and a dance, rather than any charm they exuded. When vexed, the Oregon Mare would kick her victim with machinelike rapidity and precision. Since she wore shoes with sharply pointed toes, such a tête-à-tête would leave the subject with an interesting array of cuts, bruises, abrasions and contusions. The Grizzly Bear's technique was also appallingly simple and direct: she was "a mountain of a woman" with biceps like a stevedore and would squeeze her victim until his (or her) ribs cracked and eyes popped out. Her appearance was no less fearsome because of one eye gouged out in a fight.

Morgan described her in action, both romantic and pugilistic, one night in a Dawson dance hall. The orchestra was playing that durable tune, "Casey Would Waltz with a Strawberry Blonde," and the Grizzly Bear whirled in the arms of her partner with "her single orb directed tenderly on his perspiring features." A rival who believed there was a glint of triumph in the Grizzly Bear's eye came at her shrieking and clawing. In a few seconds the whole assemblage was kicking, scratching and slugging—a fight was rarely a private affair in the Klondike. Five minutes later the Mounties came on the run and broke it up, "with no arrests and no casualties, beyond injured feelings."

Whatever the physical perils in defending her honor and dignity, a dance-hall girl received top pay for swinging around the floor with her bearded, heavily booted and often villainously aromatic patrons. The lusty dances of that period, the polkas, quadrilles and waltzes, were also rather wearing, but most of the girls were husky and healthy. "Two-fisted slammerkins in long underwear," as the late Alva Johnston so rousingly phrased it. The dance halls generally paid their girls a salary of at least $50 a week and in addition they received twenty-five cents for every dollar chip spent by their partners. Most girls, therefore, collected about $200 a week.

And there was always the glittering possibility of marrying one of the prospectors who struck it rich out on the creeks. The dance-hall girls had first crack at the newly rich sourdough staggering in from a summer of digging, washing and collecting the fine grains of gold at his claim. There was, for instance, the prospector from Chicago who became so enthusiastic about the charms of one of the girls that he hurled a sack of nuggets at her as she whirled around the dance floor. The golden missile broke her cheekbone. He hovered around during her recovery from this wound and was led to a preacher before he could escape Outside with his treasure.

Not all the dancing girls did that well.

A prospector named Dog-Tooth Harry came back from the creeks bowed down with sacks of dust and nuggets. Ugly as a pickled moose nose, he fell in love with one of the girls in a dance hall. It was a one-sided case of love at first sight. Dog-Tooth Harry proposed marriage, and the girl proposed that he jump into the Yukon. Infuriated, Dog-Tooth Harry carried her to the scales while she bit, scratched and used every epithet at her command. Her admirer calmly noted that she weighed 142 pounds. He calculated that her weight in gold was $24,424, went to a bank and obtained that amount in currency in exchange for some of his gold, and then returned to the girl.

"I will give you your weight in gold, twenty-four thousand four hundred twenty-four dollars, if you will marry me," he announced. He riffled through the bundle of banknotes in his hand.

The girl's face softened, her hands fluttered at her bosom, and she looked up into his ugly face as if he had been transformed into the handsomest matinee idol south of Seattle.

"Why, dearie," she cooed, "of course I'll marry you."

"The hell you will," Dog-Tooth Harry grunted, spun on his heel and marched away sourly triumphant.

Among the more curious feminine specimens cast upon the shores of the Yukon were Calamity Jane, the leathery-faced old terror of Deadwood and Leadville; Nellie Cashman, the toughest of the lady sourdoughs; the swashbuckling laundress of Forty Mile; and a lady who became known as Susie Bluenose. It took an adventurous woman to join the Klondike rush, it took a hardy and determined woman to make her way over the trails to the Yukon interior, and it took a tough-spirited one to stay in the Klondike once she got there. All four of these ladies exemplified in their separate fashions some of the psychological currents that had been stirring in American womanhood since the passage of the frontier from the days of its conquerors to the days of its exploiters.

Calamity Jane, of course, represented the past; she was a living ghost who could not reconcile herself to the white-gloved civilization that had blighted the frontier towns where she had become such a legendary and sometimes terrifying figure. Age and disillusion had caught up with her by the time of the Klondike rush, but she was still eager to find some new place where the churchgoers, the grocers, the mining companies and the women's clubs had not yet assumed control. A reporter for the *Nugget* noted on her arrival in Dawson that she is "as gentle and refined as any of her Eastern sisters." But a second look convinced him that Calamity was not ready for lavender, old lace and a cozy fireside. "There is a suggestion in the steel-blue eyes, however, that would warn the unwary, and a glance at the half-sad face indicates that her life has not been all sunshine." Calamity Jane took a quick look around and decided that the Klondike was not for her; perhaps the Arctic cold got into her aging bones, or perhaps Dawson just wasn't lusty enough for a veteran of Deadwood, South Dakota.

The laundress at Forty Mile was a woman of whom Calamity Jane would undoubtedly have approved. Her husband was a miner and she took in laundry to support herself while he was out on the creeks looking for a claim worth working. One of her patrons was the rather haughty manager of the local post of a big trading company. He put on such lordly airs that he was known at first as the Prince of Alaska, but that did not seem quite adequate so he was dubbed The Pope. One day shortly after the husky laundress received word from her husband that his prospects were vastly improved by a new stretch of creek he was working, the trading-company manager sent back a bundle of laundry and a note complaining that it had not been delivered in "proper condition." The laundress roared, "Tell The Pope to go plumb to hell—Jack's getting forty dollars to the pan now!" From then on, the manager's manner was much less pontifical.

For "Susie Bluenose"—a "lady typewriter" whose real name has been concealed from history—the gold rush was much too boisterous, uncouth and riddled with dissipation. She was the Carrie Nation type, the forerunner of the reformer and crusader later dominant in the women's clubs.

Susie Bluenose showed up at the mission at Golovin Bay to take over the secretarial work, according to the recollections of Jack Hines, "The Minstrel of the Yukon." Near the mission was Nelly Page's roadhouse, an establishment which became the object of Susie's reforming urge. The missionaries had no objection to the boisterous atmosphere exuded by Nelly's place. But Susie, a thirty-ish spinster who always dressed in black and wore a stiff white shirtfront under her furs, took to dropping around nights and frowning on the singing and drinking. First she demanded that, out of respect for the mission, the singers modulate their voices, and Nelly agreed.

Victory only emboldened Susie. Nightly she assumed a position at the end of the bar and delivered temperance lectures. The men tried to ignore her even when she addressed them as "sots," "tosspots," "rumhounds," "soaks" and "alcoholic wretches." She took to buttonholing them and delivering her sermons face to face. When they still tried to pretend she wasn't there, she took to dumping their drinks in the spittoons.

Nelly Page, realizing that she would soon be run out of business unless she took drastic measures, ordered her Indian boys to guard the door and lock it every time they saw Susie coming that way.

That worked splendidly until one night Rex Beach, the future novelist, his partner and two of the Seward Peninsula's principal guardians of the law, United States Commissioner Nudd and United States Marshal Lamont, dropped in for a drinking and singing session.

On this important occasion Nelly's sentinels fell asleep at their post, and Susie managed to breach the defenses. She burst into the barroom and screamed, "Stop that music!" Rex Beach had been plinking away on his mandolin, but Nelly told him to play louder and continued dancing with Marshal Lamont.

Susie jumped up on a chair and shouted, "You blackguards, you roistering scoundrels, you're all going to roast in hell, do you know that?" She leaped off the chair and shouldered her way over to Nelly and grabbed the proprietress by the arm. "Young woman," she hissed, "if this racket is not stopped at once I'm going to have this den of iniquity closed immediately. I am going to report you to the United States Marshal!"

The music, singing and dancing stopped, and there was complete silence in the barroom.

Marshal Lamont disengaged himself from Nelly's arms, marched over to Susie and bowed gallantly.

"I am at your service, madam," he said. "Would you care to dance?"

Susie fled into the night and never again interrupted the merriment at Nelly Page's.

If the men of Golovin Bay had been capable of greater insight, of course, such a brutal end to the reformist aspirations of Susie Bluenose would not have been necessary. They would have realized that a frustrated feminine heart beat beneath that starched white shirtfront and have taken the appropriate, humane measures to unfrustrate it.

Few women in the Klondike ventured from the towns and settlements in actual search for gold, the raw gold that had to be wrested from its frozen nesting places in the earth. There were some prospectors' wives who worked by their husbands' side at the diggings, and there were plenty of other women who prospected in the pockets and pokes of the miners. Nellie Cashman, a proud, tough and independent woman, was one of the few who ventured alone into the solitudes. A small figure in mackinaw, trousers, boots and fur cap, she had first appeared in the Western mining camps; no one knew her life before that. She was among the first to arrive in the Klondike, and one of the early sourdoughs remembered her being turned out of a trail camp after supper because the gallant stampeders feared for her reputation—or theirs—if she was allowed to remain in camp after dark. Edward Morgan described her as "a lone undaunted figure in the wilderness, who had surmounted all the obstacles with which nature had beset her path, and had talked out of existence all those put in her way by men." Many of the men, of course, resented the idea of a woman being able to live and work as they did.

In the winter stampede to the Kluahane district, she was one of the first to hit the trail. The perils and hardships of the Arctic winter were nothing compared to a calamitous night she spent in a tiny warm spot of civilization at Stony Creek, she said afterward. She arrived at the Stony Creek roadhouse when it was almost dusk, dined off moose and rabbit meat and washed it all down with a few quarts of hot tea. Night and sleep settled over the little roadhouse. A squaw snored behind the stove. Two male stampeders occupied the two lower bunks. Nellie was too tired to climb up to the top bunk. So she curled up on her blankets in a corner of the room. Around midnight another traveler appeared at the door; he was a robust fellow weighing close to three hundred pounds, so weary that he refused food, and climbed into the top bunk and rested his bulk on the canvas stretched tightly between two poles that constituted a mattress.

A few hours later the snoring rose to such a pitch and volume that the two sleepers in the lower bunks arose grouchily and decided to hit the trail rather than listen to it. Nellie and the squaw were awakened by their parting curses and took over the two lower bunks.

Toward dawn the fat man in the upper bunk decided to turn over, and that was too much for the tortured canvas beneath him. It gave way like a flooded dike on the Yukon in spring. The fat man hurtled down on Nellie Cashman; the canvas bottom of her bunk split also, and together they descended on the sleeping squaw. God knows what dreams were thus simultaneously disrupted. But the violent awakening, amid a smothering pile of thrashing limbs and blankets and furs, was too much for their sleep-clouded minds. They tore out of the cabin, all three of them, screaming and heading in different directions, as if ten thousand devils were in hot pursuit. Nellie never saw her two companions again, but years later she said, "I can still hear that squaw shrieking—it was the worst moment I ever knew in the Yukon."

This is but a sampling of the women who left their homes in the States for the Yukon; there were others more saintly, more depraved, more spectacular, more beautiful, and they were to exhibit themselves in the whole raffish pageant, as in this account of it, later in its unfolding.

5

Squaw Men
and Siwash Maidens

IF MANY of the "slammerkins in long underwear" were disappointed in their hopes of finding a husband among the goldrushers, they could reasonably blame the rival attractions of the Indian women, full breeds, half-breeds, three-quarter breeds and quarter-breeds, who seemed to many Americans, particularly those who had fled from nagging wives or possessive mothers, to have a most fetching amiability. If their attitude toward frequent baths and their fondness for such delicacies as boiled fish heads and pickled moose nose were a little difficult to understand at first, their submissiveness and their native charm more than balanced such racial characteristics. A trinket or a bolt of bright cloth would make them as happy as a woman with a diamond ring back in the States. They had a childlike trust, at least until experience taught them not to believe everything a Caucasian told them or promised them. They were utterly innocent of any yearning for Women's Suffrage or even the faintest knowledge of how they suffered under the Double Standard; they agitated neither for the right to vote nor for a new dress, and they had been taught to be complaisant toward their menfolk from the day they began to toddle. Thus there were frequent "certificates of marriage" published in the newspapers of the Yukon Territory, such as the following:

I, Siwash George, King of the Klondike, at Dawson, Yukon Territory, do hereby certify that, on this 27th day of September A.D., 1898, at 11 P.M., in the city of Dawson, Yukon Territory, Lewis Haber, aged 24 years, and born in New Orleans, and now residing in Dawson, and Malemute Annie, born in Moosehide and now living in Lousetown, were united in marriage before me and in my presence, by Bishop Bumpus, who is authorized by law to perform such a ceremony.

SIWASH GEORGE
King of the Klondike
Per Cupid.*

Not all such ceremonies, of course, were so weightily formal as to be performed in the presence of the "King of the Klondike, Per Cupid," with the highest prelate of his realm, the good Bishop Bumpus, presiding. Many of them were solemnized by a hand-shake or a tilt of the whisky bottle with the bride's father or brother.

On the whole, relations between the invading whites and the Indians were quite amicable, marked by much more tolerance and humanity than were shown by the settlers in the American West.

There was occasional bloodshed, but no such massacres as oc-curred among the winter lodges of the Plains Indians and the border settlements of the whites thirty years before. Arthur Tread-well Walden, the Yukon "dog puncher," told of an incident that happened at the headwaters of the Tanana River and might have led to serious consequences but for a certain amount of forebear-ance on both sides. The Indians attacked two prospectors, killing one and wounding the other. "In the old days in the West,"

---

* *The Klondike Nugget,* Dawson, September 28, 1898.

Walden said, "the Indians would have been massacred, making it a war and calling for retaliation." Instead, the whites in the vicinity surrounded the Indian village and called on the tribesmen to produce the murderer. The Indians were recalcitrant, so the whites seized the chief of the tribe, placed a rope around his neck and proceeded to hang him. While he was still kicking, the Indians pushed forward a crippled man and identified him as the murderer. Their chief was cut down while still alive and the cripple was hanged in his place. The white men knew the cripple was not the killer, and the Indians knew they knew, but "the psychology of the Indian made it seem only justice." Morally and ethically, such methods were entirely reprehensible, but they saved much conflict between the two races. It was also true that the Siwashes and other Yukon tribes were not nearly so proud and ferocious as those of the Great Plains; and perhaps by that time all Indians knew the futility of resisting "progress."

Generally the whites and the Indians were on excellent if hardly equal terms. The American mania for dancing was one of the reasons for a growing intimacy between the races. The "squaw dances," with bearded miners swinging their solemn Siwash lasses to the strains of Viennese music, may have been incongruous, especially for the gentlemen who composed them for the gallant Hussars, the high-nosed noblemen and their proud ladies; but they helped pass the long Arctic nights. The dance craze was so infectious, Walden recalls, that on a Yukon steamer the Eskimo deck hands were recruited to act as partners for the passengers. (Nowadays this would seem to hint at a streak of lavender, but actually Klondike-style dancing was more an athletic contest, in which a contestant could come out with splintered shins and broken toes.) Walden said:

As it was beneath the dignity of a male Eskimo to impersonate a woman, the white men had to tie bandanna handkerchiefs around their heads and be the women. This was rather amusing as the Eskimos ran from four to five feet high and one of the lawyers aboard was six feet seven inches tall.

Walden noted that there was no jealousy "as a white man knows it" in the Indian character. He described a dance at Circle City where there were not enough white women for partners so a number of Indians were invited.

Someone drew a chalk line down the middle of the floor, and the squaws danced on one side and the white women on the other. The men, seeing the joke, danced first on one side of the line and then on the other. The squaws danced very well, but always did so with perfectly sober faces, and, as it was beneath the dignity of the bucks to dance at all, they sat around the walls of the hall in silence.

The meeting of white men and Siwash maidens at dances soon led to greater intimacy, and since many of the "half-breed" girls possessed an exotic beauty that often follows a mingling of the races, hundreds of them were soon married, more or less formally, some of them in ceremonies performed at the Catholic missions, to the stampeders from the States. Canadians, having inherited the English tradition of staying clear of any form of marriage contract with the "natives," engaged in less permanent relations with the Indian girls. There was a certain amount of social stigma attached to such marriages, and "squaw man" was a fighting word next to none. But at least a man's Indian in-laws didn't look down on him: they not only welcomed the white men as kinfolk but bragged about their Caucasian sons-in-law and brothers-in-law and treated them with great and continuing respect, no matter how seedy and disreputable they might seem to other white men. Walden recorded that even a few Englishmen, forgetting the imperial tradition, married Siwash girls. One was an Oxford-educated remittance man, "a younger son who could quote Greek poetry by the hour when he was liquored up." His squaw dyed her hair blond in his honor, and they seemed quite happy together.

Another squaw man, who had settled down before the gold rush to a long and lazy existence of salmon fishing and allowing his amiable relatives-in-law to support him when even fishing became too tedious, was one of the founding fathers, quite by accident, of the Klondike stampede.

George Carmack, born in California to a forty-niner and his bride, jumped a windjammer in an Alaskan port in 1885, moved inland until inertia overtook him and settled down with a tribe of Siwash in the Lake Bennett country. He was a gawky, slouching fellow with a drooping mustache and a large nose; even the few photographs of him still in existence catch the indolence which was his leading characteristic. He seems to have had barely enough energy to remain erect for the photograph.

Several years before gold was discovered, he married a beautiful Indian girl named Kate, who had large dark eyes, a broad serene forehead and a graceful figure. Her brother, Tagish Charlie, an amiable loafer, and Skookum Jim, another tribesman, became his boon companions. In the Siwash dialect, Skookum means strong, and Skookum Jim won his nickname by trotting over Chilkoot Pass with 160 pounds of bacon on his back. Skookum Jim rarely used his strength, however, in hard labor. A photograph of him shows a villainous-looking character with a sinister mustache, high cheekbones and narrow menacing eyes; by the time he posed for the photographer he had also acquired an incongruous costume of tailored suit, high boots and glittering watch chain draped across his vest. Actually he was a good-natured fellow, with just a little more energy than Carmack and Tagish Charlie.

By the summer of 1896, Carmack, his bride and their shabby

retinue had moved north to the Klondike region and were encamped at Caribou Crossing, not far from the future site of Dawson City.

Early that summer Bob Henderson, a young prospector, handsome in a melancholy fashion, worked along the Indian River and
its tributaries. He found nuggets and dust in the beds of several
creeks and hurried to the Canadian government's recording office
at Forty Mile to register his claims with Captain Constantine. That
official informed him he could stake out only one discovery claim,
500 feet of creek bottom from rimrock to rimrock. Henderson
chose a claim on Gold Bottom and on his way back to start working it he came across Carmack, Tagish Charlie and Skookum Jim,
who were making a pass at salmon fishing.

Henderson felt sorry for them, he later explained, and told
himself, "There's a poor devil. Guess I ought to tell him about
what I found."

Henderson followed his generous impulse and told Carmack
there was gold farther inland from the Yukon. Carmack couldn't
get very excited; rumors of gold discoveries had been circulating
through the country for years, and nobody had got very rich yet.
Still Carmack and his two companions trailed along behind Henderson.

One September day the trio trudged along what later became
known as Bonanza Creek. The summer sun was warm and the
blood flowed sluggishly through Carmack's veins. He yawned and
suggested that they lie down and rest for a few hours. He and
Tagish Charlie stretched out in the grass and soon were fast asleep,
but Skookum Jim, with his fateful bit of extra energy, decided to
pass the time by panning for gold. He woke up his companions
with the news that there was indeed gold dust in the creek bottom.

On September 24, 1896, Carmack and his friends appeared before
Captain Constantine at Forty Mile and recorded their three claims
on Bonanza Creek, the Discovery Claim for Carmack (another

instance of Indian generosity toward the white man, no matter how undeserving) and Numbers One and Two Below Discovery for Skookum Jim and Tagish Charlie. With them they brought a Winchester shell packed with gold dust.

After registering his claim, Carmack, with his typical muddle-headedness, proceeded to get drunk in all the saloons of Forty Mile and babbled to everyone who would listen that the creeks were crusted with gold along the Indian River. Few paid any attention at first, then with a simultaneous impulse every ambulatory citizen in the region stampeded to Bonanza.

(And they neglected to share their information with Henderson, who spent a backbreaking summer panning out a mere $600 in gold dust. By the time Henderson heard that the ungrateful Carmack and hundreds of stampeders had staked out all the claims on Bonanza and Eldorado creeks, it was much too late for him to grab even a mouse's share of the proceeds. All Henderson got out of his discovery of Klondike gold was a small pension from the Canadian government. As a Dawson newspaper commented later, "And now Carmack has money to throw at the birds, while Henderson owns practically nothing but a townsite at the mouth of McQuestion Creek."*)

Carmack and his partners soon wearied of scraping gold from the creek bottom and sold out for a reputed $40,000. That was the beginning of a glorious toot for Carmack, Kate and her brother, who made a triumphal tour of the Pacific coast along with Skookum Jim. Kate, child of nature, irritated hotel managers in the States by blazing a trail to her room by nicking the banisters and other woodwork with her fish-skinning knife; it was the only way she could find her way home. The coastal cities were becoming accustomed to uproarious Klondikers scattering their profits. Car-

* *The Klondike Nugget,* September 28, 1898.

mack and Party outdid them all, particularly in San Francisco and Seattle, where they leaned out of their hotel windows and threw money to the scrambling populace. The Seattle *Post-Intelligencer* described one such incident:

Yesterday, unheralded and unannounced, George Carmack and his Indian wife and brothers amused themselves by throwing money from the top floor of the Seattle Hotel. In a few moments there was a scramble that would have put a college cane crush in the shade. . . . Men dived from the walks and off passing street-cars. . . . Butcher boys and teamsters hurled themselves in the air from their seats. . . . Hats were broken or lost . . . faces were bruised and bleeding, coats were torn and soiled.

All this time Carmack and his native Alaskan relatives were splitting themselves with laughter in their apartment at the top of the hotel. Having nothing but money, they knew of no better way of becoming popular and having amusement than by distributing it in the streets. The idea is amusing, but decidedly uncommon in Seattle.

By 1900 Carmack and Party were broke, one and all. The only residue of their fortune was a necklace of nuggets that Kate wore until her death during World War I. Carmack drifted back to the States without Kate and died in poverty several years later in New York. Kate was granted a pension by the Canadian government and all the rest of her life talked about her hilarious tour of the Pacific Coast. Along with his sister, Tagish Charlie returned to Caribou Crossing. As a reward for his share in the discovery of the Klondike bonanza, Charlie was awarded full citizenship by the Canadian government and was exceedingly proud of his non-Indian right to enter a saloon and buy a round of drinks, when he had the money. He enjoyed being a personage, and with his slender poke would enter a bar shouting, "Treats for the house." Despite these honors, Charlie also spent much time in jail for various minor offenses. One day, returning from a Fourth of July celebration in town, he staggered off the bridge of the White Pass Railroad and was drowned. Skookum Jim's fate is obscure but apparently he outlived the others.

That "Madame Butterfly" theme did not pervade all such Arctic romances, however. One of the more celebrated love matches at Cape Nome before it was discovered that the sands of its beaches were liberally salted with gold dust involved a Swede named Ole and an Eskimo maiden named Oluk. Ole's suit made considerable progress when he salvaged a barrel of butter from a wrecked whaling schooner. All fats were highly prized by the Eskimos, but butter was the supreme delicacy. "For plenty of butter Ole could marry Oluk," the girl's father announced.

Ole agreed that Oluk was indeed worth a barrel of butter and the couple was married according to native custom. A big driftwood fire was lighted on the beach, and music was provided by an accordion, banjo and native drums.

The wedding punch was a native concoction called "hootch" by the natives, who thus provided the word "hooch," popular in the United States during Prohibition. Hootch was made from fermented sourdough, rapidly deprived the drinker of his senses, wits and inhibitions, and left him with a hangover of unparalleled severity. (Experts on native concoctions, from bamboo whisky to the fearsome tuba of the Philippine Islands, say "hootch" is the most potent of all.)

The drink hit the bridegroom so hard that he began paying too much attention to another Eskimo girl, one Oo-mak.

Oluk charged into the tête-à-tête, sent Oo-mak into flight by butting her in the stomach and then plucking out her hair by the handfuls. Ole, chivalrous but unwise, tried to act as peacemaker. Oluk thereupon showed him that trifling would not be tolerated in their marriage; she blacked both of his eyes, bit off part of one ear and struck him on his nose so forcefully that it was twisted to one side. Fellow Swedes hauled Ole off to his nuptial chamber in such battered condition that a witness said it was "doubtful if his mother could have recognized him."

Possibly spoiled by the white man's slightly more chivalrous attitude toward women, the squaws sometimes asserted their rights more forcefully with their white husbands than they would dare with men of their own race.

Some of them even applied for divorces. Rex Beach told of a Siwash lady married to a white prospector "with book, bell and candle" at a near-by mission. She objected to him because of his raucous snoring. The husband, however, did not want a divorce, principally because his squaw was one of the most skillful cooks in the Klondike.

The Indian girl took her problem to the settlement's miners' court. This tribunal, as in all mining camps far removed from courts and the Northwest Mounted Police, had absolute powers, deciding claim disputes, rendering the death penalty and even granting divorces on rare occasions. The most serious offense in that barren country was stealing another man's supplies. For the person convicted of that crime, there was the choice of being hanged instanter or, if it was summer, being publicly flogged and sent down the river on a log to be devoured by mosquitoes; if it was winter, being turned out on the trail barefoot with only the faintest hope of reaching another settlement alive.

The miners' court not only granted the divorce but awarded her all the communal property—a sewing machine.

Beach explained it was her complaint of the sourdough's snoring that aroused the court's compassion. "It was not native gallantry that prompted us to grant the divorce and award her the alimony requested, it was because most of us had partners who slept with their mouths open."

Justice, rather roughly designed and executed, was rendered in the case of another Indian girl, a beautiful half-breed with a rudimentary breach-of-promise suit. The girl, who had been educated in the States, complained that a wealthy saloon owner had promised to marry her. Then his friends began joshing him about being a "squaw man," which made him "redder than his fiancée," according to Wilson Mizner. The saloonkeeper tried to jilt her.

The women of the camp, not usually sympathetic toward Indian brides, indignantly called for a miners' court. The girl's cousin, with whom she lived, declared that her honor had been impaired. Feelings ran high on both sides, particularly that of the girl. One of the toughest citizens heard that the saloon owner's lawyer had made disparaging remarks about the Indian lass. As court convened, he glowered at the lawyer and warned him, "Don't be disrespectful, mister, because if you do I'll kill you so damned dead you'll stink."

In that atmosphere the reluctant fiancé didn't have much of a chance. The court gave him two alternatives: marry the girl *and* give her $500 to assuage her injured sensibilities, or pay a $5,000 fine in gold dust and spend a year in jail.

There was no jail, of course, in that raw new settlement, so while the defendant was making up his mind which of two ghastly possibilities to accept, another miners' meeting was called to discuss plans for construction of the jail. He decided to marry the girl. Mizner noted that this wise decision put off building a jail "until civilization set in" and then it was "built and jammed in short order."

Some of these mixed marriages turned out very well, particularly if entered without duress. Jack Hines, the Arctic troubador, came across one at Golovin Bay. The proprietor of the roadhouse, John Dexter, had landed there as a member of a whaling expedition from New Bedford. While camped on the shore, he had gone inland, fallen into a hot spring in the subfreezing weather and been nearly frozen to death. He was taken to the near-by hut of the chief of the Chinik tribe, whose daughter Molly, a tall girl "straight as a lance," nursed Dexter back to health. He decided to settle down there and marry his nurse. The Chiniks built them the huge log roadhouse as a collective wedding present—further evidence of the Indians' generosity before they were embittered or corrupted by the gold-rushers. The Dexters prospered when the gold rush came along, importing gambling equipment and a bar from San Francisco. The marriage was a great success, and Molly Dexter was among the most respected women in the Far North.

To the sensitive eye of Jack London, however, most marriages or living arrangements involving white men and Indian girls, particularly if the whites were determined to clean up a fortune and then hasten back to the States to spend it, ended tragically for the girls. He wrote in his journal of stopping off at an Indian camp at the mouth of the Koyukuk River and talking to a "three-quarter-breed" girl, herself the victim of an earlier misalliance, with a "white baby girl" two years old. The girl told him sadly that "I have no man." London jokingly, he said, offered himself as a husband, but she replied bitterly, "I marry Indian. White man always leave Indian girl."

At Tanana Station he met an "ubiquitous Anglo-Saxon" living with a "beautiful half-breed woman" with Caucasian features, a delicate oval face and slender form. How much harder her lot, thought London, than the tragic half-castes of Lafcadio Hearn's writings.

Despite the salving respect and consideration of a "squaw-man's" Indian relatives, London thought his fate was almost equally unhappy. He met one Bill Moore, who had settled near Hamilton Station with an Indian wife, and noted that Moore was "satisfied to remain—ambition lost—hurry-scurry, devil-take-the-hindmost competition of civilization has no attraction—sure thing for the rest of his life—but how bleak and blank his existence."

Many a Klondiker on returning Outside had to explain to his wife that not all gold-rushers settled down with Indian brides.

London's second wife, Charmian, once remarked that he wrote so convincingly of such marriages and alliances that he must have engaged in the Yukon design for living himself.

"No, no, my dear," he replied, very earnestly. "I never was a squaw man. When I make the statement that I write only of what I know, I must not be taken too literally. . . . An artist must have some latitude to spill over into. . . . "

Few Klondikers had such an airtight system of defense when quizzed by the women they left behind them.

Wax Museum:
The Knight of the Golden Omelette

AMONG THE high rollers and big spenders of the Klondike, Swiftwater Bill Gates was a towering, if sometimes tottering, figure. It was part of the Klondike fever for a man to toss away in a night or two all the dust and nuggets he had torn from the earth in a summer's work, and then bravely trudge back to his diggings with an aching skull and trembling limbs. But none spent more gallantly—and more publicly—than Swiftwater Bill. He poured hundreds of thousands of dollars into the project of building and maintaining his reputation for profligacy. Both he and his strenuously acquired reputation, however, were ruined by that classic figure of domestic vengeance—the irate mother-in-law. For it was she who wrote his one and only biography, she who wrote with drastic simplicity that he was merely a "lecherous monster." Swiftwater Bill lived, labored and squandered with the sole aim of acquiring the fame of being the gayest dog of all; but he emerged from his mother-in-law's hands as a craven, a cheat, a thief, a harried little man dodging from one villainy to another.

Swiftwater Bill's first appearance in the Yukon Territory was in the humble role of bull cook in a squalid roadhouse—which was simply a bunkhouse with a lean-to kitchen attached—at Forty Mile on the Yukon River. That was in 1896, when he was "about thirty-five," according to his mother-in-law's later reckoning. Then known only as plain William F. Gates, he cooked, washed dishes and made bunks in the roadhouse near Circle City with no visible promise of his future fame. Certainly his appearance—except for luxuriant growths of hair—was not particularly prepossessing. He was only five feet five inches tall, keg-shaped, very deferential in manner. His beard and hair were long, black and wavy, and he grew a handle-bar mustache that would have been envied by the biggest sport on Broadway. All his energy seemed to be spent in growing those magnificent sprouts of hair.

In so lackadaisical a citizen, content to keep house for the wandering adventurers of the Arctic, it was amazing how the news of a gold strike quickly galvanized Gates into a man of action. He joined the stampede to Number Thirteen Above Discovery, Eldorado. On that golden creek he worked a rich stretch of gravel and sand in company with half a dozen others. They included the Berry brothers, who became rich and stayed rich; Professor T. S. Lippy, who also became a millionaire; Ole Oleson, who later sold his claim for $250,000; Michael Doré and Antoine Stander, a pair of French Canadians. Young Doré died of exposure in his cabin, surrounded by coal-oil cans filled with gold dust.

It was one of his partners who conferred the sobriquet of "Swiftwater Bill" on Gates. Later he claimed that the title was given him because of his daring in negotiating the rougher stretches of river, but actually it was a term of derision because he insisted on walking around the rapids while his partners rode through Miles Canyon and White Horse Rapids and their wild, frothing waters with the supply-laden canoes.

In November of 1896, Swiftwater Bill found himself a wealthy man. He had 200 pounds of gold dust and he sold his claim, having decided, rightly, that there was more money to be made faster and easier in the boom towns springing up along the Yukon. So he journeyed to Dawson City with another man who had similar ideas—Jack Smith, whose rise to affluence had been just as swift. Smith was the manager of a troupe of variety girls which had become stranded in Circle City. While he was trying to scrape up food for his soubrettes and dancing girls, news came of the discoveries in the Klondike region, specifically along Bonanza Creek, a tributary of the Klondike, and Eldorado Creek, which ran into Bonanza. Smith staked out a claim on Bonanza which he sold for $155,000.

The two partners set up a tent saloon called the Bonanza a mile from Dawson, then moved into Dawson and built the famous Monte Carlo, a combined saloon, variety theater and gambling hall which soon became to the nobility of the Klondike what Maxim's was to Balkan princes. Now the partners had the finest deadfall north of Seattle, but no whisky and no dancing girls. Gambling alone wasn't enough to amuse the newly rich prospectors and miners flocking into Dawson from the near-by diggings, although Swiftwater Bill, when asked what the house limits were at the tables, gestured expansively and announced, "The sky's the limit, boys. Tear off the roof!"

When the ice broke on the rivers, he went to San Francisco to procure the feminine and alcoholic staples for the Monte Carlo. His first move was to buy a Prince Albert, a top hat and a collection of fancy tiepins. Settling down in the Palace Hotel, he paid the bellboys in nuggets to point him out as "The King of the Klondike," and held forth among the potted palms in the lobby about the riches of the Klondike creeks and how easily they could be gathered up by men of intrepidity and spirit. He stood drinks at the bar, entertained grandly in the dining rooms. And it was not long before his heavy poke shrank to nothing but leather. He still had to buy a hundred barrels of whisky, engage entertainers and transport his cargo to Dawson.

A Doctor Wolf became his willing victim—at first. The physician, weary of his rounds, loaned Gates $20,000 on the promise that it would be returned with 100 per cent interest within ninety days. Swiftwater Bill departed with his girls and liquor, but he had not counted on Doctor Wolf's continuing and growing interest in his investment. Doctor Wolf was, in fact, waiting on the wharves of Dawson long before Swiftwater Bill and his fleet of pleasure-laden scows appeared around the bend of the Yukon; he had heard rumors that Gates was something of a highbinder, and decided to go North to protect his interests. The tales told him around Dawson while he waited for his debtor only increased his concern. Eugene Allen, editor of the *Nugget,* recalled that he warned Doctor Wolf, who was a friend of his brother's, that "Swiftwater Bill was never known to pay back any money after it was thrown away. If he made another strike somewhere, he might toss some your way, but that's about your only chance."

Then, one afternoon, word crackled through town that Gates's arrival was expected momentarily. Now almost frantic, Doctor Wolf joined the throng hurrying toward the river front. His first glimpse of the self-crowned "King of the Klondike" was hardly reassuring. At the head of his convoy of barges, Swiftwater stood in the prow of a Petersborough canoe, decked out in his high silk hat and claw-hammer coat, "his flowing mustache curled back over his shoulders, arms extended in a wide gesture of greeting to the people of Dawson City." Just behind him, throned on a keg of whisky, was a girl adjudged beautiful by current Dawson standards. An oarsman labored in the stern. And behind them came the other girls and the whisky, promising surcease against the long Arctic night.

Swiftwater Bill stepped onto the dock and bowed grandly to the multitude.

Just as he straightened up, he caught sight of Doctor Wolf with thunder and lightning in his face. Editor Allen observed that Swiftwater "began to crumble like a peacock that has looked at his feet."

"So, you're here, are you, Swiftwater?" Doctor Wolf roared. "Well, now that you're here, you've got just exactly three hours to pay me back the $20,000 which you borrowed. To hell with the interest! But don't think three hours means any more than three hours."

Swiftwater meekly replied that he would raise the money promptly, disappeared in the crowd (whose attention was now fastened on the sprightly young women being helped ashore) and, presumably with the assistance of Jack Smith, rounded up $20,000 and paid off his creditor. Doctor Wolf left at once for the less hectic opportunities of San Francisco.

The incident did not crush Swiftwater's spirit, it soon became apparent. Among the entertainers he brought from San Francisco were Gussie and May Lamore, both young, dark-eyed, plump and lively. One night he watched Gussie whirling around the dance floor with a huge Canadian, her skirts swirling provocatively an inch above the ankle.

He waited prudently until the Canadian had finished dancing with her, his libido rising with every bar of music. Then he walked over to her and calmly announced: "I'll give you your weight in gold tomorrow morning if you'll marry me—and I guess you'll weigh about $30,000."

Gussie accepted the dowry but, being a willful minx, kept postponing the marriage. Their ensuing year's courtship, if it could be so dignified, was an affair of entreaties, wheedlings, tears, cuffs, curses and vexations. Gussie was expert at keeping her suitor dangling; she managed somehow to convince Swiftwater that she loved him as well as his gold, but that they should not fling themselves into a hasty marriage. After all, there were a lot of other men from whom gold dust literally leaked like sawdust from a broken doll. Her suitor had his own way of showing Gussie that it was not an unmixed blessing to give and give and give.

Before the ice broke that spring, two crates of fresh eggs were brought in by dog sled. To the Klondiker a fried egg was like beluga caviar to a bankrupt gourmet. Swiftwater immediately paid $2,280 for the entire shipment of eggs and repaired to his favorite restaurant, ordering that the whole batch be fried in relays. He was just sitting down to his first platter when Gussie, with whom he had quarreled the night before, arrived to share in the feast. Swiftwater ignored her. As platter after platter arrived on his table, he ate one or two, then marched to the door and threw the rest to the dogs gathered in a leaping and howling pack outside. Before the entire performance was finished, a furious and tearful Gussie flung herself out of the restaurant. Between them, Swiftwater and the stray dogs of Dawson had eaten every fresh egg in the town.

For that feat of malice Swiftwater was dubbed "Knight of the Golden Omelette."

Gussie's revenge was considerably more costly than two crates of fresh eggs. Swiftwater had a falling-out with Jack Smith, his partner in the Monte Carlo, and Smith bought him out. Swiftwater announced to Gussie that he was "going Outside," and this was her last chance to marry him. The thought of all that money leaving for San Francisco without her brought the girl to her senses. She agreed to take two coffee cans filled with gold dust and bank them in San Francisco, where Swiftwater would join her.

But when they met in San Francisco, Gussie coolly announced that she was keeping the gold *and* her freedom. With that, she skipped out of his life. Swiftwater struck on a dangerous method of retaliation: less than a month later he married Gussie's sister Grace, bought her a fine home in Oakland and left with her on a honeymoon at the Baldwin Hotel in the San Joaquin Valley. There he tipped the bellboys a silver dollar apiece for telling each new arrival, "There is Swiftwater Bill Gates, the King of the Klondike."

Grace Lamore Gates was less impressed with him than the tourists, for she left him three weeks after the marriage. Swiftwater was not ready to call his encounter with the Lamores a complete loss, although his future mother-in-law estimated that the Lamore sisters took him for more than $100,000 between them. One night he sneaked into the Oakland manor he had bought and furnished for Grace and removed $7,000 worth of solid silver plate and cut glass. With much bravado, he told reporters in San Francisco: "Now that she's quit me, I'll be damned if she'll keep that."

Resilience was always a key characteristic of Swiftwater Bill. The Lamores had done considerable damage to his financial status, not to mention his male ego, but he was ready once again to search for gold—and another woman. First he journeyed to Ottawa, where he persuaded the Dominion government to grant him a huge concession on Quartz Creek, three miles long and two miles wide in some places. Then he proceeded to London and convinced the cautious financiers of the city to provide the funds for purchasing hydraulic equipment and shipping it to the Klondike. In the spring of 1899 he turned up in Seattle to supervise operations from that comfortable base.

And there it was that his erratic path crossed that of Mrs. Iola Beebe, author of *The True Life Story of Swiftwater Bill Gates*, with whom he was to become embroiled in as melodramatic a relationship as any that could be viewed in the flare of theatrical gaslight.

Mrs. Beebe, a widow and the mother of two toothsome daughters, had invested her inheritance in a hotel which was being shipped piecemeal to the Klondike. She looked up Swiftwater Bill at his Seattle hotel because she had heard he was the greatest living expert on commerce in that region, although his experience actually had been limited to the roadhouse at Forty Mile and partnership in the Monte Carlo. She found him perfectly charming and eager to be of assistance, and was impressed with his "deliciously velvet tones" and the four-carat diamond "gleaming like an electric light from his bosom." On that visit, however, she brought her elder daughter Blanche, who was nineteen, and she was somewhat disturbed by the peculiar shine in his black eyes whenever they rested on Blanche, as they frequently did.

A Mr. Hathaway, who was with Swiftwater and was introduced as a British mining expert, seemed to be eminently respectable and sedate. Later the two gentlemen were introduced to Mrs. Beebe's younger daughter, Bera. She was only fifteen, but again that odd speculative light came into Swiftwater's eyes. But Mrs. Beebe, perhaps a bit too wrapped up in her hotel venture, did not take alarm. So the shock was all the greater when she returned home late one afternoon and found a note propped on the mantel. It was addressed to "Dear Mama" and read:

"We have gone to Alaska with Swiftwater and Mr. Hathaway. Do not worry, mama, as when we get there we will look out for your hotel. Bera."

Mrs. Beebe, not at all reassured by this note, hastened to the docks and rushed aboard the steamer *Humboldt,* just about to raise its gangplank and lift anchor for Alaskan ports. With the assistance of the ship's officers, she found her daughters and their escorts in a cabin. Sailing was delayed while Mrs. Beebe went into hysterics; the two gentlemen explained lengthily that they meant no harm, really, and the police were summoned. Swiftwater talked Mrs. Beebe into not preferring charges and was allowed to sail off with his friend.

Several weeks later, her daughters safely in tow, Mrs. Beebe departed for Alaska. The first person she met in a hotel at Skagway was Swiftwater Bill Gates, all suave apology, murmuring, "Mrs. Beebe, let us forget bygones." Mrs. Beebe agreed in principle but reminded herself, "Knowing the black purpose in Swiftwater's heart, I watched my girls day and night."

Just one week later, maternal vigilance faltered, and Mrs. Beebe found another note from Bera in her hotel room. "I have gone with Swiftwater to Dawson. He loves me and I love him." The distraught mother followed at once. As she stepped off the boat at Dawson, Swiftwater and her daughter greeted her. Mrs. Beebe began expostulating wildly until Swiftwater informed her that he had "done the right thing"—by which he meant that he had married the fifteen-year-old Bera. His mother-in-law was so overwhelmed that in the next days she invested $35,000 in his mining venture.

And thus began the long ordeal of Mrs. Beebe struggling to cope with her slippery son-in-law and make him see his duty as a family man. She accompanied her daughter and Swiftwater to the diggings on Quartz Creek that winter when a son, Clifford, was born to the couple. Before the ice broke that spring, Mrs. Beebe and the infant were deserted, with Swiftwater and his bride rushing off to the new discoveries at Nome. In Dawson, Mrs. Beebe and the baby existed on the charity of the Canadian government. Swiftwater wrote that she and the child must join them in Nome, since he had struck pay dirt along Dexter Creek. On the way to Nome, Mrs. Beebe heard that Swiftwater had indeed staked out a moderately profitable claim but had gambled all his gold away at the gambling tables. A harder blow awaited the long-suffering lady when she landed on the wharf at Nome. Newsboys were shouting, "Seattle *Times!* All about Swiftwater Bill running away with another woman!"

With his extraordinary mobility, as Mrs. Beebe learned, Swiftwater had decamped with Bera to Washington, D.C., deserted his young wife there with her second child, doubled back to Portland, Oregon, and there eloped with Kitty Brandon, his seventeen-year-old niece, the daughter of his sister. Now he had two raging mothers-in-law hot on his trail. Kitty's mother caught up with the bigamous bridegroom and her daughter in a Seattle hotel but Swiftwater escaped with the girl by dashing out the rear exit and fleeing to Tacoma. Meanwhile, Bera and her second son were returning to Seattle on a charity ticket, and Mrs. Beebe was wondering "if the duplicate of Swiftwater's enormities can be found in all the annals of this great Northwestern country."

A few months later, having deserted his niece-wife, Swiftwater holed up at the Victoria Hotel in Seattle, broke and haggard, apparently unaware of the fact that Mrs. Beebe and Bera were in the city.

Mrs. Beebe battered on the door of his room. It opened a crack, and only one eye and one curlicue of his black mustache were visible. Mrs. Beebe put her shoulder to the door and plunged into the room littered with a fugitive's detritus of old newspapers, partly eaten sandwiches, tin cans, soiled sheets and cigar butts.

Swiftwater, clad only in a grimy nightgown, dove for the bed, pulled the sheets over his head and begged his mother-in-law to go away quietly, wailing that she was tormenting a broken man. He was persuaded to come out of hiding; his unshaven, hollow-eyed face touched even the hardened woman who confronted him. Seeing his advantage, Swiftwater poured out his troubles, his apologies and regrets—and spoke most intriguingly of the gold that was waiting to be removed from the earth of the Tanana country in Alaska. Mrs. Beebe promptly hocked her diamonds so he could be provided with a grubstake. All was forgiven, but definitely not forgotten, in view of her son-in-law's promises of a new fortune. She was determined to keep a closer watch on him *this* time, poor woman, and noted somewhat sourly, "Swiftwater's transformation from a broken-down tramp of the Weary Willie order to a fine gentleman was rapid after he got his hands on the money I borrowed with my diamonds as the pledge." Resilience, that was the prime characteristic of William F. Gates. Mrs. Beebe followed him to Fairbanks, the settlement nearest his claim at Number Six Cleary Creek in the Tanana district. There she found a rival claimant, Swiftwater's sister-mother-in-law, who was demanding money on behalf of her own daughter. With marvelous understatement, Mrs. Beebe commented, "It may possibly be said that as an offset to Swiftwater's phenomenal luck, he had two women, the mothers of his two wives, waiting patiently at Fairbanks for him to bring out enough money to properly provide for his families."

Swiftwater placer-mined $75,000 from his claim and ducked out of Fairbanks on his sister. But not Mrs. Beebe. Someone told her Swiftwater was on the boat, and she clambered aboard at the last moment. Her son-in-law greeted her blandly. But on reaching Seattle he gave her the slip by jumping to the deck of a smaller ship alongside, thence to the dock and up the street with the woeful cries of Mrs. Beebe rising behind him. This time Mrs. Beebe flounced to the nearest police station and had him arrested for bigamy.

To any other man, the jig would be up, but hope still flickered in the liquid black eyes of Swiftwater Bill. He somehow persuaded Mrs. Beebe to put up bond for his release. This time, he declared, all would be put aright. Again Mrs. Beebe believed him, for she permitted Bera to divorce him so he could free himself of the bigamy charge. Untangled again, Swiftwater promptly married Kitty Brandon in an entirely legal ceremony. "I want to ask now, is there no law to reach a monster of this kind?" Mrs. Beebe demanded of newspaper interviewers. Even this was not the *coup de grâce* for Mrs. Beebe, who was as determined as Swiftwater was resilient.

Next season Mrs. Beebe learned that her former son-in-law, who by this time had also divorced Kitty, had taken $200,000 out of his Tanana claim, and she promptly set out for Fairbanks. Again Swiftwater found himself grasped by the lapels by Mrs. Beebe, who shook him like a half-filled flour sack until his eyes popped out and his teeth rattled. Once unhanded, he gave Mrs. Beebe $50 and instructed her to engage a hotel room and wait for him there. *This* time he would make amends, generously, he promised her.

Alas, it was her last sight of the man who had led her such a lively chase from Seattle to most of the mining camps of Alaska. Swiftwater slipped aboard a ship for the States, converted his gold into currency and bank drafts, assigned his Tanana interests to one Phil Watson and somehow had himself declared a bankrupt. He had placed himself beyond the reach of Mrs. Iola Beebe, and even that doughty lady had to admit the rascal had outrun and out-witted her. But, of course, she had a sort of revenge with her pen a few years later. He may have been "Knight of the Golden Omelette" and the biggest sport north of Seattle, but he was also revealed as the sort of craven who hides under bedclothing at the approach of danger.

No matter. Resilient, a human pogo stick, that was Swiftwater Bill. Later he dashed off to Peru to join the silver rush, and disap-peared from written history. He would now be about ninety years old. It is rather warming to think that the great vanquisher of mothers-in-law might still be rambling around, looking for another El Dorado—and perhaps another mother-in-law.

7

~~~

The Literary Pay Dirt

UNDOUBTEDLY the richest vein worked in the Klondike was not in gold, but in human experience. Not even the luckiest, shrewdest and thriftiest prospectors could boast of heavier pokes than Jack London, Robert W. Service and Rex Beach, once they had turned their thoughts from gold-hunting to writing about what they saw and felt and endured in the Klondike. As prospectors, the literary gentry were neither successful nor particularly diligent. The literary man, in embryo or full growth, is notoriously a sedentary fellow. He toils not. But he does spin tales, once the material for them is worked over in his mind, a process much like separating ore from tailings. Even such a vigorous man of action as Jack London was content in the Klondike to be a bystander, recumbent if possible, and accounted a rather lazy fellow, as subconsciously he gathered the material for his novels and short stories and nonfiction pieces, which came streaming from his typewriter in the years following his woebegone return from the Arctic.

"The average Yukon literary artist found that the Arctic was God's Country, and then ducked out as quick as he could," the late Alva Johnston noted in his lively study of the Mizner brothers.* That was only a slight exaggeration. But it must be conceded that at least one litterateur had the gold fever bad enough to wander for more than two years through the mining camps from Skagway to Nome. He was Rex Beach, the subsequent author of *The Spoilers, The Barrier* and *The Silver Horde.*

On the theory that "Freezing is a far pleasanter death than drowning," he left a snug home in Chicago to join the gold rush. A law student in his early twenties, he talked his older brothers into grubstaking him in the Yukon. His equipment included a fur-lined sleeping bag, a rifle, a dogskin suit and a mandolin— and of these only the mandolin proved to be of any value, he recalled in his autobiography.† The mandolin "enabled me to pick up a bit of refreshment now and then," he said, by playing at "squaw dances."

Probably because his diligence as a prospector was superior to that of several other gold-rushers who were to become equally prominent as writers, Beach was the only one of the lot who actually dug out enough pay dirt to qualify as an authentic miner.

When news of the gold strike on the beaches of Nome echoed throughout the North Country, Beach quickly developed a machine to "wash those sands by the ton instead of the shovelful." The pay dirt on the beach had already been worked over by the first comers, equipped with rockers and sluice boxes, down to the low-tide line. Beach's scheme was to reach into the surf and suck up the golden dust nestling in the sands. Beach, considering himself "something of a rough-and-tumble executive," hired a crew of men to help him with the sand-sucking machine. The cold surf caused his men to "shriek like Vassar girls" and shrink from sufficient hard labor to make the dredging process pay for itself. And then

---

* Johnston, Alva, *The Legendary Mizners.* New York: Farrar, Straus & Young, Inc., 1953.

† Beach, Rex, *Personal Exposures,* New York: Harper and Bros., 1940.

a gale came up and wrecked all such machinery along the beaches of Nome. At the end of his experience as a mining executive Beach found that he had enough gold to melt down into "a button about the size of a Chicago Athletic Association swimming medal." Before he left Nome the next spring, however, Beach had worked a claim for which he was offered $30,000, he said; but he was reticent about exactly how much he did take out of it. It was enough, at any rate, to establish himself as a legitimate gold miner.

Most of Beach's experiences in the Yukon bordered on the ludicrously unfortunate; he was always at the wrong place at the wrong time. On his arrival, along with "some fifteen hundred souls, and twelve saloon keepers," he was halted at Rampart City, when the Canadian authorities announced that Dawson and other Klondike localities were undergoing a famine. Impatient to reach the actual site of the gold rush, inexperienced in living with the Arctic winter, barely skillful enough to cook flapjacks, Beach and his fellow pilgrims fretted through the long dark months and barely managed to survive that most dangerous of Northern maladies, cabin fever, the acute distaste for one's immediate companions. Beach admitted that part of his troubles that winter were traceable to his failure as a judge of human nature. He had his choice of two partners: one was formerly the steward on a riverboat, who had been fired, Beach learned, for purloining a blanket from the steamer; the other was a stranger "in whose countenance the rugged virtues stood out as prominently as his cheekbones." Beach chose the latter, and ever afterward regretted his choice. The steward turned out to have staked a claim liberally pocketed with coarse grains of gold.

On the other hand, "my hand-picked partner was indeed a louse," Beach later admitted. He had one habit that revolted Beach above all others, the ability to suck up hot coffee without touching his lips to the saucer; this prideful slurping almost drove Beach insane. A worse tendency was soon to reveal itself. His partner took unto himself a Siwash mistress, whose name was Annie but who was known in the region as "Short and Dirty," a sobriquet well earned, according to Beach. The lean-to shared by Beach, Annie and her protector wasn't nearly large enough for such an arrangement, aside from the moral aspect of the situation. Annie was a child of nature who "loved to sing and sew and boil frozen fish heads in a lard can"—and only her sewing was socially acceptable. One day the domicile was split asunder forever when Beach's partner struck Annie in the course of a quarrel, and Beach knocked him down, not as an impulsive act of chivalry but because of a long-nurtured dislike, as Beach later explained.

Annie, or "Short and Dirty," made the rounds of Rampart City telling everyone how Beach had risen to her defense, and related the final scene between Beach and her ex-lover so vividly that Beach's acquaintances thereupon saluted him as the knightliest fellow north of Seattle, and assured him jocularly, "You're a Southern gentleman, by Gad, suh!"

This courtly little gesture was so embroidered with the passing years that it became one of the more durable scandals of the Yukon. Ten years later Beach received a clipping from a Fairbanks newspaper which stated that the now-famous defender of saddle-colored little Annie had been a "squaw man" in Rampart City during the height of the gold rush. Beach investigated further and found that "Short and Dirty" was spending her summers posing for camera-clicking tourists from the States and telling the tale of how she had been the celebrated Rex Beach's common-law wife, whom he deserted on becoming "rich and famous." Annie did so well with this impromptu soap opera that she was able to spend the winters alternating between the saloons and the Fairbanks jail, Beach also learned. Poking his coffee-sucking partner in the jaw had finally resulted in Beach's learning one of the basic facts of life: it is dangerous to come between a man and the woman he is striking.

The next misadventure befell him a short time later when he teamed up with two young men who had left their studies at the University of California to seek their fortunes in the Klondike. They decided to establish a wood-cutting camp to serve as a re-fueling station for the Yukon steamers on their way to Dawson, having heard reports that the price would soon go up to $40 a cord. Seventy-five miles down-river they set up their camp and fell to chopping and sawing; daily the woodpile grew and the grub-pile diminished, until an inventory disclosed only these items: "a box of case-hardened pilot bread, some oatmeal in which weevils romped, a can of rubberoid gaskets labeled 'evaporated potatoes,' and a side of salt pork with a pay streak like Eldorado Creek."

Half starved, Beach and his companions still consoled themselves with hopes for a happy season of profiteering when the Yukon ice broke up and the river steamers resumed their runs to Dawson and other river ports. The first steamer that hove in sight slowly paddled to a halt when the pilothouse glimpsed the huge piles of wood. The captain inquired of Beach and his partners how much they wanted for it, and they told him $40 a cord. The derisive blasts from the steamer's tall stacks served as the captain's answer, and the boat proceeded downstream. As the next steamers halted briefly with the same inquiry and the same abrupt rejection, the woodcutters reduced their price from $40 to $35 to $25 to $15 a cord. Finally they sold out for $10 and even had to help load the steamer with their wood. Profiteering was a respectable enough calling in the Arctic, and widely successful, but Beach failed even at that.

No matter how hard he tried, his ventures in the Yukon were invariably unfortunate. It was little wonder that many years later he was bitterly affronted by a column written for a newspaper syndicate by Westbrook Pegler in which that hardened skeptic wrote that he always discounted by sixty per cent anything he read of Alaska-Yukon hardships in the works of Beach and Service. Beach stiffly commented, "Inasmuch as Jack London wrote the first and perhaps the most highly colored portrayals of life up there Mr. Pegler must likewise put him down as a willful exaggerator. . . . I take no offense at being called a fiction writer: I've been called worse things to my teeth but actually neither London nor any of the rest of us overwrote the hardships of life on the brown-bean frontier and I'm sure any sourdough will subscribe to that statement. . . . The average man who did not den up at the first frost like a ground squirrel and who wrestled with that country, no holds barred, went through a great deal of grief."

Jack London, it was true, wrote about the North Country with rawer colors on his palette than any of the other literary men. And it was London, especially, against whom Wilson Mizner directed his most caustic criticisms in discussing Arctic literature. His most recent biographer said Mizner had an enduring contempt for such fiction and its "supermen and superdogs, its abysmal brutes and exquisite ingénues," and even fifteen years after London's death Mizner was still capable of howling with indignation whenever he heard London praised. The biographer also noted that there was an unlovely aroma of sour grapes about Mizner's crusade against the literary men of the Yukon, that he believed he could have seized the literary laurel for himself if he had been able to endure the lonely labors of composition.

It is also noteworthy that Mizner was not entirely equipped to discuss the adventures and characters of Yukon fiction. His own experience was limited to the barrooms, dance halls and gambling dens, while London, Beach and Miller shared the perils of those who dug for gold out on the creeks and the tundra; all of them suffered from frostbite, scurvy and malnutrition. The only mishap suffered by Mizner was a tooth broken when he unwisely joined a stampede out of Dawson. Doubtless it was a great pity that Mizner did not commit to ink and paper his recollections of the raffish circles in which he moved, but that, as he once said, would be like "blowing a police whistle" on all his old pals.

London, like his severest critic, was in the first wave of gold-rushers who headed for the Alaskan ports from San Francisco in the summer of 1897. At the age of twenty-one, London was already a veteran of the world of adventure; he had been a hobo, a sailor and an apprentice revolutionary. His fierce advocacy of socialism did not deter him from joining the most individualistic of enterprises, although subsconsciously he probably was more concerned with gathering experience for his future works than trying to make his fortune as a miner. Charmian London, his widow, was convinced that the idea of using the Klondike as literary material came to London only as an afterthought. Since early in his boyhood, London and his family were haunted by poverty; he was always conscious of the necessity, somehow, to achieve prosperity and ease the burden of his mother and stepfather. It was a specter that pursued him to the tragic end of his life.

Mrs. London wrote that she had "often heard Jack say that he had no idea of using the Klondike as a literary asset, until his dream of gold fell through and he was bound out of the country, penniless to all intents and purposes. It must have come suddenly to him that the adventure had been sufficient in itself, for he had been smitten with discouragement, before leaving home, as to any success in the coveted direction of a writing future." Leaving behind him a desk clogged only with rejected manuscripts and discouraging notes from the editors who had read them, London set out for a Golconda such as few other gold-rushers discovered for themselves. His departure entailed considerable sacrifice on the part of his family. To equip her brother and her husband, who accompanied London part of the way, London's sister drained her savings account of $500 and placed a $1,000 mortgage on her home, which provided them with passage to Alaska, clothing, gear, food and tools. London was saddened by the fact he had to leave his beloved stepfather, then on his deathbed. Almost from the beginning of his quest London was dogged by ill fortune. His brother-in-law, who was past sixty, took one look at Chilkoot Pass, another at their mound of stores and equipment, and announced he would be of little use to the expedition. Just as the brother-in-law turned back to San Francisco, London arranged to join three men they met on the northward voyage aboard the *Umatilla*—Jim Goodman, Fred Thompson and Merritt Sloper, with whom he was to spend most of his time in the Yukon.

There was no doubt that the stocky London was well equipped physically for the trials ahead. Men were dropping by the hundreds as they attempted the portage over Chilkoot Pass in the summer heat of the Alaskan coast. London was one of the more cheerful spectacles of that antlike epic of thousands of men hauling their supplies over the pass on their shoulders. He stripped down to a suit of bright red woolen underwear and literally raced up and down that tortuous incline, carrying 150 pounds on his back with every upward journey. In later years London boasted about how he started at the bottom of the pass with Indian packers, none of them weighed down more than he was, and beat those professionals to the top; it was a matter of greater pride than any of his books.

When London's party came to the shores of Lake Lindeman, his sailoring experience proved valuable as he directed the construction of two flat-bottomed boats. He paused, characteristically, on the day they were finished to write poems in honor of the *Yukon Belle* and the *Belle of the Yukon,* although winter was coming on and every moment counted in the race for Dawson before it locked them out of the Klondike. At White Horse Rapids the self-assured young man again proved his versatility. Almost a thousand boats were crammed together at the headwaters of the Yukon, none of them daring to try the violent waters; every boat that had tried, London and his companions were informed, had capsized and left its occupants to drown. One look at the rapids, and London pronounced: "Nothing to it. The other boats tried to fight the current to keep off the rocks. We'll go with the current, and it'll keep us clear."

London's confidence was so impressive that his companions manned the boat while he sat in the stern and calmly allowed the *Yukon Belle* to follow the main force of the water. They landed safely in calmer waters and took their second boat through, again without mishap. London was immediately deluged with offers to pilot the other boats through the rapids. It was mid-September and there was no time to lose, but London took his eye off the main chance. His party waited while he piloted 120 of the other boats at $25 apiece. He made $1,500 for several days' work, but a truly opportunistic man in his place would have made several times that much, considering the urgency of the situation. It was more money than London ever saw again in the Yukon.

But the delay cost London and his companions whatever chance they had of a fortune in that vanguard of fortune hunters. A blizzard howled down from the Arctic Ocean when the party reached the mouth of the Stewart River, a tiny settlement called Upper Island, only seventy-two miles away from Dawson. London and his companions settled down in an abandoned cabin, chopped firewood, prepared for the long siege against the Arctic night. More than fifty other trekkers, including various professional men lured away from their practices and chambers, also settled down there for the winter. London himself never regretted it, whatever it might have cost him in the race for mining claims.

In the snow-mantled camp his hunger for debate, discussion and philosophical argument was well satisfied; the winter was one long night at the fireside, with a little time out for sleeping, doing chores (when they couldn't be avoided) and exploring the country near by. Here London met "The Malemute Kid," Buck, the dog hero of *The Call of the Wild,* and Elam Harnish, whose nickname was "Burning Daylight" and who provided the idea for London's novel of that title. Here London and his friends, both the erudite and the untutored, argued over what lay closest to his heart and mind—and to many other thinking men at the turn of the century —socialism, the Darwinian theories and the scientific approach to making this a better world, socially and materially, at least. His friend Thompson sometimes grumbled that he couldn't arouse London to a proper sense of duty toward the wood chopping and other details, because London became so engrossed in debate. In the stripped-down baggage of a gold-rusher, he had made room for his copies of Darwin's *The Origin of Species,* Milton's *Paradise Lost* and Haeckel's *Riddle of the Universe.*

Despite his youth, London was regarded as one of the intellectual and social leaders of the Upper Island camp. Emil Jansen, who provided the model for "The Malemute Kid," later wrote of him:

Jack's companionship was refreshing, stimulating, helpful. He never stopped to count the cost or dream of profits to come. . . . He stood ever ready, were it a foraging trip among the camps for reading matter, to give a helpful hand on a woodsled, or to undertake a two days' hike for a plug of tobacco when he saw us restless and grumpy for the want of a smoke. . . . His face was illumined with a smile that never grew cold.

London and Thompson wandered away from the snug camp on one occasion to do a little prospecting on Henderson Creek, which emptied into the Yukon a mile below. They dug into the frozen bed of the creek and were elated when their shovels brought up gravel with shining grains clinging to them. Gold! London and his friend ran back to Upper Island, quite unselfishly, to spread the word of their find. They were all rich . . . rich! There was a stampede to the creek in which men of all economic creeds from Marxism to McKinley Republicanism joined with nonpartisan dispatch. An experienced prospector looked over their "gold dust," laughed bitterly and told London and Thompson they had shoveled up a fine vein of iron pyrites, or "fool's gold."

The Arctic winter had been pleasant enough in the settlement on the Stewart River; it was the warmer weather that proved disastrous to London. He floated down to Dawson on a raft when the ice broke. His raft-mate was a Doctor Harvey, who said London, when his sweep broke, uttered the most fulsome blasphemy he had ever heard. "Doctor, I don't know who made this world but I believe I could make a damned sight better one myself." Conditions in Dawson only strengthened this conviction, it would seem. That tent city was hospitable only to those who could pay outrageous prices for the necessities. Laborers were paid $17.50 a day and up, but such wages were scarcely magnificent in a place where breakfast cost $3.50. London, according to Thompson's recollections (which were not always generous), "never done a tap of work" in Dawson. Thompson, of course, was unable to understand that London was doing his own kind of work in frequenting the bars, gathering a sort of oral history of the Klondike as he listened to the accounts of the first prospectors to explore the creeks where gold was found; there was no better place than a barroom for gathering the raw materials of a gold-rush history. He talked to the dance-hall girls, who apparently looked on him as a fine fellow, even though he was unable to spend money on them, and he watched men throw away their substance on the gambling tables.

One of the women he admired was Freda Maloof, a Greek dancer, who seemed to him surpassing fair after a winter in the womanless settlement on the Stewart River. His widow recorded his later disillusionment, quoting a letter London wrote her some years after his return from the Yukon: "And who, of all people, do you suppose I ran into last evening . . . rummaging around the street-fair in Oakland?—Freda Maloof, fat and forty—doing the muscle dance in the Streets of Cairo! It was good to see her and talk over old times when I, all doubled up with scurvy, used to admire her dancing and her plucky spirit in Dawson. I've promised to send her a book I mentioned her in." (The book was *The God of His Fathers*.)

Scurvy felled him early that summer, covering his face with sores, weakening the few remaining teeth in his head, bending him over like an old man. Finally he was taken to Father Judge's hospital for treatment. There he decided to leave the Yukon as soon as he was strong enough for the journey. When he was well enough to travel, he left Dawson with two companions named Taylor and Thorson in a small open boat for the 1,900-mile journey down the Yukon to the Bering Sea. On that journey he began to keep a notebook; the idea had come to him that he might recoup something from his unsuccessful venture as a gold-rusher by writing some stories for *Outing Magazine* or *Youth's Companion*. Either the debilitating effects of scurvy or his previous failures as a freelancer, it is apparent, kept his aspirations at a low level indeed. The entries in that notebook, his only visible profit from an arduous year in the Arctic, show that he had begun to consider the possibility of using his experiences and observations as literary material. Such entries as the following, as he and his companions drifted down the Yukon toward the open sea:

At Circle City:

Deserted—Mosquitoes make a demonstration in force—now, just inside the terrible (so called) 300 miles of Yukon Flats. . . . Description of Flats—not Thousand Islands of St. Lawrence nor thousands of thousands, but thousands of millions—mosquitoes, woods, sloughs, immense piles of drift, all kinds of life what we have been told about, geese and goose eggs, our experience, the shotgun, etc.

Above Fort Yukon:

Scattered Indian camps, deserted log cabins, woodyards. Beauty of the night—drifting down the river, midnight & broad daylight, robins & other song birds singing on the islands; partridges, drumming tern, seagulls & loons discordant crys [*sic*] echoing across the glassy river stretches; kildees, plover, ducks, foolish or silly cries of wild geese, Martins, owls, hawks.

At Tana River:

The camp was large and the Indians had arrived from the Tanana & were in full force, waiting the fishing. Dance in progress, white man's dances. . . . Effect—In the crowded heated room, discerned the fair, bronzed skin and blond mustache of the ubiquitous Anglo Saxon, always at home in any environment. 5 A.M. & everybody up, children playing, bucks skylarking, squaws giggling and flirting, dogs fighting, etc. . . .

At camp 100 miles below Tanana:

Lafcadio Hearn & Japanese Half Caste—Beautiful, half-breed woman saw there, Caucasian features, slender form, delicate oval face & head, describe her environment. How much harder her lot than the Japanese Half Caste. Ubiquitous Anglo Saxon White man from Sacramento living with them, brother-in-law, etc. . . .

Below Hamilton Station:

Eight miles on passed Bill Moore's. Settled down with Indian wife (years in country) satisfied to remain—ambition lost—hurry-scurry devil take the hindmost competition of civilization has no attraction—sure thing for the rest of life—but how bleak and blank his existence. Pride of Indian in calling him brother-in-law. . . .

Off Point Romanoff:

Pick up Father Roubeau on edge of surf in 3 hatch kyak. . . . Quite a linguist. Pleasant anecdotes of Jesuit brotherhood. Obedience, poverty, chastity. Alaska 12 years. Reducing Innuit language to a grammar—pride of his life. Revel for hours in eulogy of same. . . . Possessed of fatal faculty of getting lost. . . .

These were obviously the notes, not of a keeper of travel journals, but a writer storing up impressions for his future work.

With only his notebooks to show for a year's privations and the loss of the grubstake provided by his sister, London beat his way home, working as a stoker on a steamship from St. Michael to British Columbia, taking a steerage passage from there to Seattle, hopping freights from Seattle to his home in Oakland. In a few years he was mining his memory and making more money out of the Klondike gold rush than any sourdough who had struck it rich on the Eldorado.

But even after those memories, transmuted to best-selling fiction, had made his fortune, London detested the mere mention of the Klondike, according to Thames Williamson, because "it was a hell of a place; it had ruined his health." Williamson quotes London as saying, "I'm making up for it, though. I'm giving the public what it likes to think Alaska is, and I'm getting gold for it. Writing is my strike."

The only literary man who had established himself professionally before going to the Klondike—and made much less out of his adventures than his younger colleagues—was Joaquin Miller, the bearded poet, adventurer and visionary, who was known as "The Sweet Singer of the Sierras." Miller, a determined romantic, wrote so lyrically about the beauties of the Northland that many innocents came to the Klondike believing that hunting for gold was as sweetly uncomplicated as picking wild flowers. In their disillusionment, they turned on Miller and denounced him as a Pied Piper full of sinister purposes; actually he was only a poet miscast as a journalist.

Miller, always quick to assume the picturesque posture, had performed widely as a poet and man of action—one might almost say a rough-cut D'Annunzio—for many years before he saw a literary opportunity in the Klondike. It would have suited his nature to have been the issue of an alliance between a Regency buck and a Gypsy princess, for in his day a poet had to play the role grandly, Byronically; but in stern reality he was born in Liberty, Indiana, to a plain-living Quaker family. His lifelong experiment in heroics began at the age of seventeen, when, like most adventurers, he ran away from home. He was born Cincinnatus Hiner Miller, but adopted the name "Joaquin" out of his admiration for the Mexican highwayman Joaquin Murietta. It was in 1856 that he made his way to the Indian country in northern California and took up the Indians' highly unpopular cause. The tribes of the Northwest had been warring intermittently on the white settlers for several years, but that did not deter Miller from joining forces with one Joseph DeBloney, known as "Mountain Joe." DeBloney proposed the establishment of an Indian republic at the foot of Mount Shasta. The only physical evidence of the "republic" was a roadhouse constructed by DeBloney and Miller in which the latter, marking time until a more dignified office could be found, served as cook. In 1859 a posse of settlers captured Miller and accused him of joining the Indians in their horse-stealing forays. A friend sawed through the bars of his jail window and thus saved the future poet from the summary justice of the frontier. Later that year the Pit River massacre took place and Miller wisely departed for Oregon and less controversial activities.

Early in his twenties Miller became editor of the *Democratic Register* in Eugene, Oregon. It was not long before Miller was committing indiscretions again, this time in print. The federal government suppressed his newspaper when the Civil War began, and Miller departed for San Francisco and the literary life. He published two volumes of poetry and became a member of the circle dominated by Bret Harte and Charles Warren Stoddard. When he journeyed to London, Rossetti and the pale young esthetes took him up as a full-blooded specimen of the Wild Westerner. His "Songs of the Sierras," highly colored chromos of the primeval

Pacific mountains, were richly praised in England but harshly criti-
cized in the United States. The American critics, lofty in their eru-
dition, sniffed at his noted gaffe, rhyming "teeth" with "Goethe."
By the time of the Klondike discoveries, Miller had attained a fair
amount of popularity as poet, novelist and playwright, had married
for the third time, counting a Digger Indian bride, and had comfortably established himself at The Hights in Oakland, California.

At the age of fifty-six, saddened by the disappearance of the
Western frontier, Miller suddenly became restless at The Hights
with its monuments to his principal heroes, John C. Frémont,
Robert Browning and Moses, and its funeral pyre on which he had
already directed that he be given a pagan farewell, and with the
latest of his causes, the advocacy of free love. The Northern frontier, it seemed fitting, should also receive the tribute of the "Sweet
Singer of the Sierras." Since even the most poetic missions cost
money, Miller quickly arranged for the Hearst newspapers in San
Francisco and New York to send him to the Yukon as their correspondent. He moved out for the North so swiftly that Jack London
(who came to The Hights looking for financial support) missed
him by only a day or two.

Whatever qualms his editors felt on sending a poet on an assign-
ment that cried out for a Richard Harding Davis must have been
soothed by his announcement as he boarded the *City of Mexico:*
"I am going to get the information for the poor men who mean to
go to the mines next summer. If I find the mines limited either in
area or thickness, my first duty will be to let the world know." His
equipment consisted of a knapsack crammed with hardtack, bacon
and tea, his flute and a notebook and pencils. For a man determined to survey the mining situation, it hardly seemed like adequate equipment. But he added, "I will not need the usual provisions because, having got right down to the bedrock of cold
frozen facts, I shall take the next steamer leaving Dawson and
return straight to San Francisco."

In his first dispatches during the summer of 1897, Miller proved to his editors in San Francisco and New York only that the poet had triumphed over the mining engineer in his survey of the Alaskan situation. Over the miserable trail from Dyea, Miller tramped with hundreds of other men who labored under their great burdens while Miller traveled light and played his flute as a consolation for their travail. His first dispatch read in part:

I feel that the quest, so far as a poor man's getting out here goes, has been settled for me in the affirmative. Truly, if this were my own woods on The Hights the scene could not have been more pretty. The tall cottonwood trees moaned . . . water came tumbling down out of the wooded valley walls, down out of the clouds, great nameless cataracts.

Well, I trudged along over the slippery rocks and sand and saw fishes leaping in the air, and then a bank of mammoth English primroses! My boots become yellow from the blossoms, reaching almost to my knees. Think of blossoms like that in Alaska!

A kingfisher flew by. A prettier walk than I found there on the bank of that swift stream could not be found in the United States. It reminded me of Los Gatos, California, only on the hillsides there were great gardens of snow instead of gardens of grapes and prunes.

Miller neglected to mention the other strollers on that riverbank, the carrion cloud of insects buzzing over dead horses, or the water sucked up by thirsty throats from the polluted river. Yet, despite their later indignation, Klondikers could not claim they were lured north merely because Joaquin Miller so winningly described the scenery; they were there to hunt gold, not to admire the landscape. And they had paid no attention to much more widely published warnings against the hardships and dangers of the journey. Nor was Miller the only man overwhelmed by the grandeur of the North Country. A sober-minded physician could overlook the perils of a winter's day summons to call on a miner out on the tundra and write: "The creek trails were most lovely then, snow covering the trees and all the landscape so completely and so silently they seemed carved in Carrara. The cry of ravens sometimes broke the quiet, the turn of creaking windlass, or the clear music of a pack train's bells. . . . "

In his subsequent reportage, Miller persisted in describing the scenery and despite his experience in the mining camps of the West he ignored the "bedrock facts" of prospecting and mining in the Klondike. He shut his ears to the sounds of men laboring and admired the "twittering brotherhood of the forest." Not that the scenery alone obsessed him. A friend of Jack London's told of meeting Miller on the trail near Bonanza Creek and listening to the poet for an hour on the subject of the North Country's future development "when the ice-locked land would be the scene of great cities, marts of commerce reached by tracks of steel that would conquer the now untrodden valleys and mountains."

Miller was so entranced by his visions that disaster overtook him. He had intended to leave Dawson at the end of summer in 1897, having only his knapsack and a ticket to San Francisco to sustain him. The steamers did not arrive, and winter was coming on in giant southward strides. He was in the position of not being able to stay in Dawson, with thousands of other destitute and homeless men caught there in similar circumstances; nor could he leave, except on foot. Bravely enough, he took the latter course; he had too much pride for beggary. Late in September he set out for Circle City, 220 miles away on the trail homeward. The winter storms came whirling down early in October, and he could only turn back. For thirty-six days he struggled on the trail back to Dawson, his face bitten with cold, his gray beard spiked with frost. He had to crawl the last few miles into Dawson. Suffering extremely from exposure and exhaustion, he was taken to the Sisters of St. Anne; they managed to save from frostbite all but a toe and an ear. The beard he had cultivated for his role as The Sage of

The Hights had served him nobly against the assaults of the Arctic.

In May of 1898, wondering what he was going to do about getting back to the States, Miller was located by a San Francisco newspaperman, who brought him a letter from his aged mother. Enclosed was enough money to pay for steamer passage home. Miller wept and said, "I'll never see her alive"—and the prophecy came bitterly true, for she died before he reached San Francisco.

There was a last and undeserved humiliation, according to his journalistic colleagues. A newspaperman invited Miller to have dinner with him one night before the poet embarked for home. Colonel Steele of the Mounted Police stomped over to their table, shaking his finger at Miller and declaiming, "You're responsible for the death of many fine men and the ruin of thousands!" The diatribe would have continued, his host said, except that the newspaperman reminded the colonel in a frosty British accent that Miller was his guest. Steele stalked away, after warning Miller against any more excessively lyrical descriptions of the countryside. It may be significant that Steele was not so proud of this episode that he included it in his autobiography.

His friend later recalled that Miller was so disliked, so widely regarded as a literary charlatan—mostly by men looking for someone to blame for their predicament, anyone but themselves and the gold hunger that brought them to the Klondike—that "no one but myself came to wish him Godspeed on his journey."

Joaquin Miller quickly recovered his aplomb when he returned to the States in the summer of 1898. The following spring and summer he went on the road, muffled to the beard in a parka, with mukluks and mittens, and told vaudeville audiences of his adventures in the Yukon. Long ago and far away was the anger of Colonel Steele and the men who felt they had been misled by Miller's enthusiasms and visions. The vaudeville tour brought him enough money to live comfortably at The Hights until his death in 1913.

News of his vaudeville trouping quickly reached Dawson, where the *Nugget* reported this news with more than a tincture of indignation, then commented editorially:

Who of us cannot recall the poetic effusions of the ancient poet of the Sierras as he tramped over Chilkoot and floated down the mighty Yukon? His interesting accounts of the country, glowing with graphic word pictures of the beauties of this region, were eagerly devoured by millions of readers, and a percentage of those millions never rested night or day until they traveled and saw for themselves. But what an awakening. Where, oh where, are the gorgeous blossoms changing the complexion of the hills from base to crest like the blushes of a maiden? Where are the endless varieties of nature's jewels which gladden the eyes of our traveler—and the mighty game on every hand—and the mammoth trout in every stream—and the gold glittering on every gravel bed—and the—— Yes, where is the poet himself? To be practical, the only natural beauty of this land is its immensity, its grand gameless solitudes, its barren mountains and wonderful river. Mr. Miller has evidently reached the sixth age of man, when one sees "sermons in stones, books in the running brooks and good in everything."

Some of this indignation was, of course, misdirected. What of the editors who had sent a romantic poet to do a reporter's job on the biggest story of the decade? The Hearst editors learned their lesson from that experience, it should be added. When the Spanish-American War broke out a few months later, the Hearst coverage was entrusted to the career men of journalism, without a Byronic type among them. (And it should also be added, perhaps, that their accounts of insurrection and war in Cuba were often as giddy as Joaquin Miller's dispatches from the Klondike.)

The literary man whose work symbolized in the popular imagination all the melodrama, excitement and color of the gold rush was Robert W. Service. He arrived in the Klondike almost ten years after gold was discovered there. The only gold he handled was across the counter of his teller's cage in the Canadian Bank of Commerce. He heard only the echoes of the stampeders who drenched the Klondike with their sweat and tears. He saw only the ravaged creek bottoms and scarred hills where they had gouged out their wealth. He traveled from Skagway to White Horse, not under a mountainous pack with a cloud of mosquitoes stinging him relentlessly, but seated comfortably in a railroad car.

But instead of resenting him as a Johnny-come-lately, a literary grifter profiting from their triumphs and tragedies, the Klondikers took up Service and made him their poet laureate. Fortunately for him, he wrote of their experiences when memory had healed many wounds and when his audience was prepared to look back on the Klondike through a film of sentiment. Service, accidentally, caught their mood in just the right time and spirit; he remembered for them what they wanted to remember. But it was no accident, as he confesses in his autobiography, *Plowman of the Moon**, that in parlor entertainments he was an enthusiastic reciter of "Casey at the Bat," "Gunga Din," and "The Face on the Barroom Floor." His own work derived considerably from these models. How he came to write his first poems and launch himself unwittingly as the bard of the gold rush is an almost ludicrous example of a man falling into a literary career, as he might tumble into an uncovered manhole.

Service, at the age of thirty, ventured into the Yukon with the determination to live carefully and frugally—and how differently from the lively people he wrote about!—so that he could save $10,000 and retire to some more pleasurable shore than he had known since his birth in England. His superiors told him it was part of a banking career to make himself popular in the community, preferably in one of the churches of White Horse, rather

---

* Published by Dodd, Mead & Co., New York, 1945.

than its worldier institutions. By 1906, after all, much of the raf-fish spirit had disappeared; respectability was well intrenched. As a "prize specimen of that ingenuous ass, the amateur reciter," Serv-ice already had run through his repertoire a number of times at church socials. A friend, probably expressing popular exasperation at his limited resources, suggested that Service write something original for his next recitation. According to his own account, Service's creative processes worked like this on that momentous occasion:

First, you have to have a theme. What about revenge? . . . Then you have to have a story to embody your theme. What about the old triangle, the faithless wife, the betrayed husband? Sure fire stuff. . . . Give it a setting in a Yukon saloon and make the two guys shoot it out. . . . No, that would be too banal. Give a new twist to it. What about introducing music? Tell the story by musical suggestion. . . .

Inspired by these thoughts on a Saturday night, Service strolled past the noisy saloons to the bank, where he decided to start writ-ing his "recitation." The sound of revelry gave him an opening line, as he recalls. *A bunch of the boys were whooping it up*. . . . Entering the bank, he startled the night watchman into wakeful-ness. The watchman drew his revolver and fired a shot at the un-familiar shadow. "Fortunately he was a poor shot or 'The Shoot-ing of Dan McGrew' might never have been written. No doubt some people will say, 'Unfortunately,' and I sympathize with them." Service transferred his inspiration to paper but found, when it was finished, that it was highly unsuitable for recitation at a church concert.

A short time later, his creative juices now in ferment, Service attended a party at which a mining man from Dawson suddenly announced, "I'll tell you a story Jack London never got," and launched into the grisly tale of a "man who cremated his pal." The story haunted Service and a short time later, on a midnight walk, the opening line came to him: *There are strange things done in the midnight sun.* And thus "McGee" was committed to paper.

Shortly after being transferred to the Dawson branch of his bank, Service decided to have the poems, which now almost filled his bureau drawer, published at his own expense, vanity thus triumphing over Scottish frugality. He excused this self-indulgence with the thought, "Here is my final gesture of literary impotence. It is my farewell to literature, a monument on the grave of my misguided Muse. Now I am finished with poetic folly for good. I will study finance and become a stuffy little banker." That first volume became an instantaneous best-seller in the States, Alaska and the Yukon Territory. In Dawson, when he entered a saloon, the piano player would bawl out, "Here comes the bloody bard," and chant:

> "Hail poet, known as Ruddy Kip,
> Who paints for us the Yukon chip:
> Underneath a lamp of red
> Sighing softly: 'Come to bed.' "

Despite such amiable distractions, Service wandered through the streets of the rapidly declining capital of the Klondike, gathering from its haunted and ramshackle streets the material for hundreds of poems still to come and enrich him through the years. "As I pensively roamed these empty ways, a solitary and mournful dreamer, ghosts were all about me, whispering and pleading in the mystic twilight. Thus I absorbed an atmosphere that eluded all others. . . ."

And thus by an ironic coincidence, a man who "absorbed" the spectacle of the Klondike stampede from its ghostly remnants grew rich and famous through what Louis Untermeyer called "the red blood and guts style carried off jauntily." Of the four pre-eminent literary figures of the Klondike gold rush, London and Beach committed suicide, Miller died with his "sweet singer" mantle somewhat bedraggled, but Service vigorously survives them all. The moral for writers, already pointed up by the fact that Tolstoy wrote *War and Peace* without experiencing the Napoleonic invasion and Crane wrote *The Red Badge of Courage* although he was born after Appomattox, seemed to be that epic human events are best "absorbed" after the striving and suffering are done.

8

Thespis in Deep Freeze

ALTHOUGH THE theater in the Yukon was a lusty, vigorous and profitable institution, its artistic standards were on an approximate level with the traveling tent shows and *Uncle Tom* companies back in the States, and its muddy Rialtos in Skagway, Dawson and Nome were just barely glamorous enough to lure the most entertainment-starved audiences.

The Arctic tributary of the American theater was actually a strange wedding of show business with other forms of entertainment or dissipation. One form was the music hall partitioned off from a honky-tonk, with the various acts designed to dazzle the patrons sufficiently so they would eventually fall in the hands of the bartenders and "hostesses" (whose ideas of the meaning of hospitality were curiously primitive). Whisky and sex were so much more profitable than the less personal forms of amusement. Other theatrical ventures had a strong blending of the boxing arena, with an impressive left hook more highly honored than an organ-toned Hamlet. And in those settlements which could not support a professional theater there was often a sort of Little

Theater movement, which would hardly be recognized by its more pretentious descendants.

If the plays and vaudeville programs were not of a standard to impress either Aristophanes or Hammerstein, the Arctic theater at least provided the background for the careers of three of America's greatest theatrical magnates—John Considine, Alexander Pantages and Sid Grauman, who prospered in the years when show business was converting from vaudeville and the legitimate stage to the cinema palace. Between them the three men probably left more Mongolian caravansary, Mandarin palaces and Moorish seragli, all bravely disguising their cinematic dance of shadows and their devotees, than any other men in the American entertainment industry. And all three owed something of their imagination and daring—some will call these qualities by other names in esthetic distaste—to the atmosphere they absorbed in the Klondike stampede. As with lesser men, the gold rush marked them more deeply than any other event in their lives. Oddly enough, it was these three entrepreneurs who won the only theatrical fame of great consequence in the years following the gold rush; no magnificent acting careers were born there, although Marjorie Rambeau was a child actress in the Klondike for a short time. The more promising actors apparently preferred to stay closer to the managers' and bookers' offices on Broadway.

For most actors and actresses, singers, dancers and vaudeville performers, the Klondike was a rugged experience. Mining camps are notoriously critical audiences, with a harsh way of showing disapproval. Beauty is the only excuse for incompetence or lack of talent—feminine beauty, that is. The sensitive artiste had no place in those roaring dens adjoining honky-tonks and ramshackle opera houses where a restive audience and the Arctic wind and the howling of sled dogs often combined in an assault on the actor's nerves and self-esteem.

Generally speaking, it was the first comer who prospered among performers as among prospectors. After the summer of 1898, audiences had a number of attractions to choose from and became almost as demanding as those in the States—and much rougher about showing their disappointment. But the early arrivals had very little competition, and a modicum of talent was rewarded more munificently than at any time until Hollywood ushered in the literally Golden Age.

The Oatley Sisters, Polly and Lottie, arrived in Dawson during the spring rush of 1898. A few hours after their arrival the sisters began singing and dancing on the boardwalk at the corner of Second Street and Fourth Avenue, since there was no theater available. They were such an instant success that the *Nugget* sent a reporter over to review their show. He wrote that they sang and danced the buck and wing all night long, so appreciative was their audience. Their dog Tiny joined in singing a few numbers whenever the mood was on him. And the *Nugget's* reviewer gave his opinion that the Oatley Sisters had "splendid voices" and were "excellent dancers." Every night for two weeks they gave sidewalk performances, and the nuggets and pokes fell at their feet in such showers of gold that they were able to buy themselves a hall. Their mother, Mrs. Frank Monroe, arrived to establish a home for the young women. Not a week passed for the rest of that year without at least $5,000 being collected in their box office.

The variety actresses, dancers and singers almost without exception were accorded, offstage at least, all the respect they deserved and demanded. In the rougher music halls they might be subjected to lewd suggestions as they pranced around in pink tights or the daringly flimsy costumes popularized by the "Black Crook" type of presentations. But other than the blandishments that might be expected of men in a comparatively womanless country, the girls who "lived private," as they put it, were protected almost as securely as if they were back in their native villages and towns. Female performers could be divided roughly into three classifications: the rather ill-rewarded aristocracy of dramatic actresses, the flashier and much better-paid girls who sang and danced but would not mingle with the patrons as part of their duties, and the variety girls who worked in the lowest class music halls and drank "on a percentage" with customers after their turns on stage.

In Skagway, particularly, the art of "box-rushing" was developed into a highly efficient operation of separating the customer from his ready cash. After the show, the female singers and dancers rushed up to the boxes like a horde of harpies, shrieking, laughing and demanding drinks. Without invitation they rang the bell for the waiter, a thug whom it was unwise to disappoint, and ordered champagne at $20 and upward a pint. One young man engaged in hauling supplies to Lake Bennett for the Northwest Mounted Police complained to his superiors that he had wandered into one such resort in Skagway and was presented with a bill for $4,750 for a few hours of amusement. He paid $750 for a box of cigars and $3,000 for drinks brought to his box. That still left him $1,000 short, and the proprietor boldly appeared before Colonel Steele at the Lake Bennett barracks of the Mounties to demand that he force the young contractor to pay up. Colonel Steele not only ushered him to the door with scant courtesy but assured him that he would be arrested if he ever crossed the line into Canadian territory again.

Certainly there was no economic necessity for a girl to augment her income by joining the box-rushers. Entertainers of all types and talents were so much in demand that legitimate opportunity abounded, and the variety actress had only to close her ears to the seductive bubbling of champagne and the whisper of gold dust sifting out of a heavy poke. There was a surfeit of sopranos in the variety theaters, but Anna Kane ("The Nightingale of the North"), Nellie LaMarr, Minnie LaTour, Blanche LaMont and Jessie LaVore (it was the French period of vaudeville) all were paid $150 a week. There were also the usual specialty acts—knife-throwers, acrobats, trained dogs, dancing bears, magicians and tumblers. Also Lady Godiva, Little Egypt (famous in the World's Fair of 1893 at Chicago) and a "living tableau" of the famous heroines of history. An Irish tenor, who was particularly soulful in singing about home and mother, was not only tolerated but attained a high degree of popularity. Another temporary success was a man who mounted a scaffold and allowed himself to be hanged every night, thanks to the superb sinews of his neck.

Most of the popular songs had a ragtime jingle to them—"Ta-ra-ra Boom-der-é," "There'll Be a Hot Time in the Old Town Tonight," "Put Me Off at Buffalo," "She Got It Where McDooley Got the Brick," "Down Went McGinty," "Man Who Broke the Bank at Monte Carlo," "I Got Mine," "Put Your Arms Around Me, Honey," and "You Don't Have to Marry the Girl." Also the more sentimental and slower-paced songs of Stephen Foster, and "Genevieve," "Bird in a Gilded Cage," "After the Ball," "Doris, My Doris," "Just As the Sun Went Down," "Sunshine of Paradise Alley," "Somebody Loves Me" and "Only One Girl in the World for Me." The ragtime tunes called for a bouncy eupeptic delivery, while the more sentimental were rendered with many an eloquent gesture.

There were so many musicians wandering around Dawson that it was said they outnumbered the gambling-house dealers. Impoverished miners joined up in street bands, racking the summer night with their impromptu renditions. The more proficient groups played in the music halls for an ounce of gold a night for each musician.

One of the roving street bands was organized by Ikey Sutro, who opened Dawson's first pawnshop; he had a collection of instruments taken in hock and leased them out nightly on a profit-sharing basis, thus collecting on both the loan and the rental. Playing on his hand organ, he often joined the band, lending a semblance of cohesion to its efforts. Music lovers remembered that Sutro's down-

and-outers committed particular outrages on "The Blue Danube." One of the musicians, the drummer, had more talent for hammering an anvil than anything so delicate as his chosen instrument; the violinist was a walking cadaver with barely enough strength to lift his bow, let alone apply it to the catgut; the cornetist had little to recommend him except a robust pair of lungs, and the Dutch trombone player had a tendency to race the other musicians and would look up triumphantly when he finished ahead of them.

The much-traveled Arthur Walden described the state of the theater in the Klondike as "good, bad and indifferent," most of it indifferent. One troupe wintering in Dawson ran through its repertory of old plays and was acclaimed as a highly professional group, even if its presentations had been seen by most of the patrons in childhood. *Uncle Tom's Cabin,* of course, was the centerpiece of its repertory, and Walden declared that he had never seen the roles of Eliza and Simon Legree so well performed. Although the ice in the celebrated river-crossing scene was represented by crumpled newspapers, "Eliza acted her part exceptionally well . . . having seen people actually cross floating ice" on the Yukon a few hundred yards away. "I can't say as much for the bloodhounds," Walden commented. "These were represented by a Malemute puppy, drawn across the stage in a sitting position by an invisible wire and yelling his full displeasure to the gods."

A Yale-educated doctor found that his own theatrical tastes became degraded to the point that he preferred the most bloodcurdling melodramas to more sophisticated plays. He believed that was because

men who face death squarely, in their daily experience, prefer more gore than ordinary audiences. Tragedy has been at its best in periods after hand-to-hand battles with great odds. . . . The Elizabethan drama flowered after the Armada had been met and conquered. We who had encountered Chilkoot and the White

Horse could not be content with comedy. The reality of death had brushed our faces so closely, our eyes no longer blinked from gory portrayals.

Low comedy was also popular in Dawson, particularly if the comedian was clever enough to bone up on local names and places and work them into his patter. One of the masters of the comic vulgate was named Jenner, whose acting was "so terrible that it was interesting."

One of the Klondike's foremost showmen was "Arizona Charlie" Meadows, whose career had been picturesque enough for a dozen entrepreneurs in that era when a man of the theater was supposed to exude flamboyance, whatever his degree of taste and his knowledge of the dramatic arts. He was an old Indian fighter, born in a covered wagon near Visalia, California, baptized in the bloody range wars, shot up in the campaigns against Geronimo and his Apaches in Arizona. He toured the world with a Wild West show and was married aboard a ship off Singapore. The trademark of Dawson's most thunderous melodramas was "Arizona Charlie" making his sweeping bow before the curtain, sombrero in hand, and sonorously announcing the evening's attraction.

While spending the winter in Washington, one Sam Dunham wrote a poem that epitomized the Klondiker's taste in homespun entertainment:

> I want to hear the soothin' tones of Bates' old guitar
> As he sings about "The Fisher Maiden" at the Polar Star,
> And see Brick Wheaton rassle with his yaller mandolin
> As he chants the charms of Injun Hooch an' other
>   kinds of sin;
> I want to hear them songs once more an' want to
>   see my friends
> Where the swiftly rushin' Klondike with the
>   mighty Yukon blends.

The Yale-educated doctor recorded in his diary that a boy and his sister, both in their early teens, were among the star performers in the hurly-burly of Dawson's variety theaters. They were, he bluntly noted, "being exploited by their parents." "I had seen the mother making funny clothes for her children, each such being half masculine and half feminine. . . . It was ludicrous when each danced with the partner; this partner's was the individual's counterpart; one half male and the other female. The illusion was about perfect, and it brought down the house." It appeared that the "stage mother" lost nothing of her ambition and determination in the Arctic migration.

An occasional producer of shows and even more frequent performer in other men's presentations was Wilson Mizner, whenever his other occupations palled on him. He acted as a sort of unofficial booking agent for many of the girl singers, including such popular and beautiful artists—despite their sobriquets—as Glass-Eyed Annie, Flora the Ton, Diamond-Tooth Gertie and Nellie the Pig. Nellie, he recalled, "had a rather violent temper and once bit a waiter's ear off, but in the main she was a lady to the knuckles of each fist."

In the opinion of Mizner and other experts, however, the most talented actor in Dawson was no strutting human ham but a donkey known as Wise Mike. It is just possible that he was one of the ancestors of Francis the Talking Mule, who has made recent motion-picture history. Mike was the sole survivor of a pack train that had met with a tragic end. He often climbed into the windows of cabins out on the tundra at night, since he regarded Dawson and its suburbs as his personal domain; it was a bit of arrogance that sent many a newcomer fleeing into the night in terror. His usual practice, however, was to curl up and go to sleep around the potbellied stove in one of the saloons. It was a standing practical joke in the town to get a newcomer loaded on whisky and then suggest that he "kick that old donkey out of the bar." One touch of the boot in his ribs and Mike would flounder to his feet, snorting furiously, rearing up on his hind legs and wrestling with his tormentor. He also snapped his teeth so ferociously that the cheechako had an instant mental picture of losing an arm. It was all a game with Mike. Having scared the newcomer out of his wits and listening appreciatively to the laughter of his audience, Mike would kick up his heels once or twice, and then throw himself down, doglike, next to the glowing stove. Mike never assayed the more serious drama, but there was no doubt that he was the greatest comedian west of Broadway.

Amateur dramatics were a great anodyne for loneliness and boredom during the long Arctic winter. The dramatic urge springs up in the unlikeliest places and among the unlikeliest people. Rough old characters, who had long ago abandoned their lives to a round of hard work and recurrent dissipation, found something of their childhood's delight in make-believe by playing in the shows presented in isolated mining camps and in the Klondike towns. Minstrel shows, with their easily repeatable patterns, were among the favorites for amateur production; straight plays and concerts were also arranged.

One of the leading amateur performers was the future author Rex Beach, who displayed a considerable talent for clowning, according to Jack Hines. From Hines's description of Beach's standard act, however, it would seem it was just as well that Beach later took up the pen rather than the grease-paint stick.

He appeared on the stage dressed as a tramp with an oversize morning jacket that had oyster crackers in place of buttons. Around his neck he wore a lavalere [sic] of spider crabs. . . . During his monologue he pulled off a joint of the crab leg and chewed on it, and then tore an oyster cracker button from his jacket to eat with it. After ten or fifteen minutes of such clowning, he got down to the serious business of his act—singing "The Holy City," which was having a great vogue at the time. He sang it with parodied lyrics he had written himself. When he came to the last chorus, instead of singing, "Jerusalem! Jerusalem!" he sang "He's losin' 'em! He's losin' 'em!" And as he sang, his great baggy pants sagged down around his knees and finally fell to the floor. He hobbled off stage for his exit in the biggest laugh I ever heard on any stage. This sort of humor might not get a critic's award nowadays, but in Nome in 1901 it was a riot.

Somewhat apologetically, Hines explained, "Humor was broad in those days. Many of the prospectors who made up the audience were men of little education. They liked straight-forward clowning, and Rex gave it to them."

The Klondike theaters were redolent of the sweat and blood of the prize ring as well as the more delicate odors of the acting profession. At the Academy and the Music Hall in Dawson there were fight programs two and three times a week on the stage. There were several well-known pugilists in the gold fields, Frank Slavin and Joe Boyle among them, and they gladly met all comers. When the brawny but unskilled volunteers from the creeks met these professionals, there was more gore than pure science on display, but then their audiences were not squeamish, particularly at the sight of someone else's blood.

Tex Rickard, then a bartender at the Monte Carlo, was making his first appearance as a matchmaker in those days. Even then he had a sharp eye out for promising young fighters. "Klondike Mike" Mahoney recalled that Rickard sized him up and insisted that he had the makings of a heavyweight champion. And Rickard may have been right. In the spring of that year, 1898, Mahoney had hauled a piano—a small piano, granted—over the Chilkoot Pass for one Hal Henry, sole owner and manager of Henry's Theatrical Enterprises; the enterprises consisted of the Sunny Samson Sisters Sextette, who were bound for an engagement at a Dawson music hall. (The sextette was turned back at the Yukon territorial border by the Mounties on the grounds that the journey was too arduous for six frail females. Yet those tender morsels returned to Skagway, Mahoney learned later, played a six months' engagement at Soapy Smith's honky-tonk and "retained their modesty and virtue to the end." To have fought their way through half a year in the toughest dive on the Alaskan coast, the Sunny Samson Sisters must have been exceedingly tough-spirited as well as virtuous.) Mahoney demonstrated his pugilistic skill for Rickard and Boyle in a four-round match with Paddy Slavin, and Rickard was so enthusiastic he saw a world's championship glimmering in Mahoney's future. But Mahoney returned to driving his dog team, Rickard went on to bigger and better things, and Boyle drifted over to Europe, where he so impressed Queen Marie of Rumania, one way or another, that she placed him in complete control of the Rumanian oil fields during World War I.

Prize fighting in the Far North occasionally assumed a garish dignity. Jack Hines, who was studying grand opera and doing various odd jobs on the side, recalled that he refereed a fight between Stewart Carter, amateur middleweight champion of California, and Harry Pidgeon, a professional, in which all of them wore white dress shirts, black ties and black trousers. By the end of the third round all three were so spattered with blood that their shirts "looked like butchers' coats." Hines called the fight a draw, and the trio staggered out of the abbatoir.

A more ticklish matter was the fight Hines refereed between a big Irish Hill bruiser named Shaughnessy and a Negro professional who had fought throughout the Klondike. The theater was packed with Shaughnessy's compatriots from Irish Hill and, what with a $2,000 purse and the huge sums bet by the bloodthirsty Irishmen, Hines could see that any decision favoring the Negro heavyweight would make him the candidate for a Donnybrook in which his neutrality would not be considered. From the opening bell, the Negro had all the best of it, and Shaughnessy had great difficulty in staying on his feet until the final round began. "Kill him, Shaughnessy," his partisans howled at the fast-fading Irishman. Just before the Negro landed his knockout punch, Shaughnessy, bloody but gallant, turned to his supporters and uttered one of the great understatements in ring history, "Boys, this bloke is doing me no good." Shaughnessy went down for the count, and Hines was spared the necessity of fleeing across the tundra with several hundred outraged Celts at his heels.

It was one of those coincidences freakishly dictated by fate that the two men who reigned over the entertainment industry on the Pacific coast, in its most imperial period, arrived almost simultaneously in the Klondike on their separate ways to fortune— along with the mechanical monster that was to dominate their lives a score of years in the future. As early as September of 1898, the Music Hall in Dawson was advertising showings of Thomas A. Edison's newest invention, the Projectoscope, and some of his latest films—"Destruction of the *Maine*," "The Battle of Manila," "The Fall of Morro Castle" and a melodrama titled "Brocky Morgan, the Mountaineer." It was unlikely that either Alexander Pantages or Sid Grauman realized the import of Edison's Projectoscope then, for it was merely a novelty, nothing to compare with the livelier delights of theater-in-the-flesh.

Sid Grauman and his father, David J. Grauman, already veterans of the gold fields, arrived in Dawson with hopes of finally making a strike for themselves. The elder Grauman had produced tent shows in cities throughout the United States. A few years after Sidney Patrick was born on St. Patrick's Day 1870, he was carried along in his father's nomadic wake. Most of his scant schooling was obtained in a canvas school at Cripple Creek, Colorado, after he had accompanied his father in the Oklahoma land rush. But it soon became apparent in Dawson that the Graumans would not enrich themselves either as prospectors or showmen. "D.J." returned to San Francisco and a reunion with Sid's mother while the boy, now nineteen, stayed on to try his luck. The best Sid could do was peddle newspapers, he found, and even there the ubiquitous Wilson Mizner was waiting to outwit him. With public interest whipped up over the Spanish-American War, Sid's first shipment of newspapers from the States had a presold market. Just before the dog-sled shipment arrived, however, Mizner conned him into a deal: Mizner would buy the first paper for $25 provided Grauman would sell no others for an hour. The bushy-haired and bright-eyed Grauman naïvely believed Mizner merely wanted an hour's jump on his fellow citizens in learning the war news, although he should have known Mizner's concerns were always more immediate and personal. So he was stunned when he learned that Mizner had taken his copy of the newspaper, rented a store and read it before 200 citizens who paid fifty cents apiece for his primitive newscast. Grauman was disconsolate until Mizner gave him half the proceeds and assured him the public reading had only whetted the general appetite. And Mizner was right. Grauman sold out his stock in a few hours. As premier newsboy of Dawson, Sid did not fare too badly. He charged $1.50 a copy on the streets of Dawson, $2 out on the creeks. Once he took in $3,200 in three days.

Grauman joined the rush to Nome, following the example of Wilson Mizner, who had become his idol. He was a resident of the McQuestion Hotel, operated by Mizner, who granted Sid the privilege of using his comb and brush. Grauman's black mop was the only other hair in town so privileged. In later years Grauman recalled Mizner's boast of having owned "the finest library in Nome." It consisted of a table and a brightly shining kerosene lamp by which to read the seams of his hotel's sheets, which were usually lively with insects on the march.

Grauman was grateful for Mizner's patronage, variable though it was. Once when they were both broke—Sid's shipment of news-papers from the States being overdue—Mizner grandly invited Grauman to dinner. They dined on bear steaks and the trimmings. The bill was $15. With enviable nonchalance, Mizner told his companion to make a break for it, host being as broke as guest. While Grauman did as Mizner suggested, the latter lightly told the proprietor to put the meal on his "account." An hour later, when Grauman located his generous friend, Mizner had a vivid assortment of cuts and bruises.

There is no doubt that from Mizner the future theatrical magnate learned the invaluable lesson of accepting adversity with brave contempt. In his Hollywood years Grauman often told of Mizner's hopeless but never-yielding pursuit of a dance-hall girl who preferred a richer man. One night he saw Mizner slip a black mask over his face, enter a restaurant and emerge a short time later with a revolver in one hand and a cash register under the other arm. Mizner quickly put the gun in his pocket, threw away the cash register without trying to loot it and hurried to the nearest saloon, where he began singing "Sweet Alice Ben Bolt," with considerable feeling. The officers of the law soon entered in search of the bandit and noted that Mizner was about the right build. But his audience was so enthralled, a dozen witnesses sprang up and declared Mizner had been there for hours. Mizner graciously delivered another encore.

Grauman later braced Mizner for an explanation of the strange, profitless holdup. Mizner really was trying to rob the restaurant of a certain type of chocolates which the dance-hall girl preferred above all other delicacies; the restaurant would sell them only to its steady customers, and Mizner's purse was such an inconstant quality, fat one day, lean the next, that he was no one's steady customer. Robbery was the only means by which he could get the chocolates. When he poked the gun at the proprietor, however, he learned that the chocolates had been stowed away in the safe. So he grabbed the cash register, knowing that a bandit with a fixation on chocolates would not be too hard to track down.

Further experience in the quick footwork required of a theatrical entrepreneur was obtained by Grauman through producing several tent shows in Nome before he went back to the States. With this background, and his father as a partner, Sid began his climb to success. Sid was responsible for the innovation of showing a film along with a half dozen vaudeville acts. The Graumans soon owned several San Francisco theaters and a half dozen in northern California towns. They sold out and bought the then-opulent Million Dollar Theater in Los Angeles. After his father's death Sid built the two most ornate motion-picture temples in all the land, the Egyptian and Grauman's Chinese, where he introduced the "prologue," an elaborate presentation which often overshadowed the film it was supposed to enhance. Sid Grauman was the high priest of Hollywood's cinematic mosques, but he never became so lordly that he failed to credit his days as a Klondike newsboy for giving him the ideal background for such a career.

One of the principal lessons learned in the Klondike by Alexander Pantages was that a man would spend his last dollar to be amused: for a drink, a last flutter with the dice or a few laughs in a dance hall. It convinced him that supplying amusement was actually a sounder business venture than catering to the supposedly primary needs of the human race. Few men came to the Klondike with a greater instinct for acquisition than Pantages. To call it greed would be minimizing its force and the imagination that gave it direction, even distinction.

He was born Pericles Pantages on a small island off the coast of Greece. Someone told him of the world conquest of Alexander the Great, and he immediately changed his name to Alexander. Ambition, prodded by the bitter poverty of his boyhood, was the hallmark of his character from the very beginning. At the age of nine his father took him to Egypt and together they worked in a Cairo restaurant as busboy and waiter. Apparently Alexander saw that life with father would lead nowhere but to another bout with dirty dishes and ill-tempered customers, and he had not yet reached his tenth birthday when he ran away from the hovel he shared with his father and shipped out as cabin boy aboard a schooner. Three years later he contracted malaria in Panama and his shipmates casually heaved him out on the beach. He recovered sufficiently to swing a pick and shovel and run a donkey engine during the futile effort of De Lesseps to dig a Panama canal. After two years of hard labor, he was warned by a doctor that he would die of malaria unless he removed himself to a colder climate so he signed on a brig bound for Puget Sound. ("Signed on" is a euphemism, for Pantages did not learn to read and write until his prosperous middle age.)

In San Francisco Bay he jumped ship and went to work as a waiter in Walter Meyer's beer garden. Since this reminded him of the career he escaped from in Cairo, he began training as a prize fighter and appeared in a number of preliminaries on the cards at Vallejo, then the Pacific coast's pugilistic capital; he was short but husky, and fought as a welterweight with some success. He concluded, however, he was no close threat to the championship of Mysterious Billy Smith, and retired before his opponents' punches could addle that delicate adding machine in his brain.

He was twenty-six years old when he decided to join the gold rush to the Klondike and withdrew the $1,000 he had saved. On the Alaska-bound ship he lost this grubstake to professional gamblers, landed in Skagway with a quarter in his pocket—and again found himself a waiter. He went to work for Harriet Pullen, a youngish widow with four children who had migrated from Puget Sound with $7 and an indubitable talent for making apple pies. All he got was board and room. Meanwhile, men were getting rich in the Klondike. He managed to pass himself off as a guide for a party of cheechakos and thus eased himself by the Mounted Police, who insisted on all travelers for the Yukon showing they had means to sustain themselves. For a brief time he worked in Dawson as a waiter, then saw a sign in the window of Charlie Cole's Saloon: "Wanted: One Expert Mixologist, Salary $45 per day." Pantages had never mixed a drink professionally but he took on the job. Cole was well satisfied with his bartender, particularly when Pantages suggested he put on entertainment on the theory that, drinks being about the same everywhere, the saloon with the best entertainment would be the best patronized. Cole prospered.

Meanwhile, Pantages had become involved with Kate Rockwell, known as "Klondike Kate" and "The Flame of the Yukon," a former Coney Island chorus girl who became the queen of the dance-hall girls in Dawson. She received thousands of dollars a month for singing and dancing, for and with the sourdoughs, and among the gowns in her wardrobe was a Paris import that cost her $1,500. She was reputed to have collected $100,000 in cash and $50,000 in jewels during her reign.

Pantages persuaded her to finance a new music hall on the site of the Tivoli, which had burned down. It prospered for a time; then came the news of gold discovered on the beaches of Nome, and the big spenders hurried off to Nome. Pantages left on their heels—without Kate.

(In 1906, "Klondike Kate" sued Pantages on the grounds that he had run out on their partnership and on his promise to marry her. She charged in her complaint that she bought him seventy-five-cent cigars, fifteen-dollar silk shirts and other luxuries, as well as paying $40 a week for his board. In his answer, Pantages admitted the business association but denied that he had promised to marry her. He settled the suit out of court for an undisclosed sum.)

Pantages, without a beautiful woman to back him, spent the winter of 1900 working as a bartender in Nome. Somehow he persuaded a group of entertainers to finance him in opening his first theater, Pantages' Orpheum, and it provided the best show in Nome. Pantages was a demanding impresario; if the act wasn't the best available, out it went and the devil take sentiment; he was a perfectionist, even in the carefree show business of the Arctic. And if he coddled the customer, he also tapped him for all he was worth; each seat in Pantages' Orpheum cost $12.50.

From then on, Pantages shot along toward the fortune he coveted with all the speed of an express train with the green light. In 1902 he sold his Nome theater and returned to the States. Like Grauman he pioneered the combination of films and vaudeville, starting out with the little Crystal Theater in Seattle. By 1926 he owned thirty film palaces and controlled forty-two others. Three years later, his instincts as sharp as in his struggling, scrabbling youth, he sold his circuit to Radio-Keith-Orpheum for $24,000,000, just before the depression and the talking picture torpedoed vaudeville and left it to sink with barely a trace, until television many years later brought it back to the surface.

Living by his wits, rubbing up against the Mizners and other sharpshooters, competing with the pimps, con men and mine-salters of the gold rush—all honed Pantages' financial instincts to the sharpest possible edge. He never took anything at its face value. Once on a trip to New York, after he had become the king-pin of West coast vaudeville, he stopped in front of a huge electric sign which flashed just two words: JOHN DREW.

"Who's he?" Pantages asked his companion. "What kind of an act has he got?"

9

Three Kinds of Law

HUNDREDS OF MILLIONS of dollars removed from the creek beds, beaches and hillsides of Alaska and the Yukon were a constant temptation to men who preferred a short cut to affluence, who used a gun or knife instead of the honest pick and shovel, or a cold deck, a phony claim, a bottle of chloral hydrate or a seductive woman. Considering all the criminals attracted by the gold rush, and how successful they had been in previous gold rushes, it was remarkable that the whole North Country was not in the grip of crime and violence.

Miners walked around with thousands of dollars in their pokes and pack trains brought hundreds of thousands of dollars worth of gold dust from the creeks without taking any very imposing security measures. Yet there were few crimes of violence compared to what might have been expected in a wild stampede into an unsettled country. Soapy Smith's reign over Skagway showed the potentialities of organized crime, if given the opportunity, for in less than a year he was able to proclaim that *he* was the law in Skagway. And so he was until the respectable citizens saw their businesses endangered by the fact that stampeders were beginning to avoid the terrorized town.

In its early days Nome, too, was close to anarchy. The difference between these American-ruled ports and the mining camps of the interior, mostly in the custody of the Canadian law, was that the Dominion, however much the Americans resented its strict, sometimes capricious attitude toward customs duties and excise taxes, moved swiftly to establish control through its courts and police. There was no American equivalent of the Northwest Mounted Police, which Soapy Smith may have been unconsciously emulating when he organized the mounted Skagway Guards. The United States established a few wretched garrisons but neither their experience nor their police powers were adequate for the vaguely defined tasks they were given. One of the unhappy posts was Fort Gibbon on the Yukon near the mouth of the Tanana, which was manned mostly with veterans of the recent campaign in Cuba. A physician who visited the post reported:

Their equipment seemed, and was, ridiculous. They had many horses and oxen, brass cannon, and all sorts of semi-tropical clothing and clumsy military gear and truck, utterly unadapted to this country. The oxen could be eaten, but what they could do with cannon and with horses in these trackless forests was a mystery!

The enlisted men renamed the post Camp Misery.

William Ogilvie, the first commissioner and governor pro tem of the Yukon Territory, told how difficult it was for most of the Americans to grasp the fact they were under Canadian law.

At St. Michael he attended a meeting of Americans headed for the Klondike and with some amusement heard them vote into being a vigilance committee to regulate their affairs when they reached the gold fields.

Then, unable to "hold my tongue any longer," Ogilvie spoke up:

"Gentlemen, any interference of yours in our Canadian affairs will be quite unnecessary. The Royal North West Mounted Police will attend to law and order and everything else." To my amazement, they wanted to know "What the hell" the North West Mounted Police were. When I explained, they asked, "Who the hell sent them here?" When told "The Canadian Government at Ottawa," they wanted to know "what in hell" the Canadian Government had to do with it! I assure you that it took some time, and also long perusal with them of the new maps I had with me, to convince these saucy fellows that the Klondike diggings actually were in Canada.

Despite his stern lecture on the omnipotence of Canadian authority, several of Ogilvie's "saucy fellows" later were encamped at Circle City when winter closed down and the only supplies available were those aboard two river steamers ice-locked there for the winter; they voted at a miners' meeting to commandeer the supplies without reference to Canadian officials. Armed but orderly, the miners stalked aboard the boats and removed the supplies to their own warehouse, to be accounted for later.

In fact, throughout the several years when Americans were particularly numerous in the Klondike gold fields, the Canadian authorities were constantly on the defensive, somewhat shrilly proclaiming their sovereignty and hauling their tattered maps out for fresh proof of it.

The man who chose robbery as a career had little hope of longevity in either Alaska or the Yukon Territory. It wasn't too hard to pull a job, but finding a place to hide was almost impossible. Flight across the tundra in winter, with experienced men on his trail, was usually doomed to failure. Burglary, depending on the circumstances, was often a capital offense. Murder rarely went unpunished.

Still there were men who tried against all the odds. There was

even a sort of Arctic Robin Hood who made the trails around Fairbanks unsafe for travelers when that mining camp was booming.
He was called the Blue Parka Man. Once he held up a party including Bishop Rowe on an intersection of trails outside the town.
The bishop, with "a winning smile and gentle voice," expostulated
with the bandit for robbing a poor laborer in God's vineyard.

The Blue Parka Man was instantly contrite. "Of course I won't
rob you," he told the bishop. "Take your poke off that heap on the
ground, Bishop, and take that poke with the shoestring around it,
too. Why, damn it all, Bishop, I'm a member of your church!"

The Blue Parka Man was captured a short time later and sent to
McNeill's Island federal penitentiary for a long sentence, and it
developed that he was indeed a parishioner of Bishop Rowe's. The
bishop, according to Judge Wickersham, always smiled benignly
when the story was told in his presence.

The development of law and order in the North invariably pro-
gressed through three stages. First a man avenged wrongs himself
or his fellow prospectors avenged them for him if he was unable,
with "an eye for an eye, a tooth for a tooth" functioning as the
Code Klondike. As the country grew more thickly settled, the law
was somewhat roughly and often drastically administered by
miners' meetings, which elected a judge pro tem, a sheriff and a
jury to try any case brought before it; the whole camp stood by to
see that justice was then carried out. It is worth noting that the
judgments of these impromptu courts were invariably more severe
than those pronounced later for similar crimes by the legally constituted courts. The third phase was when regular police forces and
courts were established, and justice was administered more slowly,
laboriously and drably—and more fairly.

Many of the decisions handed down by the miners' courts were
so picturesque—and often so revelatory of the miners' mass preju-
dices and sympathies—that they would send the conventional legal
mind into delirium.

James Wickersham, the foremost Alaskan jurist and an able historian, came across a Klondike miners' court decision, however, which he found admirable in its swift rendition of justice. The case involved a young woman of the camp who complained that a dance-hall fiddler had wooed her with his violin, seduced her and left her pregnant. Now he refused to marry her. There was considerable indignation among the miners toward the amorous fiddler; mostly womanless, they could not understand the attitude of a fellow who would spurn the affections of a young and attractive woman.

Judge, sheriff and jury were quickly selected by the miners' meeting, and the jurors retired to consider her appeal for relief. All she asked was that the musician be forced to pay her hospital bills. A unanimous verdict was quickly reached and the girl was delighted to learn that she had been awarded all she asked and much more. The verdict:

Resolved, that the defendant pay the plaintiff's hospital bill, $500, and pay the plaintiff $500, and marry her as he promised to do, and that he have until 5 o'clock this afternoon to obey this order; and,

Resolved further, that this meeting do now adjourn till 5 o'clock.

The wretched musician fully realized that his choice in the matter narrowed down to two alternatives: complying with the judgment of the court or being strung up promptly at five o'clock that afternoon if he ventured to defy it. The miners stayed in town, milling through the saloons and waiting for him to make up his mind.

Long before the appointed hour he saw the wisdom of compliance. On hearing of his decision, the judge, sheriff and jury—all of whom would have cheerfully hanged him a few hours later, if he had been less discreet—adjourned to the bar where the fiddler and his bride adorned a celebration of their wedding a few minutes earlier, and officially offered their congratulations.

Judge Wickersham commented, with unusual grace for a professional contemplating the work of amateurs, "It would have taken my court two years, with many pleadings, hearings and arguments, instead of two hours, to give judgment, which in all probability would have been reversed on some technicality."

These informal courts, for all their crudity, sometimes dealt shrewdly with the cases brought before them, and the one at Circle City even managed to keep a genuine, rooting-tooting badman within bounds, at least for a time. The case involved a man named Allard, who had been wounded in the leg by one Buck Corvee, one of the few stampeders who fancied himself as a gunfighter. Allard had once killed a man in Montana, as everyone in the settlement knew, but he was considered a decent, law-abiding citizen by local standards. Corvee, knowing of Allard's reputation as a killer, felt he had to eliminate him in order to enhance his own sordid fame.

Court was called into session after a judge, Jimmy Belcher, and a clerk were elected. Anyone in the courtroom could cross-examine a witness or comment on testimony, since the audience constituted the jury, the prosecution and the defense. Since it was winter, the court sat in a large log building, although in the summertime the sessions were generally alfresco.

As testimony was being taken on the circumstances surrounding the shooting, Buck Corvee rose and bawled out, "I'm ready to settle this thing outside right now—with guns. If Allard is man enough to come out, we won't be keeping you gentlemen any longer."

(What Corvee proposed was the so-called "drop" procedure in gunfighting: the first man out the door would whirl and shoot the other as he came out.)

Both Corvee and Allard dashed for the door of the courtroom.

"Come back here!" roared Judge Pro Tem Belcher. The two men approached the bench, hands over their guns, watching each other out of the corners of their eyes.

"I make a motion," Belcher proposed to the jury, "that we let these two men fight. If one of them is killed, he gets a Christian burial. If both are killed, both get Christian burials. But if one survives, *we hang him!*"

"What's this?" demanded Corvee. "Why, that's a personal threat. I'll kill Allard as quick as I draw on him—and then I'll get hung!"

"Correct," Judge Belcher said. "And there's just one thing further, since I hear no dissenting vote in the room. If either of you is found dead after this day in suspicious circumstances, the other will be hung without trial."

A year later Corvee quarreled with Jake Kornstadt, a Circle City saloonkeeper, and sent word through intermediaries that he intended to kill Kornstadt. Shortly thereafter, he stalked into the saloon and Kornstadt shot and killed him before the gunfighter could even draw. Kornstadt summoned a miners' court to pass judgment on his act and was quickly acquitted. Allard admitted he was greatly relieved by the news of Corvee's death. "Not that I hated him any more, but he was a careless, drunken fool and I was always afraid I'd be hung on account of the damn pest."

Homicide, particularly in a gunfight where a man had an even chance unless he went up against a professional, was always treated more lightly by the miners' courts than larceny, especially if the latter offense involved stealing from another man's cache on the trail or at his diggings. Mizner told of an old man named Kern who admitted this crime. He was given the choice of being hanged, "with everyone in town taking a hand on the rope, a mile long," or taking a sled without dogs and trying to reach another settlement over the ice and snow. "In like circumstances," Mizner said, "Indians invariably chose to hang." But Kern chose to make a run for it. The citizens of Circle City so admired his courage that "all shook hands with him and wished him the kind of luck he'd never have."

Later they learned that he met another party far out on the trail. He was given food and warned to turn back to Circle City, the circumstances of his departure not being known to the other travelers. Old Kern merely shook his head and continued on his way. He died somewhere in the frozen wilderness.

Commissioner William Ogilvie, who was a surveyor by profession and who drew the first fairly accurate map of the gold fields, took a rather dim view of the informal courts. "At those meetings," he wrote in *Early Days on the Yukon,* "as at every other gathering of curious people, for most of them had no other motive in attending, one or two present led in the talk; it did not follow that they were the best fitted to lead in common sense, but that seldom figures. . . ."

As an example of the way emotion and prejudice influenced the decisions of such courts, he cited the case of the manager of a trading company's branch at Forty Mile. The manager had brought with him and his family a female servant, young and comely, who was under contract to serve him for one year in exchange for board, wages and the fare for her return trip to a coastal port.

Not long after the household was established, the girl began staying out late at night. She not only refused to explain or mend her ways, but stayed out even later, often not returning to her employer's house until morning. The only other woman in the settlement being her employer's wife, it appeared that the girl was engaged in a love affair of no mean proportions. She impudently advised her mistress that the contract was being fulfilled as long as she performed her household chores; it was none of the lady's business where she slept.

The manager and his wife finaly presented her with an ultimatum: either she appeared at a certain hour, early in the evening, or she would be locked out of the house permanently. When she disregarded the warning, the threat was carried out.

A miners' meeting was called to consider her complaint that she had been brutally and unjustly treated. To the miners, many of them Americans with a strong prejudice against anything like bonded servitude, a horror of the Colonial days, it seemed as though the merchant—who was disliked in any case for his aloof manner—was virtually setting himself up as a slave owner. Their prejudice was further aroused by the oration of an eloquent "professional man," as Ogilvie described him, probably a man who had turned from the law to prospecting, in which the girl's plight was painted with all the primary colors of Dickens re-creating life in a London workhouse.

The miners decided that the trader was to be ordered to pay the girl all the wages owed under the contract and her fare to the coast.

There was a general sense of shame, however, when the belief later grew that "the orator who was such an ardent advocate for unfortunate womanhood was her partner in misconduct." One of the Forty Mile miners told Ogilvie he "like the others had been hoodwinked by the story the girl told, and judging from the zeal displayed by her advocate, one would never suspect he was her partner in guilt."

In the same mining camp, Ogilvie learned of another "trial" that verged on sheer vaudeville; if the Canadian commissioner had not been such a sober historian, in fact, one would suspect he was fobbing off an old dialect-comedy sketch on his audience.

It involved a Jewish tailor, a Negro barber and an Irish prospector. The tailor and the barber had been exchanging services for some time on a sort of loose barter arrangement. Then the tailor decided it was time for an accounting and presented the barber with a bill for $4. The barber entered a counterclaim for $5.50. A miners' court was called in the town's largest saloon, and both sides of the case were presented with as much passion as if they involved millions of dollars. The court, bored to extremity by the piddling affair, nourished as it was on the red meat of much stronger dramas, must have allowed its attention to wander, for it awarded the tailor, or plaintiff, the $1.50 surplus sought by the barber, or defendant.

Before the court was declared adjourned, one of the tribunal jumped to his feet and proposed that the tailor be fined $20 for taking up the court's time with such a trifling matter. "Had it been carried," Ogilvie commented, "the money would have been spent then and there, the reader can guess how." In other words, the "fine" would have been spent on drinks for the house.

This was the Irishman's cue to speak in defense of the Jewish tailor.

"No, gintlemen," he shouted, "ye can't do that! It's absurd. This poor man has called on ye for justhice. Ye have acknowledged his claim by meetin' and decidin' in his favor, and now ye want to fine for askin' for justhice. That's nonsensical—ye can't do it!"

The tribunal sadly agreed that a man couldn't be fined for having the termerity to seek justice.

It was almost an anticlimax when the barber jumped to his feet and announced that nobody could make him pay that $1.50. Court adjourned in the disgusted realization that it had no legal power to make the defendant pay the judgment. It was easier to hang a man than take $1.50 out of his pocket.

Once the stampede to the Klondike began, it was obvious that some more effective means of administering justice must be established, or anarchy would soon take over the mining camps. A system of controlling this army of adventurers must be set up at once under unprecedented conditions. As Dr. Alfred Thompson, a member of the Canadian Parliament, stated the problem:

Ninety per cent of the people were aliens, and a hundred per cent were individualistic to a remarkable degree. There were neither mails nor telegraphs, neither roads nor bridges. The only existing mining regulations were completely inadequate. An army of officials had to be created out of the most unpromising material, from men mostly half mad from the craze for sudden wealth. Every man spoke and thought for himself. The source of all authority was at Ottawa, four thousand miles away, requiring months in which to refer a single question or to get a solitary ruling. Meanwhile the need was for instant legislation, rulings on the moment, and it was into this seething whirl that Mr. Ogilvie was cast as Governor or Commissioner. . . . An entire system had to be created. Advisers were plenty, for every man in the country considered himself quite capable of suggesting a solution of every problem. But in the multitude of counsel there was no wisdom, since very few agreed. There was no precedent. Mr. Ogilvie's powers as Commissioner were greater in many respects than the powers of a governor elsewhere, but the Federal Government of Ottawa still held the reins.

In a remarkably short time, Commissioner Ogilvie had the police system functioning so admirably that violent crime was practically unknown in the towns because of the judiciary quickly and sternly dealing with the culprits brought in by the police.

During the first thirteen years of Dawson's existence, there were exactly thirteen murders committed within its limits, a very low average considering the character and temper of the men and women who came there from all sorts of haunts and stews in their native lands. Most of them came wearing revolvers or at least carrying them in their luggage, but they quickly learned that gun and holster were out of style. British law has always been extremely rigorous in dealing with crimes where firearms were used.

Of the thirteen murderers, all were quickly apprehended, tried and convicted. Twelve were hanged; one escaped the gallows by committing suicide.

When the police held an auction of revolvers confiscated from various persons who had not been convinced that gun-carrying was out of fashion, the weapons were knocked down for only one to five dollars, much less than their owners had paid for them. The buyers mostly wanted them for souvenirs. Contrary to the impression created by Robert W. Service, there were very few unlucky Dan McGrews in the Klondike.

Out on the tundra, on the trails and the lonely ice-locked creeks, there were occasional murders, usually involving a bad case of cabin fever or the greed of one partner for the other's possessions, but these were punished almost as swiftly, although at greater hardship to the authorities.

In April of 1898 there were two murder cases whose outcome must have done much to convince the incoming thousands of gold hunters that crime did not pay in the Klondike, no matter what tales were told of Dodge City, Virginia City, Creede and other mining camps in the States. On the Stikine River three men from Vancouver, British Columbia, had spent the winter piling up a dump of pay dirt. The spring thaw was coming on fast and it seemed to Joseph Claus that their claim had such faint "colors" of gold dust it would hardly pay them for their winter's work. His two companions, Harry Swans and Richard Knight, had almost $1,000 in cash between them; he coveted that and their horses and other possessions. So one day he shot Swans, then sneaked up behind Knight with an ax and dispatched him, too. He threw their bodies into an icy crevasse and hurriedly departed. Within a few days his crimes had been discovered, the Mounties were on his trail, and he was captured between Teslin Lake and Glenora. His plea of self-defense was considerably weakened by the fact that he looted the bodies of $900 in cash and tried to flee. The court of Telegraph Creek sentenced him to hang.

That same month, on the McClintock River, two prospectors were attacked by a band of marauding Indians. Billy Meacham of

Juneau was shot to death and his partner, C. A. Fox, a Californian, was seriously wounded but later recovered. The Indians had superior knowledge of the country, but the Mounties pursued them to a point forty miles below Tagish Post and captured them without firing a shot. Jim, Joe, Frank and Dawson Nantuck were all sentenced to a quick trip to the gallows.

The Mounties were so respected that they could afford to be occasionally quixotic in maintaining order along the tough river front of Dawson. A traveler saw one officer angrily watching a barkeeper hurl a drunken man through the swinging doors. The drunk looked up from his dusty landing place with wonderment as the Mountie, instead of arresting him, stalked over to the bartender and ordered him to pick up the drunk, dust him off tenderly and take him back into the saloon until he sobered up. "You sold him the liquor which made him drunk," the officer said sternly, "and you'll keep him there safely until he recovers his wits, or I'll take you over and introduce you to the woodpile at our barracks." The drunk was escorted grandly to a bunk in the rear of the barroom.

On the American side of the Alaska-Yukon boundary, it took almost two years longer for the law to take hold and even then its clutch sometimes weakened through inefficiency, bribery or ineptitude. In Alaskan territory there was no rival slogan to "The Mounties always get their man." Sometimes, according to Hudson Stuck in his account of travels on the Yukon several years after the gold rush, the American authorities never even made an attempt to get *their* man. The trader at Mouse Point, in 1902, told him of exploring an old camp near by which had been destroyed by fire several years before. He found among the debris the body of a man whose head had been split open by an ax blow; close by were two empty pokes with a few grains of gold still clinging to them. It didn't take much of a criminologist to deduce that a murder for the purpose of robbery had been committed. The trader notified federal authorities at Eagle City, then the Department of Justice in Washington, without even an investigation being made. More than fifty years have passed, but that murder is still not only unsolved but uninvestigated.

Some measure of the problem confronting law enforcement officials in Alaska can be gathered from the labors of Judge Wickersham, one of the more constructive pioneers of that territory. To cover their vast judicial realms Wickersham and his fellow judges had to ride the circuit, much as in Abraham Lincoln's lawyering days, although under greater handicaps and with greater hardships. The Third Judicial Division over which Wickersham presided, for instance, contained 300,000 square miles—and only 1,500 Caucasian persons. It extended from the shores of the Arctic Ocean to the Bering Sea coast; its greatest lengthwise distance was from the northeast corner of the Arctic coast to the island of Attu, which was approximately 2,000 miles. Geographically, it may be seen, the Yukon was much easier to approach from the administrative standpoint, although this in no way belittles the problem confronting Commissioner Ogilvie and other Canadian officials.

When Judge Wickersham arrived in Eagle City, the headquarters of his judicial division, he found the power and majesty of the United States Government represented by two town lots—no courthouse, no jail, no other public buildings. He had to build from the ground up, literally. Nor did he have any funds at his disposal. His directive was to build whatever was necessary from license money collected from the five saloons and three trading posts in Eagle City. A couple of log structures were run up in a hurry, and Judge Wickersham took office with all the pride of a man ascending the bench of the United States Supreme Court for the first time.

His first case, however, was considerably lacking in legal pomp and circumstance. Chief Charley of the Charley River tribe came paddling down to Eagle City in birch-bark canoes with a dozen of his fiercest warriors. The "hostile fleet" landed and Chief Charley stalked over to the new courthouse "with a determination to get justice if he had to get it by force." This was the burden of his complaint:

"Eagle Jack steal my dog at Nation River. If you big chief, you get my dog—bring him me. If you not get my dog, I get my dog. Maybe some Indians get hurt. Maybe you get my dog?"

Although loath to use the federal court as a dog-collection agency, Judge Wickersham dispatched a deputy marshal to Eagle Jack's camp. The marshal brought back the dog, a possible Indian war was averted, and both tribes were given a glimpse of the omnipotence of American justice.

The first grand jury in the Third Judicial Division was summoned September 3, 1900, at Circle City, one of the principal stops on Judge Wickersham's circuit. Indictments were returned against three men: one for murder, one for larceny, one for rape. The murderer was convicted of manslaughter and sentenced to ten years in a federal prison, the thief to two years, and the man charged with rape was acquitted. Under the miners' court system, the chances were that at least two of the three accused men would have been hanged.

One of the hazards of circuit-riding, Judge Wickersham found, was being caught far away from his home base by the first winter storms. An Arctic blizzard descended on Circle City at the end of the seven-day session of court there, and the weather did not clear for ten days. Wickersham made it back to Eagle City before the permanent onset of winter.

At Circle City he found what was probably the only escape-proof jail in the world: the worst threat of punishment was to be locked *out* of jail there. A sign at the jail door read:

NOTICE: ALL PRISONERS MUST REPORT BY 9 P.M.
OR THEY WILL BE LOCKED OUT FOR THE NIGHT.
BY ORDER OF THE UNITED STATES MARSHAL.

The nearest settlement to which a man could escape was 200 miles away, an impossible distance in the twenty to fifty-degrees-below-zero temperatures. Prisoners were often let out of jail to run errands or go on work details; the sign was posted mainly to assure their prompt return. "It was entirely effective and no escapes were attempted," Wickersham remarked.

On the northern rim of his division, particularly, the multilingual problem was almost as serious a difficulty in administering justice as distance and weather. There were Eskimos and Indians of a dozen dialects; hundreds of Scandinavians who spoke nothing but Norse, Swedish, Danish, Finnish or Lapp, and Eskimo tribesmen who had long associated with the Russian traders and spoke Eskimo but wrote in Russian.

Judge Wickersham tried a triple murder case in which the bulwark of the government's case rested on an Eskimo chief's testimony. Three prospectors were murdered on Unimak Island. The government claimed a man named Hardy was the killer, while Hardy tried to shift the blame on a man named Aston.

The old Eskimo chief testified that he saw Aston at a fishing camp fifty miles away from the scene of the murder on the June 7th it occurred.

The defense attorney flashed a cunning smile around the courtroom and demanded to know how the Eskimo was so certain he saw Aston on June 7.

"Me wrote it in my log," the Eskimo replied.

"So you can write, eh?" snarled the defense lawyer, certain that he had trapped the old renegade. "Come over here and let the jury see you write!"

The lawyer thrust paper and pen in the chief's hand and watched with gaping jaw as the decrepit old fellow wrote in "a clear and legible script"—in Russian. It was quite good enough to prove the prosecution's point and lead to the conviction of the murderer.

There was a certain flexibility about the American law, especially in dealing with the Eskimos and Indians, that the Canadian law lacked to a considerable degree. The American authorities tried to take into consideration that they were administering the affairs of a native population whose evaluation of human life was much lower than that of the Caucasian's. Among the Eskimo tribes around Nome, for instance, it was the custom to tie up in canoes people too old to work and send them drifting down the river into the open sea, if it was summertime. In winter, the ancient was simply tied up in a tent removed far enough from the village so his or her cries could not be heard, and left to die of starvation and exposure.

A native of one of these tribes named Itcheruk presented a complex problem to the Nome judiciary. He shot and killed four persons with one bullet.

Itcheruk was a trapper for the Nome fur market, whose native village was on the Fish River north of Golovin. He became prosperous by Eskimo standards and decided to marry the comeliest girl of his village, handing over most of his savings to the bride's family.

The marriage had been in effect only a week, when Itcheruk's father-in-law appeared at their hut and angrily returned the bridegroom's money. A wealthier suitor, who did not regard the marriage as a *fait accompli*, offered the girl's father twice what Itcheruk had paid if he would retrieve his daughter. And the girl agreed that she would prefer being married to a wealthier man. They left Itcheruk to brood over his misfortunes. He neglected his work and drank *tonga*, a pure grain alcohol, in stunning amounts.

Finally a splendidly appropriate solution occurred to him and he sobered up completely. He went over to his former wife's new home and announced he was willing to forgive and forget. To show his amiability, he invited her and her new husband and both of her parents to a party at his hut. A few hours after the party began, Itcheruk's four guests were unconscious from the effects of *tonga*, which Itcheruk had not touched himself. Itcheruk lined them up side by side with their addled heads in a perfect line. Lying on the floor, he aimed carefully with his heavy 45-90 rifle, a weapon powerful enough to stop an elephant. With one bullet— ammunition was scarce and costly, and he did not want to waste any more money on that family—he shot and killed all four of them.

His fellow villagers congratulated Itcheruk on a noble, courageous and fitting deed: the four of them had deserved to die, from the Eskimo viewpoint.

The American authorities at Nome sent a deputy marshal to arrest him and bring him to the jail, since at first glance it looked like an inexcusably cold-blooded murder.

Once all the facts became known, however, the citizens of Nome were inclined to take a more lenient view of Itcheruk. "He seen what he had to do and he done it" was the concensus of opinion. What with the shortage of ammunition, the economy with which Itcheruk performed the quadruple assassination also seemed curiously laudable.

The court swung around to this view also, it seems, for Itcheruk was given a suspended sentence on condition that he attend church every Sunday. It was probably the lightest sentence ever passed by an American court on a four-ply murderer. Under the northern lights, however, even justice could afford its moments of inconstancy.

10

The All-Inclusive Saloon

Shortly before the great stampede to the Klondike, in the summer of 1897, there were just three saloons in Dawson. One was owned by the town's leading real-estate developer, Joe Ladue, and the others were the White Elephant and the Blue Elephant. Ladue's was a comparatively imposing structure of clapboard, while the other two were fashioned of canvas over a board framework. In that first flush of prosperity, all that a man needed to set himself up in business were some form of shelter, a few planks and sawhorses to serve as a bar, and a barrel or two of spirits.

Commissioner William Ogilvie bore witness that the rip-roaring tradition of Klondike drinking began at an early date. One June day in 1897, he recalled, the whole town seemed to go on a simultaneous bender. Maybe there was a full moon, maybe it was the vernal urge to kick up heels, maybe it was the exhilaration of being in the presence of a boom—anyway the town gave itself up to a spell of dissipation and riot. Unfortunately the authorities were not yet prepared for such a wholesale spree; the one-room jail had not yet been roofed and only the four walls were standing.

Commissioner Ogilvie dropped in at the Blue Elephant during the afternoon. His lapels immediately were seized by a Cornish miner who insisted that Ogilvie, a rather dour Scot, highly conscious of the dignity of his position, have a drink with him. Ogilvie refused. The Cornishman insisted. Finally the commissioner detached his lapels from the miner's grip and turned to leave the place, which was filled with exuberant drinkers. The Cornishman followed him, hurling every curse at his command. Feeling it beneath his dignity to knock the man down, as he explained later, Ogilvie summoned a police officer to take the miner in custody and lock him up, more or less, in the unfinished jail.

A short time later, at the White Elephant, a white man and his Indian mistress engaged in a knockdown brawl. The man had a badly cut cheek and his squaw's mouth was bleeding. She was at the point of battering her protector to the ground, however, and bitterly resented the interference of the law. Both were removed to jail as company for the sodden Cornishman.

Not an hour later an Irishman was overtaken by a seizure of indignation at British tyranny and bellowed denunciations of Ogilvie as the perpetrator of a great injustice for jailing his three friends. Ogilvie rather liked the Irishman when he was sober but had him packed off to jail, more because of the loudness of his protest than its content.

Next morning, after a night under the stars, all the prisoners except the Irishman were penitent and released with a warning. The Cornishman wept and informed Commissioner Ogilvie he had never before known the disgrace of spending a night in custody. On his way back to his diggings, the Cornishman was stopped by a sympathetic friend who suggested a pick-me-up at the nearest bar. The miner turned on his sympathizer in a blaze of anger at the mere thought of taking another drink and fled to his diggings in the wilderness. The quarrelsome white man and his squaw also accepted their release gratefully and hurried out of town.

The Irishman, however, was still in an uproarious mood. The morning air quivered with his denunciations of Canadian justice, police tactics and accommodations for their victims. He stoutly refused to leave the jail, explaining that he had a claim against the territorial government for false arrest and he did not intend to endanger it by accepting his release. He would stay there until justice was done.

"Ten thousand dollars, d'ye hear, is the last cent I'll take!" the Irishman bellowed.

He slept an hour or two more, and then the local government renewed its pleas for him to leave the jail. Workmen could not finish the roof, it was pointed out, until he left. If he insisted on delaying this work, some other prisoner might catch cold or be bitten to death by mosquitoes, or something, and it would be all his fault. With his humanity thus appealed to, the prisoner consented to being discharged. He failed to press his suit for damages, but it was observed that the Canadian police never asked him to be their guest again.

Not nearly so stuffy as Commissioner Ogilvie was the leading American official in the Klondike, Colonel James Church McCook, the United States consul at Dawson. McCook, who once described himself as "a natural-born colonel," during a banquet at which the toasts were frequent and well lubricated, became involved in a quarrel with the *Nugget* and its editor, Eugene C. Allen, which proved his undoing as the "illustrious and resplendent minister plenipotentiary"—as Allen sarcastically called him.

A heroic drunk described in detail by the *Nugget* was Colonel McCook's farewell to diplomacy.

In an exhilarated mood just after he filed a $25,000 libel suit against the *Nugget* for ridiculing his eccentric grammar and spelling, McCook embarked on one of the lordliest sprees in the intemperate history of the Yukon Territory. Well into his cups, he engaged in a butting match with a Canadian who made the mistake of admitting he was not an American and with the night porter of the Phoenix, a bar and dance hall where low company could be found at any hour of the day or night. McCook, looking forward to receiving $25,000 from the *Nugget,* gave away his watch and a pocketful of nuggets. By dawn's ugly light, depleted financially and physically, the American consul was assisted part of the way home by a pair of fellow roisterers. A block away from his chambers, his corpulent figure fell to the ground and his companions left him there in the muddy gutter. Conscious that the dignity of his position would not allow him to take more than a momentary rest there, he finished the journey home on his hands and knees. When he awakened with throbbing head and empty pockets, he found that the *Nugget* had splashed a drink-by-drink account of the night before across its front page, not to mention an editorial asserting that 30,000 Americans in the Klondike had been affronted by his "buffoonery." McCook responded by charging Editor Allen with criminal libel. Both suits were dismissed rather hastily, and by the time the ice on the Yukon broke up the following spring McCook saw the wisdom of resigning and slipping aboard a steamer for the States.

His successor was much less spectacular and much more suitable as a repository of consular dignity. Yet it was a pity, in a way, for the "natural-born colonel" was one of the few men who tried, perhaps too strenuously, to take the stuffiness out of international relations.

In the Klondike, the saloon was much more than merely a place to drink. Its all-inclusive functions could only be matched by a country town's general store. First of all, it was the chamber where miners' courts held their sessions, a circumstance which Commissioner Ogilvie held responsible for some of the more emotional verdicts handed down by such courts, for the staid official firmly believed that justice and alcohol were an unseemly mixture. The saloon also served as a sort of verbal newspaper, a stock exchange, a charitable institution, a bank and a court of arbitration.

Before newspapers were widely distributed in the Yukon, the citizenry had to come to saloons to hear what few scraps of news were obtainable from travelers passing through or steamboats which had paused in their journeys to take on cordwood. Just after the ice broke during the first spring of the gold rush, a lawyer burst into Joe Ladue's saloon with the news from the first riverboat that made its way up the Yukon. This was the news he shouted in admirably concise bulletins: "The Pope's alive! The Queen's well! There's no war! And Bob Fitzsimmons knocked hell out of Jim Corbett!" The most prominent local news to be heard in the saloons, of course, was a report on the newest find along the creeks. Many a stampede took place when some prospector dashed in from the creeks with news of a strike, and the drinkers risked life and limb rushing out of the warm stuffy saloon into the cold night and sprinting over the rugged terrain, careless of ravines, sinkholes and bear traps.

Before the easy-money sharks arrived to invade an honorable business with their watered whisky and knockout drops, saloonkeepers in the Yukon were regarded as men of the highest integrity. They served as bankers for prospectors coming to town on a spree, and as arbiters when two men were involved in a dispute over a claim. Their establishments were informal stock exchanges, where miners traded in fractions of their claims for ready cash and provisions. And they performed a service unique as it was necessary for the prospector returning from months of wandering alone or digging along the creeks: they provided the warmth of human companionship just when a man was about to crack up from the unrelenting Arctic solitudes and the final weariness of talking to oneself or one's dog. The more decent and generous saloonkeepers were also the last resort for a man down on his luck. Before

everyone went money-mad, and there wasn't enough compassion
to go around, a down-and-outer could usually get "a meal and a
flop" from a saloonkeeper, particularly if he had given the saloon
his patronage in the luckier past.

Until the big-city slickers arrived from the Outside, a saloon's
gold scales were trusted implicitly, according to a Mounted Police
noncom who published his memoir before conditions grew less
idyllic.

When a miner goes into a saloon to buy anything, he flings down
his sack on to the bar and turns his back whilst the dealer weighs
out the amount on his scales. The latter would be grossly insulted
were he to see you watching him and the man who was seen to be
keeping his eye on his sack or the weights whilst the amount was
being weighed out would be considered "no gentleman."

One slippery fellow in charge of the scales at a saloon was de-
tected at cheating and "within a very short time a bullet had
placed him beyond the reach of temptation."

With the arrival of the first stampeders, Dawson's saloons soon
multiplied, became fancier, more interested in a customer's poke
and less concerned about his general welfare. A man was expected to come in and start spending, or make room for someone
who would prove himself a real sport. The "home away from
home" atmosphere was dispelled by an invasion of female merce-
naries, sharpshooters who saw to it that neither themselves nor
their employers suffered by transactions with the gold scales, ragtime musicians and plug-ugly bouncers. No longer could a miner,
hungry for human companionship, linger in the warmth of a potbellied stove and cuddle a drink of honest whisky in his paw. Nor
was it any longer advisable for a respectable woman to have a meal
in such an establishment, unless her husband or escort was willing
to contend with a stream of insults and jeers. Mrs. Clarence Berry,
whose husband struck it rich, discovered on her way through Daw-

son that the town was "in such a rowdy state that I had to have my meals sent to me. Men and women—there were about fifty women there—conducted themselves shockingly and were carousing continually. About the worst people on earth followed upon the heels of those steady, hard-working miners. . . ." At the Pioneer Saloon that spring the rowdiness was interrupted only by a turkey auction. Dawson had endured the winter on a diet of bacon, bread and beans. On April 10 an enterprising Dutchman had sledded in from Skagway with the bird, which was exhibited for several days to whet the appetites of prospective bidders and then auctioned off for $174 at the Pioneer.

The Canadian authorities' only concern with the saloon situation was to insist on collection of license fees and to discipline any obstreperous drunks by putting them to work on the Mounties' woodpile. Boozers sweating out their hangovers kept the stoves glowing throughout the winter in the police barracks. Colonel Steele felt some qualms about allowing any sort of scoundrel with enough money to buy a license to open a saloon, but his government maintained only that "fees must be collected, the rum seller take care of himself, the dram drinker take his chances, regardless of the consequences to his morals." It was a policy that fattened the territorial treasury, for in the winter of 1898-1899 a total of $90,000 in saloon license fees was collected. Yet this was only a dribble of the gold dust pouring into the coffers of the saloonkeepers. One of the more elaborate saloons which opened in Dawson the summer of '98—and boasted a long polished bar, a dazzling display of glassware, a fancy assortment of liquors and a tropical landscape executed by a soap artist on the vast mirror behind the bar—took in $15,000 the opening night.

The criminal element among the Klondikers, which naturally found headquarters in the various drinking establishments, was kept under close watch by the authorities. A force of plain-clothes detectives mingled with the drinkers in all the saloons, their identity known only to their commanding officer, Colonel Steele, who compiled a reference library of criminals, their past crimes, methods of operating and local activities. "They were under our eyes all the time," Colonel Steele boasted. It was his particular duty, he felt, to "discipline" all those who tried to cheat the miners in the saloons, dance halls and red-light districts. In the colonel's view, an honest robber, safecracker or burglar was much less reprehensible than the men and women who used a miner's weaknesses and dissipations to get at his money, and Commissioner Ogilvie shared this opinion. "Many a sleepless night poor Mr. Ogilvie spent, thinking of what ought to be done with these unworthy creatures."

Despite Colonel Steele's undercover operatives and Commissioner Ogilvie's midnight qualms, the gold-rushers had little protection except their native wit and caution against the sharpers, drunk-rollers, short-change artists and other thieves. But it was not always the divekeeper and publican who came out on top in his dealings with the thirsty Klondiker.

One Dawson saloonkeeper who made a sport of tricking some of his best customers sold a patron a fifty-gallon barrel of whisky for $400. That bargain rate of $8 for a gallon of whisky should have warned the purchaser, but apparently he was too joyful over slickering the saloonkeeper to consult his common sense. Investigation showed that the barrel actually contained only a small keg of whisky, holding a few gallons, which was ingeniously floated in water so that when the barrel was tapped it produced its limited supply of liquor—and then only a mocking gurgle.

The whisky buyer did not complain but carefully plotted his revenge when cold weather came.

There was a shortage of candles in the Klondike and the saloonkeeper was always on the lookout for some such commodity to corner in a rising market. His victim obtained a candle mold and poured into the forms a mixture of condensed milk and water. He allowed the mixture to freeze outside, producing some excellent replicas of candles as long as they were kept in the cold. Then he took his supply to the saloon and sold them at a regretfully reduced price to the owner, saying he was leaving the Klondike and had no use for them. The saloonkeeper gleefully stored them in his back-room and waited for the most favorable market conditions; his suspicions were not aroused even when he heard the candlemaker had not left the Klondike but was working a claim out on the creeks. One day came an opportunity to dispose of his stock of candles at a dollar apiece. In the boxes stacked in his storeroom he found only sticky little puddles and soggy wicks. The whisky profits had gone down the drain with a rush and—a gurgle.

In most mining-camp saloons, the bar fly occupied a permanent if not highly honored position at the bar. He was usually an old gaffer, red-nosed, bleary-eyed, with a woozily determined smile, who had foresworn all other ambitions for the task of staying swacked until his last fiery breath. The bar fly had his uses both for the other drinkers and for the proprietor. He was a butt for practical jokes who would take any amount of rough treatment and reply only with a helplessly amiable grin. He was a target for a man with a hangover or a grievance. To the house, he was a sort of concealed asset, for when some prosperous drinker ordered a round for everyone at the bar he was there to boost the bill. For everyone he was that handiest of humans—someone to look down on. He was always the first one there in the morning, waiting for the bar-tender to open up, and could usually be counted on to help swamp out the place. Naturally there was one honorarium attached to the bar fly's position: he was always given a dram to keep him from shaking to pieces, as soon as the bartender had uncorked the first bottle.

Dawson's most celebrated bar fly was harshly treated at his usual stand one summer morning during the stampede. A new bartender came on duty, and not being acquainted with the customs of mining-camp grogshops, refused the bar fly his free drink and roughly ordered him out of the place.

Determined to obtain both revenge and his lost place at the bar, the old freeloader showed up that evening waving what appeared to be a stick of dynamite with a sputtering fuse.

"I'm going to blow you all to hell," he shouted.

The new bartender and his customers hastily evacuated the saloon and the vicinity, the former rushing to the police barracks for help. When they returned, the place still hadn't been blown up. The police sergeant wriggled up to the door on his belly and cautiously raised his head. The stick of dynamite was resting on the bar, its fuse burned out. The bar fly was pouring himself another drink from a bottle of the best whisky behind the bar.

Under questioning by the sergeant, he admitted that his dynamite stick actually was a ten-inch piece of bologna with fuse attached.

Before the night was over, with all of Dawson quaking with laughter at the bar-fly's revenge, the bartender was fired for being so indelicate in a matter of tradition, and the veteran cadger was restored tenderly and ceremoniously to his stool at the end of the bar.

Even the briefest exploration of drinking customs in the Klondike would be incomplete without mention of its "wine of the country," which was known as hootch (or hooch), a bootleg beverage of the highest potential as an agent of intoxication. It was, in fact, as blinding, benumbing and befuddling as a bolt of lightning.

There were as many recipes for hootch as for home brew in a later era, but the standard concoction was sugar or molasses, plus dried fruit or berries, plus a wad of sourdough to hasten the fermentation. In the commercial market around Dawson, there were three fittingly named brands, "Aurora Borealis," "Koprecof Dynamite" and "The Juice of the Snake."

The name and origin of hootch, it has been determined, can be credited to the Indian village of Hoochino. An American soldier deserted from the army post at Sitka many years before the gold rush and settled down among the natives, bringing with him a secret that made him a prince among men—how to distill liquor. The deserter and his friends used a species of seaweed with a hollow stem as the "worm," or coil through which the hootch was condensed. This still was crude but effective, and soon was responsible for a constantly fuddled population. Every native settlement and most of the mining camps of outlanders had its still cooking merrily away with whatever ingredients could be obtained, mostly flour and molasses bought from Yankee traders and whalers. It was a common sight, according to early settlers in Alaska and the Yukon, to see a native squatting by the side of his still, watching the slow process of distillation, collecting every drop as it fell from the "worm" and drinking it as fast as a good swallow was collected. Many of the early settlers lived whole seasons on a diet of "hootch and Alaska strawberries"—whisky and beans.

Canadian officials attempted no regulation of this pioneer form of bootlegging except to demand an excise fee if the hootch was destined for the market rather than home consumption. A miner at Forty Mile who had panned up nothing but gravel and sand made a point of asking Captain Constantine, the local commander of the Mounties, about the legality of such traffic, as he announced his intention of distilling hootch commercially. Constantine said the authorities would not interfere so long as the tax was paid.

Hootch, however, was regarded by many Klondikers as such a ferocious beverage as to deserve being outlawed. When the miners on Glacier and Miller creeks heard that a professional hootch maker was setting himself up in business, they sternly passed a resolution: "That in the event of any party or parties coming to our creeks with intoxicating liquor to sell, we shall seize the liquor, spill it and send the party or parties whence they came with a warning."

The hootch salesman, an astute student of human nature, particularly that of Klondikers, was not in the least discouraged by this resolution. "Well, we'll see," he commented. He found a vacant cabin near the mouths of both creeks and installed himself and his stock of liquor.

In succeeding days, one by one the miners in the Glacier and Miller creek settlements allowed they'd caught sight of caribou tracks and felt the urge for a little fresh meat. And one by one they returned to camp reeking of hootch and still hungry for caribou. A miners' court was called into session and this time the death penalty was prescribed for anyone selling hootch. But the bootlegger stood his ground, the miners still went hunting for caribou and many a mouth which had decried the liquor traffic still was highly aromatic. The death penalty was never imposed, and the hootch-maker went down to Dawson a few months later a wealthy man, laden with gold dust and the gratitude of the caribou.

11

Ladies Fair But Frail

ANY WOMAN venturesome enough to join the Klondike gold rush was likely to be quite a handful, not at all content with being regarded as a fragile thing, all sighs and sweetness. Influenced by the feminist spirit of the times, she was ready to assert her rights as a human being equal if not superior to any male. Whatever the frailty of her morals or character, she was contemptuous of the old-fashioned clinging-vine type of womanhood, much more independent and self-assertive than even the hardy females who participated in the California and Colorado gold rushes.

At least one of Dawson's disastrous fires was started by the combustion of feminine temper. Even the most bedraggled prostitute could become imperious if her dignity was trampled. The dance-hall girls were downright haughty until a man pressed a nugget or two in their hands or, if he were a really devilish fellow, down the bodices of their generously cut gowns. The fact that the nearest feminine reinforcements were a couple of thousand miles away gave them all an acute appreciation of their market value.

Feminine willfulness was in evidence even along the rugged trails leading to the Klondike (where a little of the old clinging-vine attitude might have been helpful)—that, and a determination not to be dominated any longer by their menfolk. Arthur Walden, the Yukon "dog puncher," told of one spirited young woman he saw among the horde of gold rushers at Lake LaBarge. A thousand boats were jammed together as the rivers and lakes were breaking up in the spring thaw. The young woman fell overboard from the scow manned by her husband.

She was drowning in the ice-choked water, with her husband dashing up and down his deck trying to work up the courage to jump in after her. Near by were two men in another boat. One of them jumped into the icy lake to save her. He hauled her to his boat and noted that although half drowned she was a sweetly formed young thing.

As soon as she was dried off, the gallant rowed her to her husband's scow, where she announced: "If this man will have me, he can have me."

Both her husband and the hero's partner protested bitterly. Drawing a revolver, the rescuer forced the husband to throw her possessions over into the boat. To the complaints of his partner that "you're letting a woman come between us," he replied with an order for the partner to split up their joint assets and take himself elsewhere. These two bills of divorcement were pronounced at gun point, but were accounted legal enough to suit the encampment at Lake LaBarge. Later, Walden said, the young woman obtained a more formal divorce and married her rescuer; "she had the admiration and he the envy of all the people who knew the circumstances."

Another young woman determined to work out her own destiny was Milley Lane, an eighteen-year-old described as being of "respectable" German parentage, and pretty in the bargain. According to the Dawson newspaper accounts, Milley was a member of a "well-fixed party" en route to Dawson when their steamer rammed into a rocky outcropping at Thirty Mile River and sank in the boiling waters. All the passengers lost their baggage and other possessions as the steamer sank in a few minutes, and they had "hardly enough clothes on their backs to protect them from the mosquitoes."

With only her bedraggled dress to her name, Milley Lane tried for three days to obtain a respectable job. People were too busy to pay much attention to yet another waif caught in the stampede, and apparently no one was clever or charitable enough to disregard her attire and give her a chance. She went down to the banks of the Yukon and considered the alternatives: "she could either jump into the river or go to board with one of the Madams in Dawson's White Chapel."

However sordid the prospects, the girl decided on survival and walked across the footbridge to Lousetown, where employers were not so particular about surface appearances. "Within an hour the girl was seen bathed and dressed in satins and laces, her beauty enhanced by handsome apparel and the hairdresser's art."

The *Nugget's* somewhat moralizing account closed with "Trail acquaintances were shocked, and when spoken to, the girl broke down completely in tears." Where these same "shocked" acquaintances were when the girl was looking for an honest job, or a little help to make herself more presentable, was not stated. And it seems likely that once she dried her eyes, she felt a lot more grateful to her blowsy madam than those appalled personages across the river in Dawson.

Another young lady who knew her own mind was sixteen-year-old Mabel Nummelin, the daughter of a couple who kept a road-house on one of the Klondike creeks. She eloped with one John Orton, a former Montana cowboy, in an open boat in which they drifted down the Yukon to Nome. Her father swore out a warrant, according to the newspaper account, because "he loves his daughter dearly" and besides he was "the more incensed when investigation disclosed the fact that Orton had carried away other property belonging to him."

A girl intent on making her fortune in the Klondike without either marrying a rich miner or starting up a business of her own had several alternatives. She could become a sort of courtesan bestowing her favors on a strictly limited clientele, usually one man at a time, with eligibility decided on the basis of his wealth. Only those with youth, beauty and a measure of brains succeeded in this category. Then there were the girls who worked in the music halls, theaters and dance halls as entertainers, or "hostesses," or combined the two occupations, singing and dancing on-stage and drinking with the patrons off stage. In this type of endeavor the girl always reserved the right to bestow her affections, if any, where she chose. The patron was buying a piece of her time, not an option on her unemployed hours. Then there were the plushy bawdyhouses of Paradise Alley in Dawson, where there could be no doubt of what services a girl was expected to render, and slightly lower on the social scale were the parlor houses and cribs across the river in Lousetown.

An English traveler was impressed with the flamboyant style of one of the courtesan class. She was "brilliantly handsome, with an admirable figure and a charming toilette." The girl, barely out of a Sacramento high school, had drifted from California to Oregon and then to the Klondike. The traveler learned that she had paid off a $10,000 mortgage on her mother's ranch near Sacramento, wore a thousand-dollar belt fashioned of nuggets and was reputed to be worth $50,000 in cash. "She never went up the creeks: it was not necessary. She was the most distinguished woman in town and held high court with her admirers."

Her distant admirer watched the self-assured young woman buy whisky for all the men at the bar and casually drop $1,000 in an hour's play at the faro tables.

"Come up, boys, and have a drink with me," she called out heartily. "There's my poke!"

It was one of those ironic instances of the whoring profession's axiom that the less a woman gives, the more she is paid.

To a Dawson physician who studied them from the purely professional viewpoint the town's light-o'-loves ranged in character and comeliness from "the elegance, the social intelligence and the regal courtesanlike charm of two or three 'queens,' brilliant though venal," to the "crudely painted creatures such as mud-stained miners seek and knew, from Coolgardie to Cripple Creek." Some he met on his professional rounds were gentle and refined—or seemed so in comparison with their tawdrier sisters—and redeemed themselves in later life. One girl who sold herself on the streets of Dawson in 1898 was "later the nurse-heroine of the most devastating epidemic I ever knew." Nursing seemed to be the profession that attracted them more than any other, once they had decided to quit prostitution, he noted.

The "scarlet woman," the physician observed, was an inescapably prominent figure in the community, no matter how desperately the eyes of the few local moralists tried to blink her away from their vision. "A blind man could have sensed their constant presence and their influence. . . . In a wide-open town such as Dawson boasted itself, no man or woman or child but some time, in some way, must come in contact with 'the oldest profession,' be forced to contemplate in some degree its personnel and ethic." It was widely believed that some government officials worked with the ladies of the evening in cutting themselves into the millions being made out on the creeks. Miners trying to stake out claims that seemed to be exceptionally promising were invited to assign part of their interests to one of these feminine holding companies, in which the grafting official naturally retained a large interest. On a February day in 1899 the physician wrote in his diary that an intermediary "introduced me to an official recorder and a Dawson whore. I was told that by assigning a half interest to the latter I would be permitted to stake a claim on Hunker Creek. . . ." It seemed ironically inconsistent to the observant doctor that the Canadian officials indignantly rejected the "democracy of the miners' meeting" and the vigilance committees, which Americans tried unsuccessfully to establish in the Yukon, and yet fondly smiled on the unregulated liquor traffic and the white-slavery system of the American mining camps. Thanks to this inconsistency, he noted, the women of the town provided a flourishing business for importers of Paris frocks and diamond jewelry.

The only official interference with the prostitutes of Dawson was imposed when Captain Constantine ordered them to stop wearing bloomers—once flaunted by the emancipated woman back in the States as a badge of her freedom—as a readily identifiable uniform. The whore ladies protested just as violently as their emancipated sisters against this male prejudice, which may well have been founded on esthetic grounds, and "strange tales were told about the sometimes forcible means employed to 'debloomer' the protesting females." They were still allowed to maintain other trademarks, scarlet curtains in their windows and red lampshades.

Few Klondikers stood on middle ground in their opinions of the dance-hall girls. To some they were harpies who gathered around a man only when he displayed a fat poke; Jack London and others leaned to the theory that tender hearts beat beneath their gaudily brocaded bodices. Outside of the attention he got at Father Judge's hospital, London was most grateful for the friendship shown him by the dance-hall girls despite his lack of funds; but that may have been more a tribute to his masculine charm, his talent for listening and his ability as a tale-spinner, than the kind hearts of the girls. "Those dance-hall girls got sort of a bad name," wrote Gene Allen, editor of the *Nugget,* "but they had hearts of gold. They'd give their last ounce to help anyone who needed it." According to

Allen, even the bartenders in the tough dives were good-hearted lads: ". . . I've been in a saloon when someone was freezing on the trail, and seen a bartender throw off his apron and get into his parka and mukluks and with a supply of whisky start out with a dog team to rescue the one in trouble." Most Klondikers would find that a spectacle hard to believe, unless the frozen one was extremely well heeled.

The hard-bitten view of dance-hall girls prevailed among most veterans of the Yukon mining towns. Younger and more beautiful girls came in from Outside during the spring of 1898, and Henry Woods described them as he found them in one of the larger dance halls on the river front:

They were of the "chippy" variety, the *fin de siècle* designation for women on the border line between veteran prostitutes and what some years later they were known as "flappers." They were young, pretty, and beautifully dressed. Even at that early date they had all the hallmarks of their profession, which later were to become "respectabilized" by adoption by their virtuous sisters. They were rouged within an inch of their lives, and many of them wore their hair short. Their skirts were abbreviated, their forms uncorseted, and their frocks close-fitting. They wore silk stockings which, although black, was enough in itself in that era to mark them as at least trifling with the occasions of sin. Furthermore, they smoked cigarets unashamedly and tossed off whisky neat with all the ease and *sang-froid* of a he-man sourdough with a copper-lined stomach. Their badinage and persiflage, the wit and wisecracks they exchanged with their male companions were all below-the-girdle stuff. All in all, the atmosphere was as modern as if there had been a projection into the future, say, 1935, and the place a night club.

Jeremiah Lynch, the perceptive Englishman who spent three years in the Klondike, noted that the girls were not regarded as matrimonially out-of-bounds, thanks to that wonderful ratio of men to women, which was probably something like ten to one.

Prizes were distributed quite impartially in the shape of rich mining husbands, and more than a dozen of these same dancehall girls are today enjoying married happiness at London, Paris, New York and other places. And I make no doubt that they are quite as moral as the traditional Becky Sharp. . . . Those who have lived and are not altogether lost make excellent exemplars of virtue. Of good women there were few; of bad women plenty. So your lucky miner with cans of gold in his dilapidated cabin, pining in the cold winter days for women's society, dropped down to Dawson and engaged . . . a housekeeper. The housekeeper soon became a wife if she handled the gentleman rightly.

Some of the girls, impatient of the delays and obligations attendant on marriage as the way to a miner's heart and poke, were more direct in their methods.

One miner with more luck than discretion fell headlong in love with a charmer who sang, danced and wangled gold dust out of the patrons in a Dawson music hall. She rejected his advances with a terrifying hauteur. The only thing left to propose, the miner reasoned, was marriage.

"Tell you what, dearie," she said, "I'd be glad to marry up with you, but I've got to protect my interests. How do I know you won't get tired of me and run off with some other girl?"

"Why, sweetheart, I couldn't do a thing like that!"

"You men are all alike," she said archly. "A poor girl don't have a chance if she don't protect her interests."

Her counterproposal almost stunned him, although he had been expecting rather stiff terms. "You give me my weight in gold dust, and then I'll have a nest egg in case you run off with some other girl."

Her suitor was so smitten that he agreed to this dowry-in-reverse, which would cost him at least $30,000. It is doubtful that he was so love-stricken, however, that he would have agreed to marriage on any terms if he had known his fiancée was not only mercenary but unfaithful. Working behind the scenes was a fellow who lived by his wits and off the earnings of the music-hall girl. He counseled her to go through with the marriage, and even added a touch of his own: he filled her corset with twenty pounds of buckshot. The $5,000 this added weight would bring was to be his bonus for being such a bright lad.

The weighing-in ceremony and the anticlimactic wedding that followed it took place, at the bride's request, on the stage of the music hall where she had performed with more energy than talent. The bride got her $30,000, her lover was given his $5,000 bonus, and the bridegroom was still in a happy daze, although he was somewhat surprised that his lady weighed twenty pounds more than he estimated at the outside.

The party that followed the two ceremonies was one of the livelier and more expensive in Dawson's history, with the bridegroom providing champagne at $20 a bottle as long as his guests were able to lift their elbows.

Disillusionment did not keep the husband waiting too long. When the ice broke up on the Yukon that spring, his wife and her carefully concealed lover took passage on the first steamer for St. Michael and the voyage back to the States where they could enjoy her dowry without a suspicious husband to spoil their fun.

Another young and comely dance-hall girl decided to auction herself off for the slack winter season; men didn't spend much money contemplating the icy earth, with all their prospective wealth frozen into it. She advertised it all over Dawson that she and the man who bid highest for her services were to "act in every way as a married couple for the duration" of the agreement. She reserved the right to reject even the highest bidder if she didn't like his looks. The money was to be deposited in a bank, and could be withdrawn by her only after she had fulfilled the contract at the end of the winter.

The auction took place in the dance hall where the girl was regularly employed. She was dressed for the occasion in a gown of "the latest Paris fashion." To her audience, it did not appear that she was in the slightest degree embarrassed in the process of being ogled, appraised, commented on (with what vulgarity can be imagined). She merely stood on the platform, serene and confident in the potency of her charms.

The bidding was as businesslike as a livestock auction.

A member of the audience said later that she was "knocked down for somewhere around five thousand dollars." Klondike Mike Mahoney who knew both parties to the transaction was of the opinion that they would be mutually disappointed—the girl wasn't worth $5,000, even with her services as a cook and housekeeper thrown in, and the high bidder was such an unbearable fellow that she would more than earn her money.

Wealthy miners often had their favorite dance-hall girls brought out to their claims by dog sled. One owner of a rich claim on Bonanza Creek fell hard for a Dawson dance-hall favorite and suggested that she accompany him to his cabin for the spring cleanup.

She was not affronted by the impropriety of the proposal. Her only demurrer was "Business gets awfully good in spring, and I'd be giving up a lot of money."

"I'll take care of that," the miner said.

He was taken aback by her demand, however, which was for $1,000 a day and all the nuggets she could pick up around his claim in her spare time.

Still, it was undoubtedly cheaper than marrying the girl, and he agreed to her demands. She stayed a month, and returned to Dawson with $30,000 and enough nuggets to have a belt made for herself.

A dance-hall or music-hall favorite being given the whirl by a free-spending admirer could enjoy herself almost as expansively as a Broadway chorus girl being given the same treatment. Even in

those surroundings, French champagne flowed freely. Gowns from
the great fashion houses of Paris, costing hundreds of dollars,
could be cozened out of an ardent pursuer. Some of the fancier
restaurants were offering menus to tickle the most jaded palates. A
fairly typical menu in the winter of 1899: Baltimore oysters, Con-
sommé Imperial, Klondike grayling, Salade Homard, Pâté Poulet,
roast beef, ptarmigan with mushrooms, omelet au rhum, Fromage
Rochefort, with the appropriate wines and liqueurs.

Working conditions, however, were generally on the squalid
side. Henry Woods observed:

Mackinaws, blue denim shirts, and rough canvas breeches were
de rigueur for the men. Gingham and calico frocks, little more
modish in line than Mother Hubbards, or at best faded and shape-
less silk gowns, were the women's ballroom costumes. Men and
women danced in moccasins, and several of the dancers of both
sexes in their stocking feet. . . . The men were a rough-looking
lot—Berry Wall himself would have looked tough in a sourdough's rig—but they evidently were not of the bad-man fraternity. . . .

Another on-looker thought it "was not an edifying spectacle
toward the early hours of the morning, men being congregated
there in all sorts of outlandish costumes, some engaged in dancing,
others standing about watching and smoking pipes, filling the room
with fumes of bad tobacco. . . ."

When the music stopped, the male patrons were naturally expected to quench their own and their partners' thirsts as expensively as possible.

At the end of each dance the couples retired to tables in stalls or
boxes at the edge of the floor, and the men bought drinks. Champagne at thirty dollars the pint was the favorite order, for each
girl got a commission of five dollars for every bottle of fizz her
partner bought. The women had terrific thirsts out of all propor-

tion to their dancing exertions. A few hours' work in a dance hall paid a girl well, for she had no time for any partner except one with a full poke. When she finished with him much of the gold had found its way from his poke into the house's till, and some of that to the girl's stocking bank.

What irked this observer was that the girls turned over most of their earnings to their "cadet" or pimp—particularly if they were veterans of the Barbary Coast or some other district where the practice was generally in effect. Yet it was remarked that any girl without "that unspeakably vile counterfeit of a man" was in risk of losing "caste among her sisters as a cheap skate." The dance-hall girls vied with one another in seeing which one could dress their "protectors" the most expensively; the cadet gave them a curious sense of pride, perhaps subconsciously in having found someone lower than themselves. No sourdough cavalier had more than the faintest chance, no matter how much he spent on her, of coming between a girl and her human parasite.

The dance-hall music was generally of a low quality, even for the ragtime music that was favored then above the waltzes and other energetic dances; the patrons "did not expect too much of the dissolute-looking youth who provided the music, for in the rough society of that day the term 'piano player' was one of con- tempt implying a status somewhat akin to that of a cadet."

Tragedy and melodrama sometimes visited the dance halls, aside from the transitory love affairs, the occasional brawls, the spectacle of miners spending the substance of a season's work in a few hours of riot and drink.

The Honorable Stratford Tollemache, an Englishman who spent a dozen years in the Yukon, wrote of a dance-hall girl who lost out in a love affair and made the rounds of the bar announcing she intended to commit suicide. No one took her seriously, but a few minutes later she went up to her room and took a fatal dose of strychnine. And there was an Englishman, Tollemache recalled, who managed a mine for someone else and came into Dawson with several thousand dollars belonging to his employer, intending to deposit the money in a bank the next morning. Instead he tossed it away across the bar and over the gaming tables. Shortly after awakening the next morning, he considered his position. He knew of no one who would lend him the money and expected little compassion of his employer. So he calmly loaded his revolver and fired a bullet into his brain. Actually, it seems, few other Klondikers took anything seriously enough for suicide.

A somewhat less grim tragedy afflicted Arizona Charlie Meadows' dance hall at Christmas time in 1898. The centerpiece of the establishment was an oil painting of Arizona Charlie's girl, a member of the singing and dancing staff, which had been executed by Julius Ullman, a fairly well-known painter who visited the Klondike in search of material, gold and a good time—not necessarily in that order. Meadows promised to pay Ullman $1,500 for the painting and was highly pleased when it was finished after a month's sittings. It was ornately framed, placed in Meadows' Palace Dancehall just before Christmas, and was the subject of many toasts in Tom and Jerries and other seasonal libations.

Ullman was not so pleased, for Meadows, in a temporary financial bind, had to forgo paying him. The painter had done very well in the Klondike, selling wealthy claim owners oil and crayon sketches of themselves, but he was fond of champagne, dollar cigars and delicacies of the table. He, too, was broke—and resentful. One day he walked into the Palace and stood by while Meadows and his girl showed off the painting to several admiring visitors; Ullman had done full justice to the voluptuous charms of the girl, a blonde whom he dressed in a lacy gown for the portrait. The artist cleared his throat and once more demanded his fee. Meadows offered to pay him $500 on account, but Ullman rejected it. A few minutes later, while Meadows' attention was momentarily diverted, Ullman advanced on the painting with a knife and slashed it to pieces. Meadows was speechless with grief, his girl fainted, and Ullman stalked out, his sense of integrity finally satisfied.

Just as luckless was the dance-hall girl who was involved in some of the less respectable business ventures of Wilson Mizner. One of his side lines was the ancient badger game, in which he played the sinned-against husband and she the erring wife. On one occasion, Mizner lingered too long in a saloon and went back to his quarters to sleep off the effects. After all, he had to break into the girl's room in time to catch her in a compromising situation; timing, it may be said, was of the essence.

Mizner awoke late for his appointment; not only that, his revolver was missing.

Cursing his hangover and his defective sense of responsibility, he hastened to his "wife's" room. Along the way he picked up a tomato can and ripped off the label.

He broke down the door and confronted his "wife" and the well-heeled newcomer suddenly cast in the role of interloper. Raising the tomato can on high, Mizner announced that it was crammed with nitroglycerin and that he was of a mind to blow them all to bits.

The interloper begged Mizner to reconsider and mentioned the fact that his belt was salted with $10,000 worth of gold dust.

After a mighty struggle with his emotions, Mizner agreed to take the money and let the wretch go. The trembling home wrecker having departed, the girl suggested they divide the loot. Mizner handed her the tomato can with a bemused air.

"What good will that do me?" she demanded.

"I don't know," Mizner replied, "but it just earned me $10,000."

If the dance-hall girls of the Yukon were a haughty and temperamental lot, compared to their sisters in the States where the law of supply and demand operated less favorably, the "painted ladies" of Paradise Alley and other red-light sections were also capable of asserting their independence on most occasions. They were treated with unusual chivalry by the Canadian authorities, the Northwest Mounted Police rarely bothering them unless they took up such side lines as drunk-rolling and the administration of knockout drops. Merely plying their trade, they were quite safe from interference by the law. One of the few measures taken against them was in the spring of 1898 when they gathered in such numbers at Dawson that all the unattached prostitutes were herded across the Klondike into Lousetown. Jack London observed that although their patrons had to cross the river over a shaky footbridge a block long swaying a few feet above the water with only hand ropes to guide the pleasure-seeker, there were few who considered the crossing too dangerous to attempt.

Lousetown, of course, was a much less desirable address than Dawson's Paradise Alley. The former was largely a shanty settlement occupied by unsuccessful miners, roustabouts who worked on the river front, criminals and all sorts of gentlemen of leisure. The gentry of Lousetown was rather lackadaisical toward the stampedes that frequently sent large sections of the Dawson population rushing across the tundra to the scene of a rumored gold strike. The only stampede that took place in Lousetown was comfortably close at hand. A wag passed the rumor around that a miner had lost $300 worth of gold dust from his poke and that it had spilled out on the principal street. A crowd quickly gathered and watched the joker solemnly panning out the dust of the street. When he found fifteen cents worth of gold in his pan, everybody else joined in the operation, and the rumor grew until it was widely and wildly reported a mother lode was found in Lousetown's streets. Practically the only hard-working residents of Lousetown, it may be readily believed, were the prostitutes in the parlor houses and cribs.

The girls of Paradise Alley boasted of being younger, prettier and more expensive than their sisters in Lousetown; they were also more volatile and caused the respectable citizens of Dawson more than their share of trouble.

Their arrogance was particularly shocking to the management of the *Nugget*. One day a friend stopped Editor Gene Allen and remarked, "I see you've opened an office on Bawdy Row."

"What do you mean?" the editor demanded.

"One of the houses down there has a sign reading THE KLONDIKE NUGGET," his informant said.

On Third Street, Allen found the bawdyhouse and its offending sign. He confronted the madam with an informal injunction to tear the sign down.

"If you don't like it, tear down your own sign," the madam of the house said. "I like it for my own business."

Major Walsh, commanding the Mounted Police barracks in Dawson, received Allen's complaint and immediately issued an order that all bawdyhouses remove their signs, thus giving the profession of journalism a signal victory over the profession with which it has so often been compared in moments of vexation.

There was no doubt that the whore ladies had an unfortunate affinity for fire, which the ministers doubtless used for allegorical references to the brimstone of the regions supposedly waiting to receive such sinners.

For comic relief, there was the conflagration at Belle Mitchell's establishment on Third Street, which was one of the two main arteries of commerce in female flesh. Belle, a girl named Tony and two gentlemen callers became involved in a dispute during which various pieces of furniture were thrown, including lighted lamps. The draperies caught fire and in a moment the house was burning briskly, with the women fleeing into the street with very little clothing to protect them from the crisp September night air. A neighbor, Charlie Kimball, doused the flames with a pail of spring water, then with the only other liquid at hand, a barrel of vinegar, but the place burned down. Mrs. Kimball provided the women with enough clothing to satisfy the demands of modesty, and Belle proceeded to salvage what she could from the ruins: about all that was left was her "welcome" sign.

The excitement had barely died down, when a man appeared with a pan and deliberately began sifting through the ashes, working his way to the spot where the gold scales had stood and where a substantial pay streak was obviously located. Just in time Belle caught sight of the prospector and gave him such a terrific slap across the face that he "sought the dreary solitude of his own cogitations," as one reporter wrote. "He probably thought some of the hanging logs fell over on him and is probably 'cussing' yet that a 'cavein' overwhelmed him just as he had located the streak."

Much less humorous were the results of another quarrel between two bawds in a "house of ill fame" along Paradise Alley on the night of October 13-14, 1898. One hurled a lamp at the other, and the house quickly burned down. Wind carried the sparks to the tightly packed stores and other establishments of Front Street and soon the center of Dawson was a mass of flames. Forty buildings were destroyed and the total loss amounted to more than half a million dollars.

The citizenry was now aroused over two matters: (1) the inflammatory tempers of the light-o'-loves and (2) the inadequacy of the town's fire equipment, in spite of the fact Dawson was likely to be ravaged by fire as long as most of its buildings were flimsy wooden structures. The first problem was dealt with by the police, who ordered the removal of all prostitutes to Lousetown, where real-estate values were lower. The second was "solved" by election of a fire chief and the enlistment of 100 firemen.

The solutions may have been admirably empiric but six months later, on the evening of April 26, 1899, another fire roared through the business section and some of the residential streets.

This time the damage was twice as severe as the first fire. Banks, hotels, stores and warehouses were destroyed before the flames could be brought under control. (At the Bank of British North America the heat caused a safe containing thousands of dollars worth of gold dust to burst. For several days, surrounded by a police cordon, bank officials searched through the ashes with gold pans to recover the precious dust.) This time it was determined that the fire had started in the room of a young lady living over the Bodega Saloon. The board of inquiry was so vexed that it forgot the traditions of Klondike chivalry and closely questioned her as to whether she had left a cigarette or a curling iron burning in her room. A woman who smoked or curled her hair was, of course, under immediate suspicion of belonging with the other light ladies in Lousetown. Eventually the board decided it could not be determined that the girl's negligence started the fire but "recommended that all women-of-the-town be excluded from all public buildings other than licensed hotels."

Adventuresses of all sorts were finding it difficult to get along, aside from the harassments of the Mounted Police and boards of inquiry which did not hesitate to ask a lady if she smoked or curled her hair. The reason was that respectable women were arriving in such numbers that even the dance-hall girls were becoming supernumeraries on the scene; wives and women who would settle for nothing short of wifehood were making the primrose path thornily uncomfortable. A half-dozen Dawson ladies of unassailable reputation assumed the function of a socio-moral "vigilance committee," and gained such power that no one held a ball without submitting all applications for tickets to them. "No Grand Chamberlain of a Queen's levee scrutinized names more closely and made more inquiries," Jeremiah Lynch, who was something of a Dawson social historian, noted. With the greatest diligence, they learned the history of every woman who pretended to or yearned for respectability. According to Lynch, some of their conclusions were disastrous to the aspirations of a number of ladies:

It then transpired that Miss Larkin was a divorcee from Seattle; that Miss Bertrand had a husband and two children in San Francisco; that Mrs. Charles was not married to her husband; and that the husband of Miss Godchaux had come to Dawson from Ottawa in the fall and she had bribed him to go away and leave her unmolested. These were women who held respectable positions in town and were supposed to be as good as anyone else.

There was no doubt that by autumn of 1899 the city of Dawson was becoming impossibly civilized. The old lusty entertainments of the dance halls, bawdyhouses, music halls and impromptu routs in Lousetown were with the "snows of yesteryear."

It should not be imagined that all the gay young ladies who yearned more for champagne and Paris gowns than the dreary anchorage of marriage, all the brawling bawds and their fine-feathered male dependents, all the blithe young ladies who preferred the enchanted footlights to darning socks in a miner's cabin—not all these creatures departed from Dawson with sad or shamed faces at the advent of the respectable females. No, indeed; even as Dawson was succumbing to whey-faced piety there came news of other gold strikes to the north, beyond the reach of all but the most determined wives and fiancées.

12

Wax Museum:
The Arctic Saga of Wilson Mizner

To HEAR many veterans of the Klondike tell about it, the gold rush was a sort of glorified Boy Scout expedition. In the passage of the years certain raffish memories have been washed away. One gets the impression from many published recollections that it was a pure-hearted crusade in the wilderness by a band of heroes, square of jaw, clean of mind, high of purpose, who loved their partners and their sled dogs and despised all forms of villainy. The pattern of their recollections is neatly superimposed on the works of their poet laureate, Robert Service, who arrived in the Klondike several years after the stampede was over and the ribaldry had died down, and who allowed only an occasional ragtime tinkle of the dance halls and a shooting scrape or two to suggest the lusty nights under the northern lights.

There is a certain shuddering refusal, altogether human, to recall such matters as the informal marriages, or living arrangements, of prospectors and Siwash lasses, the painted charmers of Lousewn, the squaw dances, the revels in the Dawson dance halls where frostbitten beauties allowed miners to compete for their favors with champagne, gold dust and gowns imported from the great fashion houses of Paris.

History can be grateful to Wilson Mizner in this respect: he never left any doubt in his auditors' minds—unfortunately he rarely committed his thoughts to pen and paper—that the gold rush was a free-for-all spectacularly devoid of Victorian sentimentality. It is difficult to describe the talents of Wilson Mizner and the use he made of them. Above all, he was an adventurer, a splendid exemplar of what a friend of his called "the cockeyed age of golden-hearted rogues." After his wayward career in the Yukon, he functioned variously as a cardsharp on trans-Atlantic liners, as prince consort of the widow of a Chicago traction magnate, as a successful Broadway playwright (whose collaborators, of course, did all the writing while he supplied the wit and bounce for their efforts), as a Florida land boomer, as the leading raconteur of Hollywood in its most imperial period. Best of all, he was an oral historian to rival Scheherazade. There was no false reverence in his recollections of himself and others in the gold rush; his greatest fault, perhaps, was to deprecate all forms of virtue as being masks for truly sinister behavior: there was only one man in the Yukon and Alaska to whom he was willing to assign a degree of disinterested humanity, a Jesuit priest whose deeds were saintly. Of his own brief but lucrative career as the employee of a Dawson saloon-gambling house, he frankly stated, "I got fifty per cent of everything I stole, and did pretty well." No doubt it is significant that one of the few heroes of his life was Soapy Smith of Skagway.

Mizner had only the deepest of contempt and purplest of curses for the London-Beach-Service school of Arctic literature. Gold-rushers were no strong, silent men but "the worst sissies of earth." Nor were they so beautifully loyal to their friends: "I never knew the meaning of ingratitude until I had one of those Arctic pals," he said. In the stream of anecdotes, smoking-car stories and end-less reminiscence with which he regaled café tables for years after-ward, Mizner always decried the belief that the Frozen North was a breeding ground for heroes and sages, and he was particularly outraged when he heard praise of certain writers who insisted on spreading such fatuous propaganda.

Wilson and his three older brothers, Edgar, William and Addi-son, were in the vanguard of the rush to the Yukon; none of them came out very wealthy, except in experience and in tall tales which lasted them a lifetime in dinner-table conversation. The Mizners had advance information on the Klondike discoveries because Edgar, the eldest, was a sort of roving executive for the Alaska Commercial Company, and when he was assured that the finds were really of gold-rush size he immediately sent for his younger brothers, who had been engaged in various adventures in Cali-fornia, Hawaii and Guatemala. The unruly Wilson, in fact, had run away from Santa Clara University and become a singer, of sorts, in a Barbary Coast dive. There he met a rowdy but beautiful young woman named Rena Fargo, who sang, danced and drove men wild in a place called the Crenmore, of profane memory. Wilson and Rena hit it off splendidly, being of the same carefree temperament.

It was Wilson's duty to gather up William and Addison and accompany them to Dawson, then a tent and shanty town of about 1,000 population which would grow fortyfold in less than a year, where Edgar's headquarters were located. On the train to Seattle, Wilson proposed a plan of operations: they would land at Dyea, pack over the Chilkoot Pass, then build iceboats and await the big freeze. Sailing over the chain of frozen lakes and rivers to the Yukon, thence to Dawson, Wilson expansively told his brothers, could be accomplished in "three days at the longest." Less ebul-lient but more experienced men estimated it would take at least a few months to make that heartbreaking journey, if bandits, diseases and natural hazards could be overcome swiftly, but they did not have the benefit of Wilson's youthful imagination.

On the train Wilson introduced his brothers to the brunette and volatile Rena Fargo who, he explained, was "just going as far as Seattle." Addison, who regarded himself as his brother's guardian angel, was taken aback when they boarded the steamer *Topeka* at Seattle and found Wilson and Rena cozily installed in a cabin; this time Wilson blandly announced that she was "just going as far as Juneau," where she had a job waiting in a honky-tonk. "Being a Mizner, I showed no surprise," Addison recalled years later.

While they waited in Juneau for another steamer to transport them to Dyea, Rena went to work in one of the honky-tonks and to "save expenses" shared a room with Wilson, as the younger brother blithely explained to Addison. "Even now I thought that she had come to Juneau to work and was going no farther," Addison said. And he could not conceal his surprise when Rena again appeared on the ship for Dyea in Wilson's company. "Were Wilson and Rena married?" was the question that haunted Addison. "Or was it better if they were not?" She did not seem to be the ideal addition to the proud Mizners of Benicia. His concern was only natural, he felt, as "I had been a mother to him [Wilson] all my life. He seldom wrote a letter home and for years I had lied for him in mine. At heart, I expected him any minute to turn to the dullness of righteousness and become a God-fearing, outstanding character. He had always been his own worst enemy, thinking it smart to know the doings of the lowest characters and, generally, getting the blame for their indiscretions, where generally he was absolutely innocent. So, it was with this delusion that I always wrote to mother." Despite his disapproval of Wilson's taste for low company, Addison then and always stood by him protectively, and usually affectionately.

And then they landed on the beach at Dyea, crowded with prospectors desperate to get their thousands of tons of supplies and equipment over Chilkoot and on the trail to the Yukon before all the best claims were staked, Addison had to admit that fiery little Rena made herself very useful, in the only way she knew.

They had no sooner landed when they were approached by a black-bearded rascal named V. R. Betterled. Betterled had twelve horses—which were, of course, in great demand—and offered to help the Mizners haul their supplies over the pass for "nothing but friendship." Since their equipment included the heavy steel runners for iceboats, this would be a considerable advantage. It developed that Betterled mistook Wilson for his brother Edgar, who, as manager of the Alaska Commercial Company, had laid claim to some very promising plots on the Klondike tributaries; and it was Betterled's scheme to obtain a share in these claims. It soon became known to the Mizners in its full flowering. Betterled had approached Rena with the proposal that she induce Wilson (Edgar, as he thought) to put the claims in her name; then they would depart with the deeds and Betterled would marry her. Rena immediately told Wilson about her suitor's plot. When he discovered that the Mizners had learned about the scheme, Betterled dumped their supplies at Sheep Camp, six miles from Chilkoot Pass, and let them struggle on without his horses.

It was while they were laboriously packing over the pass that the Mizners witnessed the workings of the law—without benefit of Blackstone—on the lawless frontier. Three men were accused of stealing another's food. One was proved innocent, another committed suicide, and the third was flogged by a sadistic dwarf on the decision of a drumhead court and sent staggering back to Dyea with his lacerated back bearing a sign lettered: "THIEF! PASS HIM ALONG!" The suicide was buried along the trail, with an itinerant minister quoting over his grave, "But he that maketh haste to be rich shall not be unpunished." The brothers thought it an odd text to be sprinkled over the heads of hundreds of gold-rushers whose only thought was to "maketh haste" for the Golconda far inland.

The party finally surmounted Chilkoot, past the bones of horses, mules and men who had been less fortunate, and camped on the shores of a lake at winterset. They built Wilson's iceboats with the steel runners made to order in Seattle and with planks sawed out of trees felled at the lakeside. After much hard labor, mostly performed by the earnest Addison, while Wilson and William sat around encouraging him and marveling at his strength, they found that the iceboat idea was only another of Wilson's bright but futile dreams: the boats would not sail over ice deeply covered with snow, and it was hardly practicable to sweep a path of hundreds of miles for them.

There was nothing to do but settle down for the winter, build boats and wait for the waterways to thaw in the spring. The Mizners, Rena Fargo and a few other companions, disgruntled over the quick collapse of Wilson's iceboat scheme and the irritations of living together at close quarters for months, were soon suffering from an acute attack of cabin fever. Only Rena and Wilson were on speaking terms, but they obviously had better reason for amiability than the others.

Wilson and Addison became bitterly estranged while whipsawing planks for the boats. Spruce trees were felled and trimmed, then placed on a scaffolding, with one man on top pulling the saw upward and another at the bottom pulling it downward. Sourdoughs have been arguing for half a century over whether the top or the bottom man had the hardest job: the bottom man was continually afflicted with a stream of sawdust falling in his eyes; the top man had the grueling job of pulling the saw upward. Friends often quarreled and split up on the trail over which job was the least miserable, and one pair known to the Mizners even cut their tents and sacks of flour in half to be rid of each other quickly.

Now that Wilson, in disgrace, could no longer ease out of his share of the work, it was inevitable that he and Addison would come to blows over their whipsawing chores. They changed places at top and bottom a dozen times an hour. Finally one day Wilson called Addison "a big stupid dumb brute"; further insults were exchanged, and Wilson struck his brother over the head with a calking iron. Brother William, who was almost as lazy as Wilson, bestirred himself to intercede and spare them the mark of Cain.

Brotherly relations were further damaged when Rena and Addison, left alone in the camp one afternoon while the others made an excursion into the woods, mixed a punch consisting of twelve bottles of Jamaica ginger and six of lemon extract and became thoroughly drunk on the fearsome beverage. "We cemented our friendship but did not commit incest," Addison said. But Wilson glowered with jealousy and suspicion. When the ice began to break up, the winter camp was ready for the psychopathic ward; "each day we did something more foolish than the day before, but, as we all hated each other, anything was better than sitting there scowling and thinking of new things to fight about." The party broke up and the brothers bitterly went their separate ways. William and a friend departed in one boat, followed by Rena and Wilson in another, then Addison and a character called "Och Gott Louie" in a third vessel. The three brothers vowed not to cross paths in the future.

By the first of June, Wilson and his traveling companion had arrived in Dawson, and the young man with a taste for low company was soon active in the less respectable circles of the tent town on the Yukon, the jumping-off-place for the creeks, whose population was increasing by the thousands every week of that delirious spring. The sedate Addison went to work for Edgar as a clerk in the company store. William pronounced himself disgusted with life in the Yukon and headed back to California remarking, "This is a country for the young, strong and stupid."

In his first days in Dawson, Wilson made an equally important decision: the indoor life of the saloons and sporting houses was much preferable to scrabbling for nuggets in the frozen bed of a lonely creek. Dawson, after all, was merely the Barbary Coast with gold dust instead of silver dollars the medium of exchange. He was only twenty-one years old, stood six feet three inches tall and weighed 200 pounds, but hard labor, in his considered opinion, was something for the peasants. And his experiences elsewhere convinced him that the company of outlaw and outcast was much more interesting than that of upright citizens. Perhaps, also, his lifelong pleasure in associating with easy-money men and demireps was a form of revolt against his family. The Mizners were ultra-respectable; they had founded three cities in California, had gone into the more dignified professions with the ease of birthright. One brother was a clergyman, the Reverend Henry Mizner of Christ Church, St. Louis. And there was always his guardian angel, the irritating Addison, to urge him along the path of rectitude.

So, with a lusty enthusiasm, Wilson plunged into the sporting life of Dawson. He and Addison were still not on speaking terms but the latter learned that Wilson "lived over the Dominion, which was the swellest hotel in town. Needless to say, he was not alone." For a short time he sang in a café where Alexander Pantages was working as a waiter and laying the foundation of a multimillion dollar theatrical fortune. Pantages wore leather pockets in his trousers, according to Mizner's recollection, and in them smuggled steaks out of the kitchen to sell outside. Pantages gave Mizner a valuable tip when he volunteered to act as night porter for the restaurant at no extra wages. Mizner wondered why, until he found Pantages sweeping up all the sawdust on the floor, carefully washing it out and collecting the gold dust which had spilled from the pokes of carefree miners.

Soon Mizner found work more suited to his talents than braying "You Would Not Dare Insult Me, Sir, If Jack Were Only Here" to an audience of bibulous sourdoughs. It was especially embarrassing, no doubt, when his turn would be announced: "Mr. Wilson Mizner will now sing," and a voice from the tables jeered, "To hell with that jackass."

"*Nevertheless*," said the master of ceremonies firmly, "Mr. Wilson Mizner will now sing."

The retired songbird, who always believed that he had a splendid voice and blamed adverse reactions consistently to the public's uncultivated taste, went to work as a weigher at the celebrated Monte Carlo, where one of his bosses was that prince of roisterers, Swiftwater Bill Gates. Weighing gold was a position of some dignity and trust—often misplaced—with the weigher stationed behind impressive brass scales and measuring out the dust to be converted into whisky, poker chips and the favors of dance-hall girls.

Like most weighers, Wilson received three ounces of gold a day as his wages, but he found ways to increase his income after a study of his fellow practitioners and recollection of Alex Pantages' methods of placer mining. Some weighers let their fingernails grow long to collect the golden grains; others kept their hands moist to pick up the particles and then dust them off into the leather pockets which were an unauthorized part of the uniform, and some oiled their hair and frequently ran their fingers through it, ending their shifts with a metallic coiffure. Mizner adapted the Pantages technique: he placed a thick carpet under his feet, he later told a New York newspaper interviewer, and once a week burned it and bought a new one. The weekly smelting process netted him $2,500 a week, he claimed; but then Wilson always had an airy attitude toward figures, usually adding a cipher or two to make his anecdotes more impressive.

In his spare time, he produced various shows which were, he claimed, "packed to the doors at five dollars in gold for a seat." One particularly successful production was *Uncle Tom's Cabin*.

That autumn Wilson and Addison were reconciled for a short
time. As Addison succinctly recalled, "Poor kid got the mumps,
and they weren't all in his neck. My heart and sympathy went out
to him." Addison was leaving town to work one of Edgar's claims
that winter, although "I did feel qualms of conscience in leaving
my baby brother behind in this den of iniquity." Wilson promised
to join him as soon as he felt better. But "Mama's Angel Birdie"
had no intention of subjecting himself to manual labor, as his
brother should have known. Virtually his only physical exercise
was joining the stampedes out of Dawson whenever a rumor circulated that baseball-sized nuggets had been found in an outlying
creek bed. With hundreds of others, he would go flying across the
tundra to the scene of the supposed strike, until a mishap showed
the folly of indulging in these cross-country gallops over the spongy
Klondike moss. Invariably the rumor would be found to be without substance or was much exaggerated; finding gold was a matter
of hard digging rather than following up barroom gossip. On his
last such dash into the wilderness, Wilson was reduced to gnawing
on a frozen doughnut he carried along as iron rations. He broke
a tooth, and when he limped back to Dawson he was given the
sobriquet of "The Yellow Kid," after a popular comic-strip character who also had a front tooth missing.

By the time Addison returned to Dawson from the family claim
in the spring of 1899, he found his "baby brother" involved in a
scandal which horrified the somewhat priggish Addison.

The tale going around Dawson was that Wilson had been working in various faro houses as a dealer. Rena Fargo would appear
at his table, apparently a stranger to him, and leave, a heavy
winner. One night he dealt her such excellent hands that she broke
the bank. Wilson's current employer did not suspect that his
jovial dealer was improving her luck, but was somehow convinced
that Rena had cheated. The proprietor, it was said, picked up a
large piece of wood, walked over to Rena and bashed her over

the head with it. Whatever the truth of the story, the romance between Wilson and Rena ended about that time; perhaps she felt he should have protected her skull, if not her honor.

Addison unburdened himself in a letter to their older brother, the Reverend Henry Mizner, in St. Louis, recounting at length Wilson's waywardness since they had come to the Klondike. Addison beseeched the counsel of his senior, since Edgar was in the States at the time and could not exercise fraternal authority. Henry replied that he had known of Wilson's conduct for some time but piously declared, "We must stick to him as long as we can—come what may. Someday this may all be forgotten, horrible as it is now."

According to the story Wilson told about himself later, in denouncing the theory that all sourdoughs were loyal to the marrow of their bones, he was thrown into the Dawson jail in a misunderstanding over the "borrowing" of a typewriter.

It all happened, Wilson would relate, over his misplaced confidence in a friend.

I had faith in that man. He made the first set of burglar's tools ever turned out in Alaska. I elected him chief of police. I paid his expenses and managed his campaign and organized a reception for him the day he took office. I even pinned a gold star on his vest.

And the first man he arrested was me! At that time, there was only one typewriter in town. Somebody had stolen it and sold it to a butcher, who thought it was a cash register. Three friends of mine were in danger of being put away for life. We needed the typewriter to draw up an appeal, and in the emergency I borrowed it from the butcher shop when the butcher was out. My new chief arrested me—and that was the true-blue comradeship of the Frozen North for you.

By that time Edgar Mizner had returned to Dawson, and now it was his turn to attempt to straighten out the family delinquent. The Northwest Mounted Police were becoming intensely interested in any character devoid of visible—or conventional—means of support. Edgar sent Wilson out to one of his claims and appointed him foreman of the crew. Perhaps responsibility would sober him and bring him closer to maturity. Wilson's first measure was to persuade the men that they were all working too hard; then they settled down for a marathon poker game, hoping to while away the long night of winter. Edgar showed up one day in the midst of this siege and with deep regret fired his foreman.

Wilson bore his elder brother no ill will. It was time to be leaving the Yukon anyway, what with the blue-nosed attitude of the Mounties and the paralyzing influence of civilization. Among the signs of its encroachment was a society column running in the *Nugget*, a sure sign that deterioration was setting in, and its wonderfully explicit column of police-court news had been reduced in proportion. Besides, news had come of an important strike at Nome, which was in the Territory of Alaska and out of the red-sleeved reach of the Mounties.

Thirty thousand men and women landed on the beaches at Nome in the summer and autumn of 1900, a rush rivaling that of the Klondike. At Nome gold mining was even simpler than on the Klondike creeks, for the dust was sprinkled in the sands of otherwise dreary beaches, as well as creeks inland. Mining was simply a process of rocking the sand in wooded contraptions and waiting for the gold to settle at the bottom. Wilson had somehow accumulated $20,000 during his stay in Dawson but he felt no temptation to try his hand at mining, for all the talk of fabulous strikes; "never was I diverted from my intention of setting up a gambling shack in a hurry and giving the boys an outlet for their gold dust or a chance at my $20,000," he said.

By August, despite the fact that lumber was selling at $700 a thousand feet on that treeless tundra, he had built his ramshackle casino. He called it the McQuestion; the odd name may have been his way of emulating Soapy Smith and his Caveat Emptor. On the other hand, it may have been named for Leroy Napoleon (Jack) McQuestion, a Klondike pioneer.

The McQuestion was combination saloon and gambling house, with a bunkhouse at the rear for drunken, weary and bankrupted patrons. It had strong competition from Tex Rickard's Northern Saloon and Wyatt Earp's Dexter Bar, where the big-time gamblers gathered. At the McQuestion the innocents were not only up against the house's luck but the scientific devices which guaranteed it. Naturally the profits were huge, and Mizner increased them by making a couple of successful mining investments. But he liked the company of celebrities and could not stay away from the high-rolling games at Rickard's and Earp's. It was a classic example of the wise guy being taken, through his own weakness, by wiser guys. In a few months he had lost his fortune and the McQuestion along with it.

Neither sadder nor much wiser after his comeuppance at the tables, Mizner turned to dealing faro, managing a hotel and handling prize fighters. Rickard already had begun his career as a fight promoter. One of Mizner's fighters was an eager young fellow destined to become as celebrated as Rickard—Jack (Doc) Kearns, later the manager of Jack Dempsey and Mickey Walker. Kearns had arrived in Nome so determined to get his share of the nuggets said to be lying around on the beaches that he refused to wait for a lighter but jumped overboard from the steamer and swam ashore through the icy waters. Kearns learned almost as quickly as Mizner that the indoor life could be profitable, too, especially since mining was a little more complicated than bending over and picking up nuggets.

Kearns joined Mizner's stable of fighters but was too intelligent to be satisfied with the hard knocks and low pay in the ring of 1900.

He decided to become a weigher in one of Nome's gambling palaces and was quickly initiated into the mysteries of his new calling by Mizner.

"Come with me, son," Mizner said, after watching his protégé fumble with the brass scales.

He took Kearns to his cabin out on the tundra and ordered him to sit down. Then he poured a jug of corn syrup over Kearns's hair, which fortunately had not been cut for some time, and plastered it down.

"Handle the dust all you can," Mizner directed him. "Then run your fingers through your hair."

By the end of a shift at the scales, Kearn's hair would be stiff with a golden cement. A shampoo would usually net him close to a hundred dollars. Mizner "could make a pair of scales do anything," Kearns has recalled with reverence.

Wilson was perhaps the only *boulevardier* in Nome, which as a matter of fact had no boulevards, only spongy straggling streets where a clean shirt was the height of elegance. When he was in the chips, Wilson would send to San Francisco for the finest tailoring and linen. (One tailor's bill did not catch up with him until many years later in New York, and then only with the assistance of a deputy sheriff.) It was his custom to meet the steamers arriving at Nome, clamber aboard from a lighter and make the first and usually the best impression on any feminine cargo being discharged there. Once he hired a brass band—on credit—to welcome ashore an especially dazzling group of actresses and dancing girls. He had "all the parlor ladies in a daze," recalled James Bain, who was known as Newsboy Red in Nome. One actress who was the toast of the town in 1901 afterward claimed that Mizner had married her, but he always said, simply if ungallantly, that he couldn't remember any such occurrence.

Before returning to the States with a modest bank roll from his two years in the North, Addison Mizner journeyed to Nome to visit Wilson and determine, for the information of the family council, if he had mended his ways. Addison learned shortly after arriving in Nome that Wilson had been appointed a deputy sheriff and that his courage in tracking down evildoers was widely admired. Hopeful but only half believing, Addison hurried out to Wilson's cabin which was so oddly constructed, as Wilson said, that it "resembled a small cathedral built by an inebriate," its ridge joints being cut at such a narrow angle that it was "all gable and two-thirds attic."

Addison then learned that Wilson's prowess as a man hunter was not all it seemed to his fellow citizens.

About three o'clock one morning Wilson was awakened by friends hammering at his door, three characters known as "Scurvy Bill," a name applied to his character rather than the state of his health, "Two-Tooth Mike" and "Mit." They had been involved in a robbery and Two-Tooth Mike had been wounded. Wilson had been a deputy for only a month; he rather liked wearing the silver star and saw his duty clearly. Saw it and shied away from it. Pursuit could not be far away so he quickly hid the three men in his capacious attic. A few minutes later the sheriff arrived at the head of a posse, bearing the information that a gang of desperadoes had tried to jump a claim on Anvil Creek, had been dispersed and were now holed up in a cabin on a near-by hillock. The sheriff told his deputy to dress and join the posse.

The cabin was surrounded and the man hunters excitedly pointed out white faces and rifle barrels at the windows. It was decided that the whole mob should rush the place, but Mizner calmly intervened. "One man should walk up there and tell them to surrender and save bloodshed," he proposed.

"Fine," said the sheriff, "but who's going to risk getting shot between the eyes by those robbers?"

"I will go," Wilson said, squaring his shoulders and thrusting his jaw out heroically.

Mizner marched up to the cabin door, while the posse waited breathless with fear and admiration.

"Come out, you rats! Or I will shoot you out," Wilson shouted.

There was no answer, of course. Wilson kicked in the door and sprang inside. A moment later, after lighting a cigarette for effect, he strolled out and announced, "There's nobody there, sheriff—just some blood splashed around."

From then on he was known in Nome as the "bravest man in Alaska." The three guests concealed in his attic, who were unwittingly responsible for this heroic legend, managed to make a safe getaway. Addison went home sadly unable to report that Wilson had learned anything but a surface respect for law and order.

Wilson himself returned to the States early in 1902 but found Benicia much too tame and the admonitions of his family much too irksome. Early that spring he boarded the steamer *Portland* to return to Nome. On May 7 the steamer became frozen solid in an ice floe and drifted helplessly toward the vicinity of the North Pole. For almost two months the ship was held in the Arctic's clutch and the outside world held little hope its passengers would be alive when it was finally released by warm weather.

Mizner's high spirits were greatly appreciated on that hapless voyage. A large assortment of costumes consigned to Nome theaters was included in the ship's cargo, and Wilson did his best to alleviate the fears of his fellow passengers with a daily revue in which he was the producer, director, sketch writer and star. Routine labor fatigued Mizner quicker than almost any living vertebrate but he always seized energetically at any chance to entertain people—a fortuitous streak of ham for the *Portland's* worried company who gratefully applauded even his deafening baritone raised in ballads and sea chanteys. It was indeed a captive audience.

Not the least of his kindly offices was performed for a Professor Blankenshrift, a roving practitioner of astrology, hypnotism and other occult arts. The passengers denounced him for a charlatan because he had not foretold their fate in the stars and jeered when his attempts to mesmerize various subjects failed, possibly because they were already paralyzed with fear.

The professor's plight aroused Mizner's sympathy. One day, when the ice began breaking up, he leaped overboard into the freezing waters, swam to a neighboring ice floe and howled for help. After he had been rescued, Mizner accused the professor of having hypnotized him and ordering him to jump overboard. This heroic evidence immediately restored the professor to the somewhat fearful esteem of his fellow passengers.

The *Portland* arrived in Nome on July 2, 1902—three months after leaving San Francisco—and was greeted by bonfires on the beaches and lighters loaded down with food and drink. A wild celebration followed in the streets and bars of the town.

That was the last bit of Arctic excitement for Wilson Mizner. He found that Nome had grown respectable, too; all the symptoms that made Dawson unworthy of his continued residence had appeared, and like Soapy Smith in Creede he recognized that "there is a time to go." He would find other places to enliven. Life would never be dull for Wilson Mizner.

13

~~~

Friendship on Ice

ONE OF THE legends dearest to creators of Arctic fiction was that
every Klondiker loved and valued his friends, human and canine,
above all else—even gold. Sled dogs, being necessary to a man's
survival on the trail, may have fared well enough; but the friendship of human for human was generally a most expendable luxury.
Men went North to get rich rather than win friends. Wilson Mizner became almost rabid whenever a non-Klondiker in later years
remarked how wonderful it must have been, all that comradely devotion under the midnight sun. A more sentimental observer, Jack
London, wrote warmly of the quality of friendship in the Yukon,
but he must have been looking back on that congenial winter camp
on the Stewart River, where men had to band together against
adversity and boredom and the atmosphere was not clouded by
avarice, the gold fields being far across the frozen tundra. Surely
London was not thinking of that scurvy-ridden summer he spent
in Dawson, when his teeth fell out for lack of a little help from
his pals.

Along the trails to the interior men died by the hundreds of hunger, disease, exposure and exhaustion, well aware in their last moments that their fellow humans would withhold a helping hand if it delayed them an instant in the race for the golden creeks. Others died in the mining camps and towns because men were loath to share their food, which would lessen their own chances of survival, and, besides, food was worth its weight in gold. There was a certain Code of the North but it had nothing to do with any sentimental regard for humanity. A man who stole another's food or other possessions was very harshly treated—sometimes hanged or otherwise done to death—but that was because a cache could mean life or death to a man far from any other source of supply, not because a man's property rights were regarded as sacred. The widespread prevalence of claim-jumping was an indication to the contrary.

The only time a man could be assured of a surfeit of friendship was when he struck it rich. Well-wishers flocked around him, bore him off to the nearest bar and insisted on toasting his future health and prosperity—with drinks bought by himself, of course. Anyone who did not establish a reputation as a free spender, whether he was so inclined or not, was reviled as a cheap skate, tightwad and sour-faced miser. The warm friendships that sprang up around a man in the barrooms usually diminished in exact ratio to the size of his poke. Good-fellowship was based securely on his ability to keep the glasses filled.

Compassion for the down-and-outers was almost unknown in those same tabernacles of comradeship. Miners swaggering into the saloons, fresh from a profitable session of digging, would throw nuggets into the cuspidors, just for the laughter and feeling of superiority the gesture aroused when the swampers, near-derelicts hired to keep the spittoons clean and shining, would dive into the snuff and tobacco juice to retrieve them in the Klondike version of ground grabs.

The tendency to fleece a fellow prospector was also quite prevalent, with the nimble-witted and smooth-tongued doing a brisk trade in unproductive claims among newcomers and other easy marks.

To bolster the hopes of the naïve, however, there was always the story of Charlie Anderson and how he was swindled into a fortune. Anderson was a strong-backed Swede who arrived too late to stake his own claim on Bonanza Creek, so he went to work with pick and shovel in a mine. When he had saved up $600 from his wages, he came into Dawson for a few days of relaxation, which he began, as was usual, with a fine roaring drunk. He invited two old friends, who were working a sterile claim up on Eldorado Creek, to join him over a bottle of whisky. In the course of the revelry the pair persuaded Anderson to hand over his little sack of gold dust, the pay for months of hard labor, in exchange for what they believed to be a worthless claim. Other prospectors would have agreed there was little possibility of a profitable pan-out on the upper Eldorado: the lay of the land was all wrong in the little valley traversed by the creek, and the timber leaned in the wrong direction.

Next morning he woke up with a horrible hangover and the feeling he had done something distastrous. Backtracking on the previous night's events, he learned that he had bought a mining claim. He begged his two drinking companions to give him back his gold dust, but they insisted a deal was a deal.

"Well, I better go to work," Anderson said stolidly, and trudged up to the claim he had bought on the upper Eldorado. He carried with him a sack of flour, a slab of bacon, a few pounds of sugar and coffee, which he had obtained on credit, and his mining tools. Along the way he picked up two other Swedes who agreed to help work the claim on a percentage basis.

The two highbinders who had sold him the claim came up to gloat over their victim. It was probably the last day of their lives they could feel the slightest self-satisfaction. Charlie was testing a pan from the dump of pay dirt he had heaped up. The pair asked how he was doing.

"Think I've got something here," Charlie said.

The pair left, snickering at his optimism. Later they learned that pan contained $1,400 in gold dust.

By that time Charlie Anderson had become something of an opportunist himself. He said nothing about that first pan to the other Swedes but signed a contract with them in which he agreed to pay them $25,000 in ten days. He paid them off within the stipulated period, and they left in a hurry, before he could change his mind.

Afterward Anderson disclosed that if the previous owners and his former partners had dug two feet deeper and struck bedrock as he did with his superior diligence, they would have shared in what became one of the most important discoveries in the Klondike.

Anderson then settled down to work his claim in comfort, building a large cabin and installing steam heat. He constructed a steam plant to thaw the ground and make mining quicker and easier. Getting rich became almost as tedious as working with the pick and shovel in earlier days, so he turned from the merely comfortable to the sybaritic, importing champagne, dance-hall girls and drinking companions from the Dawson saloons. Stories of Anderson's high living out on the creek fascinated a number of people in Dawson, among them officials of the North American Trading Company. They asked Anderson how much he wanted for his claim. Five hundred thousand dollars, said Anderson. The company officials hooted with laughter.

Laughing at Charlie Anderson was becoming a most expensive pastime, for six months later the company offered him $750,000 for his claim, and he rejected it. In three years he dug a fabulous amount of gold dust and nuggets out of that 500-foot stretch of bedrock; estimates on the total range from $1,250,000 to nearly $2,000,000. The trouble was, Charlie played as hard as he once worked. He took his drinking companions and several dance-hall girls with him on a deluxe tour of Europe, and in Paris his spending reached such a peak that Argentine cattle barons, Mexican generals and Balkan princes seemed like so many skinflints by comparison. He tossed the money away as fast as his mine produced it. The last big check was for $100,000, paid him when a big dredging company moved in with its massive earth-chewing equipment and was supposed to have taken out additional hundreds of thousands of dollars.

Charlie Anderson wound up broke but still a happy man. When Henry F. Woods, one of the Klondike's livelier historians, last saw him, Charlie was earning $4 a day as a sawmill worker in Ballard, Washington. Perhaps that mysterious happy smile never left his face because he could always contemplate the fact that he experienced half a dozen years of affluence only because he had been hornswoggled into it by a couple of false friends; if ever he felt miserable, he could always think of how they must feel.

The prime example of ingratitude, of course, was the fate of Bob Henderson, who first discovered gold in the Klondike. A small pension from the Canadian government was his only reward. George Carmack and his Indian friends, whom he had tipped off to the presence of gold on the creeks, were striking pay dirt on Bonanza while Henderson was washing out barely enough to buy beans and flour on Gold Bottom, a bitter misnomer if ever there was one. Carmack and his companions simply forgot to tell Henderson about the richer strike on the Bonanza.

In after years there were much sentimental reminiscence and fiction writing about a Klondiker's devotion to his "pard." But, as previously mentioned, many partners, driven to distraction by "cabin fever," would break up over some trivial disagreement, such as whose turn it was to chop the firewood, and split up their jointly owned possessions. In a fury of petulance, they would cut tents in half, saw sacks of flour in two and split sides of bacon with an ax, to be quit of each other on precisely equal terms.

A Dawson freight-line driver recalled an instance of uncomradely behavior when he was summoned to haul a miner named Sullivan to Father Judge's hospital from the junction of Diamond Creek and Twelve Mile River. Sullivan's partner promised the dog-team driver $500 for transporting Sullivan, whose legs were frozen from his toes to six inches below his knees and were threatened with amputation. Despite Sullivan's desperate condition, his partner insisted on frequent stops to rest. And when finally they reached the camp, he announced he did not feel up to accompanying the dogsled ambulance back to Dawson, although his help was necessary.

"Won't come, hey, the yellow bastard?" the driver roared. "We'll see about that."

He grabbed an ax, and with that as a persuader Sullivan's partner was coaxed into accompanying the stricken man back to Dawson. The malingerer had a sort of revenge, however, for he bilked the freight line out of its $500 and vanished from the Klondike.

Friendships could die as well as flourish on the winter trails, when men were thrown into one another's company for days on end in the solitudes. There was the bitter tale, for instance, of how Mike Mahoney, the dog-team driver, and Angus MacTavish, a Dawson bank manager, became bitter enemies after mushing it to Nome together at the beginning of the stampede to the Seward Peninsula. The Irishman and the Scotsman had been fast friends in Dawson, when their relationship was not tested by adversity or constant propinquity. The amiability between them began to vanish during negotiations on how much Mahoney should charge MacTavish for the 1,100-mile journey. They finally agreed on $250. There was also the matter of MacTavish's luggage: the dapper little banker insisted on carrying 200 pounds of clothing with him, although Mahoney pointed out that the last 300 miles of the journey would have to be negotiated over the treacherous shore ice of Norton Sound.

The first issue that arose between the two friends was the starting time in the morning. Mahoney already held the Dawson-Skagway record and aimed at breaking the Dawson-Nome record (which he did, by making the journey in forty-seven days, but he believed he could have made it in thirty days without MacTavish). Mac-Tavish, however, was a slave of habit, particularly the habit of "attending to the call of nature," as he put it, before beginning any sort of activity in the morning. Mahoney was not particularly amused by the way MacTavish, at the outset of their journey, made his wishes known: "I've been a man of regular habits all my life and I don't propose to change them to suit you or a bunch of dogs. You'll just have to wait here patiently until nature gives her summons."

From then until their rather abrupt parting, there was a ludicrous test of wills between Mahoney and MacTavish. MacTavish kept harping on the importance of what he called, with a quaintly professional touch, his "internal economy." Mahoney grumbled constantly about being "hog-tied by another man's bowels" and accused MacTavish of attending to them with "a kind of self-indulgent deliberation." At first Mahoney's thoughts were centered on homicide, he admitted, but then he concentrated on means of hurrying MacTavish along and making him suffer, in addition, for the slow time they were making.

Mahoney refused to halt for a hot noontime meal, as MacTavish proposed, but fed his passenger on "a handful of frozen beans," and "all afternoon fought down the longing for a can of boiling tea in the hope that his self-denial was causing his difficult guest discomfort." Most of his waking hours were spent in trying to devise means of getting MacTavish's "internal economy" in shape for an early start the next morning. Once he threw a dynamite cap into the fire, hoping that fright would accomplish what persuasion could not. The result was that they could not get under way until noon. That evening Mahoney mixed a quarter of a pound of Epsom salts into the flour for their sourdough biscuits, but next morning found "the experiment was so successful that they had to lay up for an entire day."

At Forty Mile, where they made an overnight stop, Mike had his revenge for a number of indignities he had suffered along the way. They put up at the cabin of a woodcutter, Pegleg Reilly, whose hospitality was strained at the outset of their stay by MacTavish's complaints about the food, the cramped quarters, the stuffy atmosphere inside the cabin and the fact Mahoney brought the seven sled dogs in to spend the night. The hut would accommodate two persons nicely, so MacTavish suggested that Mahoney and the dogs sleep outside in the snow. Their host's comment to Mahoney was "If you don't murder him some morning, it'll be a miracle. May God give you strength and patience, but if you have to do it, there's not a jury living that won't say it was justifiable."

That night MacTavish paid for his sins against good-fellowship. He climbed into the cabin's only bunk with Reilly and Mahoney on either side of him; the seven dogs were piled together on the floor; the noise and the odor were almost unbearable, especially to a man who had been accustomed to the amenities of living in Dawson. Worse trials were ahead for the banker. He had just dropped off to sleep, finally, when Mahoney and Reilly began to have a series of violent nightmares with arms and legs flailing at the man caught between them. The paroxysms become so violent that MacTavish was hurled out of the bunk and onto the pile of sleeping Huskies. Suspicious of this seemingly joint effort, MacTavish struck a match and examined the faces of his two compainons; they were sleeping as "innocently as babes," with beatific smiles. MacTavish climbed on the bunk again and was violently dispossessed a second time. He spent the rest of the night sleeping with the dogs on the floor, although their nightmares were almost as frightful as their master's.

At Fort Yukon, where MacTavish spent a whole day reminiscing with the manager of the Alaska Commercial Company's post, Mahoney plotted further harassments of his passenger. MacTavish had become more lordly and arrogant with every mile of their journey, insisting that since Mahoney was being paid he should be "part musher, part wetnurse and part Pullman porter. . . . This went on interminably and punctuated everything they had to do in common from choosing a place to stop at night to deciding who should put the next log on the fire." Every day, from then on, Mahoney ditched some item of MacTavish's extensive luggage. And when the Scotsman unbraided him for not looking after his possessions, Mahoney bellowed, "From now on you can look after your own goddam bags. I've been lugging them in and out of every stopping place we hit, rummaging out dry socks you couldn't find yourself . . . and all the thanks I get is a dressing down. . . . I'm through! I'm a musher, not a third-rate chore boy. Starting now, my friend, you can be your own goddam valet."

By the time they were crossing the Yukon Flats, MacTavish had only a satchel left of his baronial baggage. Bickering so incessantly they had no eye for the grandeur of nature, the ill-suited pair drove on to Norton Sound, passing the Ramparts, great palisades running for fifty miles, the mouths of the historic Tanana and Koyukuk rivers, the mission villages, the old Russian trading posts. All that Mahoney could ever remember of that journey, he said in later years, was "a small, purposeful, fur-coated figure floundering through the deep snow toward a nearby clump of brush."

The two travelers were within sight of the Nome beaches and the tents and huts which lined them when they had their final quarrel.

MacTavish brought up the fact that most of his baggage had disappeared along the way and announced he did not feel bound to pay the $250 agreed on. "All things considered," he told Mahoney, "I think $185 would be a liberal settlement."

Mahoney halted the dogs and glowered down on MacTavish, riding comfortably on the sled as he had most of the journey.

"I wouldn't make that trip again with you for $10,000, and by the holy old baldy, I'm not dragging you another inch," Mahoney shouted.

He suddenly twisted the hand grips of the sled and turned it over, dumping his old friend into a snowbank. "Mush!" he yelled and continued to Nome, leaving MacTavish stuck headfirst in the snow; he felt "like a free man after weeks of servitude." Their friendship had foundered, as had so many other Klondike comradeships, on a series of trivial irritations which would have been ignored in more civilized surroundings.

Wilson Mizner had uttered a bitter judgment on the rapid deterioration of friendship in the North Country—"I never knew the meaning of ingratitude until I had one of those Arctic pals"— and it was this same hard-bitten figure of Dawson's and Nome's live-without-work society that provided a couple of classic examples of rascality. The trouble with Mizner was, as many men and women discovered throughout the world, that one couldn't help laughing at him even while he was committing some outrageous villainy. Perhaps the word "outrageous" was the key to his actions. He never committed small, carefully calculated misdeeds solely for purposes of self-aggrandizement; there was always a belly laugh concealed in his enterprises, characteristic of a man who could never take anything very seriously, especially himself. Mizner was a sort of artist in crime, who converted a lawless act into a sardonic little comedy. Any young man contemplating crime as a profession, rather than a mere stopgap, could study Mizner's career with profit: the law goes lightly with a fellow who can make it laugh, and like all the world it hates a solemn villain.

Perhaps that's why Mizner never became acquainted with the interior of a prison.

"Outrage" certainly was the word to describe his treatment of the late Key Pittman, then a lawyer in Nome and later an able and distinguished member of the United States Senate.

Pittman shrewdly ordered several tons of coal shipped to him the summer of his arrival in Nome, kept it in a mountainous heap behind his law office and sold it at a fancy figure when winter came. It became so valuable that he mounted a constant guard over it, watching it out of his office window with a shotgun over his knees.

One winter afternoon Mizner came to Pittman's office with a long face and a sad tale. It seemed that Rose, one of the town's doxies, was in the hospital and needed an operation. Mizner was trying to borrow $200 from the bank but needed a cosigner on his note. Pittman was "familiar with the Yellow Kid's [Mizner's] wiles, but he also knew that on occasion the Yellow Kid could be genuinely unselfish." The coal business was prospering, even if the law wasn't, with the town swarming with legal sharks; so Pittman signed the note.

As Mizner dashed down the stairs, Pittman turned back to his guard mount. Four of Mizner's closest associates were hauling away two tons of coal on a sleigh and disappeared around a corner just as Pittman swiveled around in his chair. There was another shock to Pittman's faith in humanity. He met Rose, the supposedly ailing young woman, at Tex Rickard's bar that afternoon. Pittman asked about the operation, and heard her reply, "What operation?" And when the note fell due a few months later, Pittman had to pay it. In less than five minutes of a winter's afternoon he had been bilked out of $200 and two tons of coal.

Mizner also figured prominently in an extralegal matter which should be of interest to all lawyers and judges: he presided over the lightning probate of the estate of Jim Wilson, one of Nome's more substantial citizens. Probate cases can take years in legally constituted courts; Mizner's distribution of the estate was accomplished overnight, and it was never contested in one of those distasteful courtroom dramas where the deceased man's relatives claw each other for his possessions.

"Diamond Jim" Wilson was the owner of the Anvil Bar, the finest in Nome, next to Rickard's and Earp's. He weighed 300 pounds and in further emulation of Diamond Jim Brady decorated his swollen body with diamond rings, tiepin, cuff links and studs. Among his more troublesome possessions was a lady named Ione, a peroxided blonde, who had been his consort for three years and watched him grow fatter and richer in the Dawson and Nome booms.

It was the day of Christmas Eve 1900, and Jim and Ione were bickering in their lavish suite over the Anvil Bar. Wilson smoked his post-breakfast cigar and played a game of solitaire while Ione complained that her favors were ill rewarded, particularly since he had neglected to buy her a twenty-five-hundred-dollar diamond tiara for Christmas. "You can spend God knows how many thousand on a Christmas party for your whisky-swilling friends," she pointed out. "But when it comes to the woman who's loved you and stuck to you through thick and thin, that's something else again. Back in Dawson you used to spend five thousand on me in a single day. I could have had any man in town then, and why I ever took a tight-fisted fat old butter tub like you, I'll never know." She also pointed out that Wilson had just bought himself a six-thousand-dollar ring, and was about to harp on this subject in several keys, when he sharply reminded her that it was time they joined their friends in the bar downstairs.

Ione held her tongue as he went out the door, but her thoughts, as she finished making up her face in front of the dressing table mirror, were anything but Christmasy.

Downstairs she joined Wilson and the cream of Nome's demi-monde: the Yellow Kid (Mizner), the Double-O Kid, Single-O Kid, the In-and-Out Kid and the Hobo Kid, along with such sprightly lasses as Frisco Sal, Shady Sadie, Nellie the Pig and Diamond-Tooth Lou, a tall blonde young woman with what has been described as the most beautiful figure in Alaska, whose nickname derived from the fact that she had a diamond filling in one of her incisors.

They had gathered for Diamond Jim's annual holiday binge, on which he drank twice as much as usual, truly a heroic feat for a saloonkeeper who did not believe in the stuffy old adage that a man should not patronize his own bar. Twenty cases of champagne were uncorked for Diamond Jim, his friends and his best customers; and when the wine ran out, they resorted to whisky, gin, rum and beer. Jim held court in his alcove-office, where a specially built chair had been placed to accommodate his bulk. One of the most popular characters in Nome, he was toasted a hundred times, and kept up drink for drink with the stoutest guzzlers in the North. Except for a fat man's usual internal discomforts, he was a proud and happy man that Christmas. In the strongbox near his desk was a fortune, at least $100,000 in gold and paper money. He wore the key to it on a gold chain around his neck. Banks, he had observed, were untrustworthy.

As the festivities in the Anvil Bar came to a close, Jim's face had assumed a purplish color that would have alarmed his physician; his eyes bulged out, and he swayed in his chair. A half-dozen empty bottles were on the table next to him.

Surrounded by his friends, Diamond Jim then made his annual pilgrimage along Front Street, stopping in every halfway decent bar and buying drinks for the house. It was a hilarious procession; the women dressed in satin gowns, all the jewelry they had managed to acquire and fur coats; the men singing, whooping, dancing and capering. At every bar that Jim and his troupe entered they were greeted with a rendition of "He's a Jolly Good Fellow." Thus they passed triumphantly through Tex Rickard's, Wyatt Earp's, Boozer Brown's, Gus Seifert's, Joe Jourdan's, and Jim Wilson's Nevada (Diamond Jim was not related to his namesake). Then they descended on the Café de Paris, the finest restaurant in Nome, where they washed down the food with whisky cocktails and wine.

"More champagne!" Diamond Jim would bellow, beaming with good will to all men. "Bring my friends more champagne!" And the corks would pop like a battery of field guns.

But the Hobo Kid, slightly soberer than his companions, was alarmed by Diamond Jim's apoplectic complexion, which had become the color of port wine.

He suggested to Ione, "I figure Jim's had about enough to drink—it might be a good idea to get him home."

Ione not only ignored the suggestion, but proposed a toast in which Diamond Jim joined heartily.

A rum omelet and a round of cognac finished off the supper party, and Jim and his intimates straggled back to the Anvil Bar. Jim had to be helped along through the snowdrifts with Ione on one side of him and Wilson Mizner on the other.

Back at the Anvil, Diamond Jim ordered his chief bartender, Blackie, to kick out the late customers still clinging to the bar. "We'll have a little private party, just me and my pals," Jim said, easing himself into his reinforced chair. Ione had bottles of champagne, bourbon and rye brought to the green-baize table and placed a box of Jim's favorite cigars at his elbow. Jim looked as though his veins were about to burst like a system of rotten fire hose, but he called on Mizner to sing one of his favorite ballads, an old Civil War number titled "Tom and Ned." Mizner pulled out all the stops as he sang the verses of the old tear-jerker:

Tom and Ned were next door neighbors
    In a little country town;
Two better pals than they were seldom seen,

Till the pretty face and roguish smile
And the laughing eyes of brown
Of the little village beauty came between.

The ladies sniffled a little at these tender sentiments, and Diamond Jim poured a tumbler full of whisky to drink a toast to Mizner. He wobbled to his feet with a great effort.

"To the Yellow Kid, my oldest friend—and the best damned songbird in Alaska!" he saluted Mizner.

Diamond Jim knocked it back, that last hearty drink of a full and hearty life.

His face darkened with the engorged blood flooding his system; he swayed for a moment like an elephant with a bullet in its brain, and then he toppled backward into his chair, which was smashed by the force of his fall.

His friends clustered around the fallen figure. He was still breathing, and the Hobo Kid suggested someone run for a doctor at once.

Ione bent over him for a moment, and said, "No. I've seen him like this many times before. He'll come out of it."

The Hobo Kid shrugged. Along with Mizner and two of the other Kids, he accepted Ione's suggestion that they carry him upstairs to the bedroom.

A few minutes later his labored breathing stopped.

As if waiting for her cue, Ione flung herself on the body and wailed, "Oh, my poor darling! Oh, poor, poor Jim!"

"Poor Jim," echoed Mizner, thoughtfully.

They all drank a toast to the corpse, and an immediate wake was about to commence, when Ione remarked in a steady, reasonable voice: "Well, we all have to die. Jim was lucky—he died among his friends. And we were his friends, all the way back to Dawson in '98. You know, Jim often told me that if he was taken unexpectedly like this, he wanted his friends to share in the effects. You've all heard him say that, haven't you?"

There was a murmur of assent. Ione removed Jim's diamond-studded watch, with its heavy gold chain and jeweled charm, and handed it to Mizner.

"He wanted you to have this," she murmured.

There was a hurried distribution of other items of the estate: the diamond stud to the In-and-Out Kid, the cuff links to the Single-O Kid. The diamond ring, which Ione decided was Jim's bequest to the Hobo Kid, provided a bit of trouble and refused to budge from the dead man's pudgy finger. Finally it was wrenched off. Blackie the bartender came up the stairs, learned of his employer's death and was about to become irksome over the propriety of the informal probate court gathered around the corpse, but he stifled his protests when Ione announced that, with his dying breath, Jim had bequeathed Blackie $1,000 and his job in perpetuity.

As Mizner put it, "Jim's last words were that he wanted Ione to have the Anvil and 'Don't fire Blackie—he's the best bartender I ever had.' "

Next morning, when the authorities looked into Jim Wilson's death without any undue snooping and prying, Ione had already installed herself as proprietor of the Anvil Bar. She had also taken possession of the strongbox, its key and contents. No will was found, she said, and there were no relatives back in the States to lay claim to his estate.

The day after Christmas, Diamond Jim Wilson was borne to his grave, hacked out of the frozen tundra, with several hundred persons following the sleigh carrying his coffin. Since Jim was fire chief of Nome, among other civic responsibilities, a large wreath of paper flowers bore the somewhat sinister prophecy on its white ribbon: "Poor Jim, gone to his last fire."

There was considerable snide comment around town about the

swiftness with which his estate was distributed, but what finer tribute could be paid to his generous spirit than sparing his name and memory the ignominy of protracted legal wrangling? Not many men are so fortunate as to die among friends who will take time out from their grief to constitute themselves a probate court.

Friendship wasn't a sacred thing, even in church, it was observed by Federal Judge James Wickersham. He recalled in his lively history, *Old Yukon,* the Sunday he attended services at the church of Bishop Rowe in Circle City.

The deacon, a young attorney, was passing the collection plate. When he came to another young man, sitting near Judge Wickersham, an embarrassing little scene occurred. The parishioner, a merchant of Circle City, dropped a five-dollar gold piece in the plate with a smug air.

The attorney rattled the plate peremptorily and said, "Come again."

"What do you want, you blackmailer?" the merchant asked in an angry whisper.

"I want the whole twenty-five dollars you beat me out of in the poker game last night," the attorney demanded in a slightly louder tone.

The whole congregation was staring at them now, and the merchant, reddening with anger and chagrin, put twenty more dollars in the collection plate.

Judge Wickersham, possibly concerned with the honor of the local bar, heard the attorney's explanation the next day: "Joe [the merchant] needed a little Christian chastening, the church needed the money, and I needed the happy glow of righteous satisfaction which I failed to get in the poker game." It was obvious that if the honor of the poker table could be treated so lightly that a man could be blackmailed out of his winnings in church, friendship was too tender a blossom for the Arctic blast.

14

The Big Sports

ALONG THE ragged crescent of Nome's beaches, whose dark sands were washed by the Bering Sea, there sprang up the most lawless mining camp in the world. Even men who had experienced the boom towns of the American West, Australia and South Africa were appalled by the uproarious contempt for law, order, decency and justice that prevailed from the beginning of the stampede. The majesty of American law as represented at Nome suffered extremely in comparison with the stern but usually fair administration of Dawson and other Klondike settlements by the Canadian territorial government. In several months the few hundred persons then settled at Nome were increased to 7,000 in August of 1899, and more than 12,000 by the following summer. Eight million dollars in gold were extracted during the two years of Nome's greatest prosperity, when some of the luckier prospectors made $1,000 a day working the tidal silt. Naturally these statistics attracted the gentry with fancy vests, silk cravats and claw-hammer coats, with the shrewd eyes and carefully calculated air of opulence—the big sports, ever so expert at persuading others to drink, gamble and be merry. Others but never themselves. *They* needed a clear head for business, after all.

The news of such a rich strike quickly made Nome the "paradise of thieves, thugs, cheats, outlaws and the most degraded types of sporting women and their parasites." United States infantry was landed there but made little headway against the lawlessness and corruption. It was Skagway all over again, but without the centralizing influence of Soapy Smith—an ignoble example of that curious contempt for the law that sometimes comes over us, such as during Prohibition, or in periods of material prosperity.

The crooks, sporting gentry and prostitutes swarmed in a new migration from the big-city underworlds. Nome, being on the seacoast, was much easier to reach than the Klondike far inland, much more convenient for the invasion of the sedentary, but no less sharp-toothed opportunists from the States. Also it was well known that racketeering was comparatively simple under the American flag, while in the Yukon Territory a miscreant faced quick arrest, summary justice and a long stretch on the Mounties' woodpile. Contemplation of that noble institution, the woodpile, had an amazingly sobering effect on the potential lawbreaker; he could face incarceration, but blistering one's hands and working outside in sub-zero weather had no part in the calculations of any sensible crook. In Nome, however, the only demand made on the law was that it refrain from interfering with the business of getting rich.

Nome's underworld was dominated by a gang known as the "Wag Boys," possibly because of their sanguinary sense of humor. Rex Beach called them "the most extraordinary group of undesirables that had ever invaded the North." Nobody knew where they came from, how they were organized or who directed their operations; "the full extent of their skulduggery has never been appraised," Beach said, just as Soapy Smith's gang and their depredations are still considerable of a mystery. Four of the gang's more prominent members were known as Big Jack Frost, Little Jack Frost, Deaf Mike and the Hobo Kid. "They possessed a bitter collective sense of humor. . . . their motto seemed to be 'Anything for a laugh.' " Guided by something like the Robin Hood principle, they preyed chiefly on the luckier prospectors, the more successful gamblers, stores and mercantile companies. Typical of their grisly humor was the revenge they took on another unsavory character who had offended one of the Wag Boys. They watched while their enemy lay down on the bunk in his cabin and carefully chalked a target on the wall of his cabin. Later they blazed away with rifles from a near-by hillock, and their enemy was neatly drilled through the kidney. Thieves, robbers, burglars and professional strong-arm men, they banded together for mutual security at a time when "an alibi was worth more than a horse."

Yet they had a rough sense of chivalry and an almost overwhelming gratitude for any kindness shown them. Miss Edith Crater (later the wife of Rex Beach), who operated a small hotel in Nome, became acquainted with several members of the gang when they announced they liked the looks of her dog. "If you won't sell him to us, we'll take him anyway," they told her. Miss Crater went to a girl named Big Hulda, who was Big Jack Frost's mistress, and told her the threat. Big Hulda flexed her muscles and warned the gang to stay away from Edith Crater's dog because "she's a square little guy and the dog's her pal." A short time later one of the gang was wounded in a nocturnal foray that misfired, and Miss Crater gave him first aid. From then on she was taken under the Wag Boys' formidable protection, despite her protest, "But I don't want to be adopted by a gang of crooks!"

But the Wag Boys could not be brushed away once they decided someone was worthy of their good will. One night Miss Crater became annoyed with a couple of hoodlums who were loitering in her lobby and refused to leave. Two masked men entered and announced they were going to loot the safe in her office. Her two

protectors pounced on them, heaved them outside into a snowbank, hauled them out and came close to committing mayhem on
the spot. Later when Miss Crater contracted typhoid fever and her
doctor prescribed milk—if possible—the Wag Boys stole the only
cow in Nome and stabled her in the cabin occupied by Big Jack
Frost and Big Hulda. They fed her on canned corn, the only fod-
der available, and muffled her with quilts whenever she tried to
moo in protest against the unaccustomed elegance of her accommodations. Big Hulda milked the cow and delivered the milk
which nourished Miss Crater back to health.

One of their biggest coups was pulled off later that winter when
butter was almost literally worth its weight in gold. The only
sizable stock in town was stored in the canvas-walled annex to a
mercantile house on Front Street.

For the getaway vehicle, a dog team was required, preferably a
stolen one, since the Wag Boys believed in investing nothing in
their projects except brains, brawn and an occasional touch of
sardonic humor. A couple of the boys tied a soup bone to a length
of cord, dragged it through the streets and grabbed enough dogs
for a team from the pack that took up pursuit of the bone. Another
member of the gang stole a dog sled and harness. Dogs and sled
were hitched together; the canvas walls of the butter cache were
slashed open, and every pound of butter was hauled away for later
sale to anyone discreet enough not to ask questions about the
source.

The atmosphere was sinful even before the Wag Boys and other
miscreants arrived. Polygamy was an old Eskimo custom, and
only when Nome began feeling its growing pains did anyone think
of abolishing the practice. One judge was particularly vigorous in
prosecuting Eskimos who felt the need of more than one wife;
oddly enough, he was a bachelor. One of the wealthier Eskimos on
Seward Peninsula was brought before him on polygamy charges

and explained his situation: "First wife old and crippled. Took young wife to look after her while me on hunting trips."

"A commendable thought, but polygamy is against the law, no matter what the circumstances," the judge said.

"You live alone in big igloo?" the Eskimo asked.

The judge nodded.

"All right, you take the old klutch [wife] and me take young one. Then me and you each have one wife."

The courtroom exploded with laughter and the judge hastily adjourned court to take the matter under advisement.

The same legal light shone much more brightly in another case indicative of the lighthearted attitude of Nome's citizenry toward the laws. By this time the judge had turned his reforming talents from Eskimo polygamy to the red-light district. He ordered the arrest of landlords renting premises for the purpose of prostitution, as well as the prostitutes, their agents and procurers.

One landlord with more than his share of the prevailing contempt for the law had been arrested and, knowing the usual fine for his offense was $1,000, he packed a grip with 1,000 dollar bills, chuckling to himself over the joke he would play on the judge. Unfortunately for the joker, someone had tipped off the judge about the landlord's intentions.

The judge fined the landlord the expected $1,000 and quietly watched while the clerk of court dumped out the avalanche of currency and his courtroom again rocked with appreciative laughter.

When quiet was again restored, he addressed the defendant: " . . . And one year in prison. Have you got that in the grip?"

Subsequently there was much more respect for the court if not for the laws it administered.

Crime, violence and dissipation only increased as the population of Nome rose toward the 30,000 mark. "On the board sidewalks at night you had to step around the sprawled-out figures of men.

Sometimes they were asleep. Usually they were dead drunk. Once in a while they were dead." Confidence men arrived from the States with such unlovely schemes as cornering the winter's fuel supply—which could have been a serious matter on that treeless tundra—and renting latrines in a town where the most basic necessities commanded luxury-scale prices. Holdups on the trails leading inland were only part of the daily hazards of living. No one paid much attention to a sudden outburst of guns, even in the town itself. On the beaches prospectors were often chloroformed in their tents and robbed of their gold dust. Promoters sold hundreds of thousands of dollars worth of worthless claims; sometimes the same claim would be sold to a dozen different men with little experience in gold-field trickery. As for claim-jumping, that became a racket on the grand scale, with the thieves protected by a conspiracy that extended to the federal judiciary and to the United States Congress. (This most ingenious and complicated swindle in Arctic history will be described in the following chapter.) Except for a later attempt by the above-mentioned judge to control prostitution, the traffic in women was open, shameless and extremely profitable. James Wickersham, whose knowledge of the law fortunately exceeded his grasp of the public-health problem, was one of the few who took an optimistic view of this situation, with his curious statement, "The sporting women were of a more robust class than usual among their kind, hence there were fewer cases of venereal . . . diseases among them."

In that wanton atmosphere, even a man who had been accompanied to Nome by his wife was not entirely safe from moral contamination. A prospector who came to Nome early enough to pan out $60,000 worth of gold dust on the beach was one of the victims of Nome's nightly saturnalia. With a glimmering of good sense, he divided his fortune in half and gave his wife Grace, "a beautiful and excellent woman," $30,000 to cache out on the tundra. Grace, realizing her husband's character had the tensile strength of wet cardboard, misled him as to the location of the cache.

Her fearful intuition proved to be well grounded. Nimbly avoiding the lesser pitfalls of bar and gambling table, her husband devoted himself to the more or less unattached women of Nome; he met every ship anchoring offshore and greeted every female entertainer before she could even step into the lighter which would land her on the beach.

So-called "masked beauties" were the principal attractions in many of Nome's musical halls and saloons. The mask often concealed a face of appalling plainness or even ugliness, but a girl could get by for months, working the boxes and inflaming the imaginations of the amorous males they sheltered, before she was unmasked and the true extent of her charms became generally known.

Grace, the long-suffering wife, decided to take advantage of the "masked beauty" charade to teach her husband a lesson he would never forget.

She placed a red wig on her head, bought herself a particularly gaudy gown and donned a mask which concealed most of her face. With little difficulty, she obtained a job in one of the resorts frequented by her husband. He showed up that first night and began drinking more heavily than usual, but with unerring taste for feminine perfection he monopolized the time of the masked redhead. None of these hussies had ever appealed so much to him or displayed so much sympathy and understanding. She was charmingly indignant when he babbled about how his funds were sinking low and only his vixenish wife stood between him and another $30,000. Together they decided to go out on the tundra and kill his wife, if necessary, to lay hands on his cache of gold dust.

On the way out to their cabin, the masked beauty ripped off her disguise. The mask and wig lay at her feet in the moonlight. So did her husband, when the shock of her deception struck him a moment later. On being revived, he took an oath he would never, never succumb to the attractions of another woman. It seems quite likely that he kept his promise.

If this tale seems to be slightly tinged with De Maupassant, it should be remembered that the man who told it, Wilson Mizner, maintained his title as prince of raconteurs by never hesitating to take literary license in the interests of captivating his audience.

Among all the grifters and grab artists who so quickly infested Nome, the professional gambler was accounted a man of comparatively high integrity and unusual probity. Quite often he deserved this reputation. Perhaps the most trusted citizen of Nome was Tex Rickard, proprietor of the Great Northern saloon and gambling house.

Rickard had been the stripling town marshal of a tough little settlement in Texas, a job which gave him an unmistakable air of authority among the riffraff of the gold fields, before he joined the rush to the Klondike. He had no intention of prospecting or mining for gold; that was for the suckers. He would cater to their need for relaxation and amusement. In Dawson he operated a gambling house, apparently along "square" lines, for he went broke and left town with little but a reputation for honesty. He opened a small gambling and drinking place in Rampart City, which was where his long friendship with Rex Beach began. The "Grand Opening" was a notable night in the future novelist's memory. There was a program of boxing matches with the contestants slugging it out in the middle of the dance floor and "belting each other in the bosoms of us standees." And there was a ball during which the supply of Siwash beauties ran out and some of the men tied handkerchiefs around their arms and became "ladies for the evening." As Beach recalled, "For the first and only time in my career as a dancing man I waltzed with a partner who wore hobnails and a beard. . . . We made the splinters fly."

Beach described Rickard as a "slim, dark, likable young fellow" with a quick warming smile and a soft Southern accent. But if anyone tried to take advantage of him, Beach noted, Rickard could become "grim as an Apache."

Rampart City went through a hard winter, with most of the miners barely able to provide themselves with food and shelter, let alone fling money on the bars and gaming tables. Again Rickard went broke, and in the spring of 1899 he left with exactly $21 in his pocket. Word was flying around the mining camps, however, that gold had been discovered at Cape Nome, and Rickard joined the stampede with his determination to become a successful gambler and fight promoter undiminished. Beach said he heard that Rickard stopped off at St. Michael, managed to obtain a barrel of whisky on credit and opened a tent saloon on the beach at Nome. Beach was so inspired by this report of Rickard's neo-Horatio Algerian coup that he joined with two partners, also in St. Michael, to invest $5,000 in whisky. The syndicate and its liquid assets were shipwrecked en route to Nome, and thus died their dream of becoming "liquor barons," as Beach put it.

Beach found that Rickard had continued to prosper amid the uproar of booming Nome. He had used his tent-saloon's profits to erect a square-front building, the Great Northern, on Main Street. Epidemics, claim fights and drunkenness contributed to the upheaval caused by thousands of newcomers with no principle to guide them except "root, hog, or die." As the usually imperturbable Mizner commented, "It was sheer raving chaos!" But Rickard kept his balance, and men began turning to him for counsel and protection. He was called on to settle claim disputes and his decisions were accepted with all the force of a high court; and he fought as best he could the pack of shysters, many of them disbarred in the States, that descended on Nome, lean and hungry as timber wolves, to feast themselves until honest courts could protect honest men. After Nome's "consent government" yielded under the Act of Congress of June 6, 1900, to a municipal administration chosen by the electorate, Rickard was voted into the city council as a token of the public esteem.

Rex Beach testified as a character witness for Rickard near the end of the latter's life when Rickard was discharged of responsibility in a paternity suit. "The jury seemed impressed," Beach said, "by my assertion that in Alaska and many western frontier communities no odium had attached to either [being a gambler and a saloonkeeper]. Gambling was not illegal, the liquor business was considered as respectable as others and some of the squarest men in the country were engaged in it. Tex, I told them, had never been accused of crooked dealing."

With the onset of wealth and his growing sense of dignity as a leading citizen of Nome, Rickard learned to control his "Apache" temper and shed his belief that gunfighting was the only honorable means of settling a grievance.

Mizner told how a man named Jack McCloud was cleaned out in a poker game at the Great Northern and convinced himself that he had been cheated.

McCloud sent Rickard the traditional gunfighter's challenge— "Come out, and come out smoking."

Rickard grabbed his gun and started for the door, then halted. "Tell Jack I can't afford it," he said. "Here I'm worth $300,000 and he's broke. I won't stack up $300,000 against nothing. It ain't business."

McCloud saw his point. "Tex's right. It ain't business." He headed back to his claim, resolving to pan out enough gold to shoot it out with Rickard on an equitable basis.

Gunfighting was not encouraged on the premises of the Great Northern. That sort of lethal rowdyism was all right for the hell-holes on the back streets, but Rickard's drinking and gambling emporium had a respectable place in the community. It was the Union League Club, Delmonico's and the Ritz Bar as far as Nome was concerned; a place where the well-heeled and influential gathered to relax and/or talk business. Urbanity was the keynote of the Great Northern and its proprietor.

Rickard definitely did not approve of a bloodless shooting incident involving Willus Britt, who later became one of the top fight managers in the United States (Stanley Ketchel was among those he guided into the ring). Britt suddenly dashed out of Rickard's bar one evening and fired several shots at a stranger, who escaped in the darkness. His companions asked Britt why he had shot at the passer-by.

"Why, the dirty dog insulted Nellie!" Britt bellowed.

Nellie was a young woman whose reputation was generally considered impervious to insult.

Wilson Mizner, among the onlookers, croaked, "He *what?*"

"He insulted Nellie," Britt repeated.

"For God's sake, *how?*" demanded Mizner.

Despite Rickard's determination to run a "square" gambling joint, some of his customers were content with lower standards of honesty, according to Mizner. To show up the double-dealing gentry, Mizner gathered a "larceny-haunted set of faces" around a poker table one dawn in Rickard's. He dealt from a pack containing fifty-two aces. Each tinhorn, with five aces in his hand, figuring he had struck a bonanza through an imperfect deck, tried to figure out how to ditch their extra ace on the draw.

"Your pleasure, gents?" Mizner inquired.

Each discarded one card and struggled to maintain composure as they received another ace in the draw.

There was a stunned silence.

"Well, boys, what are you betting?" Mizner demanded, interrupting their desperate cogitations. "Time flies—you thieves!"

The players suddenly realized they had been tricked by the dealer and "we laughed for an hour."

To Jack Hines, the young singer, Rickard's was the most glamorous place north of Seattle; it not only had a long mirrored bar but crystal chandeliers.

Six bartenders were pouring out drinks as fast as they could work. Everybody drank whiskey with beer chasers. Placer miners in hip boots carelessly tossed moosehide pokes of gold dust across the bar to pay for their drinks, and bartenders weighed out the change. Mining officials and bankers stood beside confidence men and gamblers and dance-hall girls. Somebody was playing an upright piano that was on a platform, but you could hardly hear it over the noise and confusion at the bar. . . . The pianist was an old fellow in a long-skirted Prince Albert with a dropping cigaret in the corner of his mouth. There was also a young, white-faced, effeminate-looking violinist. A crowd of prospectors and percentage girls, drinks in hand, had gathered around the piano and were singing.

A little of the glamour wore off for Hines on a later occasion when one of the staff houris allowed him to buy several drinks: her attention wandered when she saw another young man carelessly toss a hundred-dollar bill on the bar. A few minutes later Hines and the other man were slugging it out for the dubious affections of the percentage girl. Rickard and one of his bouncers broke it up and the proprietor told Hines, "Do your fighting outside, Jack," adding under his breath, "Boy, what a punch. I hope you clean up on him." Rickard's new insistence on decorum always melted a little whenever he saw a lad with a likely punch.

Hines and his opponent decided not to pursue the matter, shook hands instead and introduced themselves. The other man turned out to be Tom Wood, the son of Major General Thomas J. Wood, a celebrated Civil War commander who had led a division at Chickamauga and Atlanta, a corps at Nashville. (Another controversial figure of the Army of the Cumberland, General Jefferson C. Davis, commanded the Alaskan Department, with headquarters at Sitka, and was rather remotely concerned with preserving law and order at Nome. His troops were as helpless in dealing with the situation as the company of infantry stationed at Dyea while Soapy Smith was ruling Skagway. General Davis must have felt fairly at ease on that wild frontier. In the middle of the Civil War, he had shot and killed Major General William "Bull" Nelson in a Louisville bar.)

Tex Rickard had no distaste for the saloon and gambling-house business, which was bringing him thousands of dollars weekly in net profits, but his heart and mind were increasingly diverted to the possibilities of prize-fight promotion. It seemed clear to him that prize fighting, after years of being outlawed and accounted a sport for the underworld, would soon reach great heights of popularity—and affluence—in the United States. The turn-of-the-century fighters were probably the greatest crop ever raised: Jim Corbett, Jack Johnson, Jim Jeffries, Bat Nelson, Ad Wolgast, Bob Fitzsimmons and several others whose names are still garlanded in sports-page type. Far away in Alaska, men followed the news of the various fights through the newspapers and the rudimentary newsreels with as much or more interest than the military dispatches from Cuba and the rebelling Philippines.

Even the clumsiest amateurs, provided they showed the required willingness to give and take a punch until they or their opponents dropped, found standing-room-only audiences in Nome. Rickard began promoting matches, with both amateurs and whatever professionals had strayed into Nome, every Saturday night at the Standard Theater. The audience, whenever it was pleased with the performance of one of the battered gladiators, would shower him with coins, which he would collect and carry off in a rubber boot.

Science was largely disdained in these bouts; a fighter who feinted, parried, jabbed with his left and crossed with his right, as the boxing masters taught, was jeered as a Fancy Dan, a toe dancer, a dirty sneak.

The pugilistic type beloved of the Nome fans was the Irish longshoreman who learned that his designated opponent would be unable to appear, being in jail, and who bellowed from the ring, "I came here to fight and fight I will. I'll meet any man in the house, but there's one dirty dog I'd like to lay me hands on. Is Paddy Ryan present? If so, I'll dare him to show his cowardly length."

There was an enraged roar from the rear of the theater, and Paddy Ryan rushed toward the stage, "shedding his foliage like an autumn oak" as he plunged down the aisle. He was stripped to red woolen underwear as he hoisted himself to the ring. The whole stage crew was called out of the wings to keep the fighters apart until the stakes could be collected and the bell rang. The referee wisely refrained from instructing the fighters on fair play. With the "headlong charge of two buffaloes," the two Irishmen met in the center of the ring and each swung mightily. Both blows landed, and both fighters fell to the canvas, mutually poleaxed. It was the only double knockout in Nome's prize-fight history.

Rickard staged other bouts in the back room of the Northern, one of the more memorable being that between Klondike Mike Mahoney, the brawny dog-team driver who had caught Rickard's eye back in Dawson, and Tommy Burns, who was soon to win the heavyweight championship of the world. Burns, a professional middleweight at that time, sailed for Nome with Brocky Bray, a freewheeling sport who owned a claim and asked Burns to accompany him to find out whether it was gold-bearing. A fight was arranged between Burns and Mahoney, with a $100 purse going to the winner. It was agreed, on Mahoney's insistence, that each fighter was allowed to punch or kick, in the French style called *la savate,* which Mahoney had learned from the French of his native Canada. This was Burns's description of what ensued:

We wore six-ounce gloves, and for two rounds I hit him with everything I had. He was bleeding from the mouth and nose at the start of the second round, but big Klondike Mike still kept boring for more. I was always shifting to my right side and boxing him all the time, as he had too much weight and height on me. I kept forcing the fight and peppering him with everything I had, sure that it would be a cinch to win the hundred dollars.

The last part of the second round I got careless. He kept shifting to my left and never letting me rest. All at once, like a shot out of a gun, it seemed to me, he sent his right foot into my solar plexus and I went down. I could hear everything but I was paralyzed for a few minutes. . . . It dawned on me that I had forgotten that we could kick with our feet, although I doubt if it would have made much difference. What a kick that was!

Rickard was even more impressed than Burns, who believed Mahoney "would have been a world's heavyweight champion if he had followed up the boxing game." Two years later, when Burns lost the title to Jack Johnson in Australia, Rickard still remembered that bout in the back room of his saloon; he urged Mahoney to join the parade of "white hopes" who went down before Johnson's fists, and offered him $50,000 to enter the ring with the Negro champion. Mahoney had struck it rich on an Alaskan creek by that time and rejected the offer.

Another colorful figure in the pugilistic world of Nome was the young fellow who changed his name from Leo McKernan to Jack Kearns. He was the son of a Seattle sports editor. This wiry lad had been so eager to start amassing the allegedly plentiful Alaskan gold that on arrival he had jumped off the ship and swum ashore. But in spite of earnest, not to say frantic, digging, he found no gold dust in the ground. Then he sought other avenues to riches. For a time he tried boxing, under Wilson Mizner's management. Enjoying only qualified success, he turned next to the sporting life indoors, still as a protégé of Wilson Mizner whose tutelage of the young man has been related in a previous chapter.

In his last fight, Kearns was matched with a bigger and heavier opponent. Mizner decided to try to equalize the situation by wrapping strips of lead around Kearns's fists. During the first round, Kearns, whose punch previously had been of the love-tap caliber, suddenly developed a fearsome kick in both fists. Every time he landed a punch it raised a welt on his opponent. But in the second round his arms became so weary from throwing the weighted punches that he could barely raise them in self-defense and was quickly knocked out. That experience decided Kearns on becoming a manager and letting someone else stick his chin out in the ring. With Tex Rickard and Jack Dempsey, he was a member of the triumvirate that dominated the boxing game in the twenties, when expert ballyhoo made the million-dollar gate a common enough occurrence.

Two names spangled with Western legend were those of Elias Jackson "Lucky" Baldwin and Wyatt Earp. Baldwin made a fortune in Nevada silver some years before and decided to try his luck with Alaskan gold. His luck didn't hold out in the Arctic. When the Nome boom was well under way, he arrived from the States and found that all the most promising claims had already been staked out. Baldwin didn't need the money so badly that he was willing to undergo the rigors of prospecting inland, so he left Nome for his California home without making much impression in the high-rolling circles of Nome. Compared to some of the local sports, he seemed almost a piker. It took more than buying the house a few rounds of drinks to maintain a reputation of living in the grand manner. Apparently Baldwin needed more money almost as little as he needed added fame as a big spender, for he left an estate of more than $10,000,000 when he died in 1909.

Among the talismans Lucky Baldwin brought to Nome with him was an ornate chased-glass partition, one of the few things he salvaged from the bar of the Baldwin Hotel in San Francisco when it was destroyed by fire in 1898. Baldwin brought the glass with him on the vague possibility of establishing his own bar in Nome, but instead he sold it to Sol Warren for the latter's saloon, one of the more elegant drinking places in the town.

The glass partition figured in an incident which illustrated the nonchalant attitude of the gold rush's big sports. Jack Hines, the wandering minstrel, was spinning the roulette wheel, just having placed his last $5 on a number. The ball slipped out of his hand and smashed the partition, which was worth hundreds of dollars. Warren calmly ordered the debris swept up and gave Hines another whirl at the wheel, although Hines fully expected to be presented with a bill for $1,000 damages or at least heaved out into the nearest snowbank. Before the evening was over, Hines had won $1,400 and "not a line of Sol Warren's face changed."

Wyatt Earp, proprietor of the Dexter Bar across the street from Tex Rickard's Northern, was another man who could face bad luck or danger with the professional gambler's icy nerves. The rowdiest sourdough in the North Country quieted down when the calm little gunfighter flicked his eyes over anyone presuming to disturb the peace. Like Tex Rickard, he was one of Nome's most respected citizens, and little wonder. Any man who had worn the marshal's star in Tombstone, Dodge City and the mining camps of Nevada was entitled to respect, especially the man who, with his brothers, had wiped out the homicidal Clanton brothers.

His reputation alone saved Earp from any gunfighting incidents in the gold fields. No man in his right mind was going up against the man who was rated the equal or superior of Doc Halliday, Bat Masterson and Wild Bill Hickok. Although he was in his early fifties, Earp was still a tough customer, with all his cold courage intact from the days when a man slow on the draw had every prospect of a quick one-way trip to Boot Hill. Shortly after he left Nome he was the armed referee of the Tom Sharkey-Bob Fitzsimmons fight in Oakland, the only man whose decision could be trusted and respected by the riotous and wildly partisan crowd in the arena.

15

~~~~~~~~

The Hundred-Percenters

NOT ALL the skulduggery, trickery and thievery in the gold rush was committed by various rugged individuals or colorful little bands of like-minded opportunists, although it may seem that way from the foregoing accounts of the less organized knavery. To leave such an impression would not be giving the so-called respectable people their due. The last shot in the locker therefore has been reserved for the pious politicians and bland lawyers who combined in an operation known as the Nome Claim Steal. "Steal" is much too mild a word for their sharklike gobble at the golden sands. As usual when such respected folk got together for an assault on the public interest and the sanctity of the law, they far exceeded the criminal class in scope, imagination and capacity for plunder. No dedicated thief could help being overwhelmed with admiration and awe, viewing the artistic conception of the Nome Claim Steal. Later generations might grow indignant over five-percenters in Washington; these lusty antecedents reached for 100 per cent.

Their audacity was matched only by the prehensile minds which conceived the Credit Mobilier, the rigging of the gold market during the Grant administration and the Teapot Dome conspiracy. It was "the most flagrant prostitution of American courts in our history," in the opinion of Judge Wickersham, who was given the task of cleaning up the Nome judiciary after its odors drifted across the continent to the District of Columbia. The conspirators, whose influence extended to the White House and was especially strong in the United States Senate, failed to anticipate the "inflamed passions which lashed like a Bering Sea blizzard round the seat of justice," Wickersham believed.

There were, however, excellent reasons for the piratical self-confidence with which the leading figures of the conspiracy pounced on Nome and its then-priceless real estate. In the first place, most of the original claimants were Scandinavians, "dumb squareheads," who were believed incapable of putting up much of a fight. The conspirators, not very well grounded in racial psychology, overlooked the fact that a "berserker" rage often lies under the placid exterior of the Scandinavian. They also counted too heavily on the belief that the intended victims, being mostly foreigners, would win little sympathy from their fellow miners. Another favorable factor, in their estimation, was that Nome was tucked away in the extreme northwestern pocket of the continent and looked delightfully remote and inaccessible. The conspirators, it may be imagined, saw themselves swooping down on Nome and its treasures, bundling it all up in red tape and spiriting it away before anyone knew what had happened.

Instead of operating in a cozy inaccessible vacuum where the cries of their victims would be stifled, however, they found that the sacking of Nome took place in an echo chamber. Wilson Mizner, in fact, was contemptuous of the victims because, instead of a manly resort to the anarchical rope and torch, they wailed so loudly and effectively the government was forced to save them from plunder. Mizner confided:

Most of the fellows up there were the worst sissies on earth. I was in court when two hundred of them were robbed of their claims by a crooked judge and a set of thieving politicians. Did they string up the judge, as the forty-niners would have done? Did they tear the politicians limb from limb? No. They just sat there crying into their beards. Then they slunk back to their cabins and had to be treated with smelling salts.

Most of the claims along Anvil, Ophir and Dexter creeks, as well as on the beaches, were originally staked out by the Scandinavian prospectors and Lapp reindeer herders who settled the dreary Seward Peninsula. T. A. Rickard, the mining expert and historian who later investigated the causes of the Nome troubles, said the careless methods of staking claims were partly responsible for the disputes. Out on the tundra there was no wood available for making proper stakes, so the prospectors marked their claims with sprigs of willow, which were often uprooted by the Arctic winds. When the stampede started, many claims were jumped because the markers had disappeared. Then the jumpers were jumped. And what had been a fairly innocent matter of inept prospecting became a vicious round of thievery.

Every red-blooded American stampeder was suddenly subjected to attacks of xenophobia, violently objecting to the fact that a pack of "lucky squareheads" had been on the ground first and staked out the best claims. Foreigners were going to become millionaires while 100-per-cent Americans took the tailings. (They conveniently ignored the fact that most of the Klondike millionaires were Americans who had been "lucky" on Canadian soil.) As early as July 10, 1899, a meeting of the American miners was called to consider how to evict the Scandinavians from their claims. Soon it was every man for himself and the devil take the hindmost Scandinavian. One Robert Chipps, who was to become a prominent member of the conspiracy, even jumped the Discovery Claim on Anvil Creek. A voracious gathering of lawyers in Nome abetted the declaration of the claim jumpers that only American citizens were entitled to stake claims on Alaskan soil. Not all Americans were claim jumpers or supported their pretensions. Many realized their own claims, if they panned out, would also be subjected to land piracy; others were fair-minded enough to realize that the jumpers were acting out of criminal greed rather than exalted patriotism.

The scene shifts to Washington, a national capital exultant over the victories against Spain in the Caribbean and the Pacific and not at all immune to the fever of corruption that breaks out in the aftermath of an easily won war. To enlist the sympathies of ultranationalist politicians, who were naturally having a field day for themselves, a delegation from Nome, headed by Chipps and a lawyer named Hubbard, the senior member of the firm of Hubbard, Beeman and Hume, which represented the Anvil Creek claim jumpers, approached influential lobbyists, administration hangers-on and members of the Senate. It was not long before they had raked up a sympathetic audience, and in the fall of 1899 an intensive campaign was under way to change the federal mining laws, with the objective of excluding noncitizens from staking and working their claims. Soon included in the Washington axis of the conspiracy were, as Judge Wickersham listed them, "influential members of the United States Senate and certain national politicians, Senator-makers and a group of their jackals"; it was devoutly hoped that the boodle would be sufficient to nourish all these eager mouths.

Almost from the start, command of the operation to corner Nome's gold was in the large capable hands of Alexander McKenzie, a North Dakotan with almost as potent politico-financial connections as Mark Hanna, the intimate adviser of President McKinley. McKenzie was a barrel-chested Scot, with a leonine mane and compelling dark eyes, a sort of one-man holding company for political power in Minnesota, North Dakota and Montana. He had been the receiver for the Northern Pacific Railroad—an experience which had evidently taught him much about the methods of fishing

in troubled waters—and chief lobbyist in Washington for a number of other railroads. "A past master of the art of controlling
weaker men in high office," Wickersham described him. Whatever
his villainies—and their full extent has probably never been ade-
quately explored—he was also courageous, intelligent, imaginative
and bold, a fellow who would have done splendidly on the Spanish
Main; it was that touch of the archaic about him, perhaps, that
proved his eventual undoing.

The maneuvering of McKenzie and his henchmen to provide a
quasi-legal springboard for their pounce on Nome was the trickiest
Washington had seen in many a drab day since the hearty buckos
of the Grant administration. A bill providing civil government for
the Territory of Alaska was passed in June of 1900; it included a
code of laws giving the district judges unusual powers. Originally
the bill also provided that United States mining laws apply to
Alaska, which meant the citizenship of a claim owner could have
no bearing on the legality of his claim. Senator Hansborough of
North Dakota—the state that provided most of the leading members of McKenzie's clique—proposed an amendment making it
illegal for aliens to locate claims in Alaska; this became the chief
issue of an extremely rancorous debate on the floor of the Senate.
One day's issue of the *Congressional Record* was charged with such
violent language and recrimination that, "after the Senators had
cooled off," it was withdrawn and reprinted without the "unparlia-
mentary and bitter language." Partly because of a counterblast of
propaganda from the other side of the Nome controversy, a number of influential Congressmen combined to defeat the Hansborough Amendment.

This, of course, meant that somewhat less legal means would be
necessary for McKenzie and his group to seize the gold flowing out
of Nome's mines. There was still that joker in the Alaska code
giving excessive powers to the man presiding over the Second
Judicial Division at Nome. The solution of the whole vexing prob-

lem—all because a few Congressmen had turned finicky—was to find a suitable man to sit on that bench and rule as McKenzie wished, no matter what storms raged around his head.

McKenzie decided that the most suitable man available was another North Dakotan, Judge Arthur H. Noyes, whose moral and ethical senses, such as they were, could always be numbed by relatively inexpensive applications of whisky. To make sure that the forces of justice at Nome would be completely paralyzed, McKenzie also appointed the district attorney, choosing one Joseph K. Wood, a political hack whose talents as a prosecutor could be kept within discreet bounds.

Before he left Washington, McKenzie also arranged for the financial structure to handle and distribute the expected proceeds of the bold venture. He established the Alaska Gold Mining Company, an Arizona corporation with an authorized capital stock of $15,000,000, with himself as president and general manager. It held title to the property of the claim jumpers, who were to receive stock in exchange for their stolen claims along Anvil Creek. McKenzie organized the Golden Sands Mining Company to handle the beach claims. Complimentary bundles of stock on these companies were passed around in the houses of Congress, naturally, and others were given politicians and lobbyists who were to protect McKenzie in flank and rear while he advanced to Nome in person. A mere wirepuller would have stayed comfortably in Washington, but McKenzie was a man of action, a real cutlass swinger who could not resist taking command of the operation in person.

It was a cozy little group that sailed aboard the appropriately named steamship *Senator* for the Alaskan ports early in July of 1900. On board were McKenzie, Judge Noyes, Attorney Hubbard and Chipps, the chief claim jumper. They arrived off Nome on July 19, Judge Noyes closeting himself for two days in his stateroom while McKenzie went ashore and began putting his plans into effect with commendable speed and energy.

His first visit was to the offices of Hubbard, Beeman and Hume, where his audacity took the breath away from even those blasé gentlemen. McKenzie's company, they were informed, was not only taking over title to their client's claims, but the new district attorney was to be given one-fourth interest in their law firm as a silent partner! Cold comfort, indeed, was McKenzie's afterthought: one of the partners would become deputy district attorney under Wood. It was becoming obvious to the lawyers that they had swum joyously into the mouth of a shark, for they had exchanged their one-half contingent interest in the disputed claims, received as their legal fees, for a handful of beautifully engraved stock in a company controlled by McKenzie.

On July 23, only four days after he landed and before any documents had even been filed with the clerk of the court, McKenzie had himself appointed receiver for all the disputed claims by Judge Noyes. The receiver's bond was fixed at $5,000 for each mine, although a number of them were taking as much as $15,000 a day in gold out of the earth. The next day Judge Noyes empowered McKenzie to seize, in addition, all personal property and even the gold already extracted at the confiscated mines—a measure later described by the Ninth Circuit Court of Appeals at San Francisco as "so arbitrary and unwarranted in law as to baffle the mind in its effort to comprehend how it could have been issued from a court of justice." In his determination to benumb the opposition and prevent it from attempting to defy his measures, McKenzie became boastful and let it be known that his plunderbund was under the protection of the biggest men in America.

But some men refused to be overawed; they organized themselves to fight back, secure legal relief through the higher courts in the United States.

The leaders of the opposition were Charles D. Lane, head of the Wild Goose Mining Company, which had purchased a number of claims from their original and legal owners, and Jafet Linde-berg, head of the Pioneer Mining Company. Both, in their different ways, were men to reckon with, whether McKenzie knew it or not. Lane was a veteran of the California frontier, a robust old gentle-man with a sword blade of a nose and a patriarchal beard; he looked like an avenging ancient out of the Old Testament. Linde-berg was physically unimpressive, a Laplander who only a few years ago had been content to tend his reindeer herd; but he was shrewd, determined and could not be bluffed by McKenzie's pre-tensions. One of the lawyers they engaged to carry their fight to the appellate court in San Francisco was Key Pittman, mentioned ear-lier, who later became Senator from Nevada and chairman of the Senate Foreign Relations Committee during the Franklin D. Roose-velt administration.

Meanwhile, Nome was in turmoil; "local industry was paralyzed as by a Central American revolution."

There were threats of mob action against McKenzie, Judge Noyes and other members of their clique. An angry group of min-ers invaded the chambers of Judge Noyes and he unwisely bellowed at them, "You get the hell out of here!" One of the miners shout-ed, "Let's lynch the damned skunk," and another produced a rope. They dragged Judge Noyes out of his chambers and down to the sidewalk, looking around for a lamppost to serve as the gallows. Judge Noyes blustered, then begged for his life. His critics found a beam jutting out from a building and were just about to string him up when a squad of United States infantry came down the street on the double and rescued the quaking jurist. The judge hurried to his hotel through the back alleys and stayed in his room for three days straight.

A short time later the same mob, its numbers growing every minute, chased McKenzie down the street and into the bank where he was sequestering most of the confiscated gold. The crowd began heaving rocks through the window and looking for a battering ram, when the soldiers appeared again. An army captain addressed the mob with an eloquence rare among the military:

"Fellow Americans! And this is America, don't forget that! We're here for you, not against you. We're your hired men, here to do your job, and protect life and property—everybody's property.

"We're here to protect lives and property even at the risk of our own lives or—God forbid—the lives of others. This is no threat. If you have patience no man will lose his gold, and that's a guarantee."

Once again violence was averted, but there was obviously enough emotional dynamite lying around to cause a terrific explosion of anarchy.

Among the many prospectors who did not merely weep into their beards, as Wilson Mizner said, was a man known as the Terrible Finn, whose epic defiance of the McKenzie ring was told Thames Williamson years later and recorded in his *Far North Country*. The Finn and an Irish shipmate, with whom he had sailed for several years, staked out a promising claim on Badger Creek. Working out on the tundra, the pair had heard rumors that claim jumpers were extremely active and they themselves might be victimized next. The Irishman rushed into town to join a vigilante mob, but the Finn stayed at their claim, calmly proclaiming, "Them fellows can't do anything. This is American territory, and Americans are good people. One time down in Portland a man I never saw before loaned me a dollar to eat on. That's the kind of people Americans are."

The Finn's faith soon sustained a terrible shock. While he was in Nome getting supplies, five undersheriffs seized his property, the claim and the cabin on it. From then on, McKenzie and his henchmen had to deal with a berserk Finn who had lost his faith that *all* Americans were good people. The Finn smashed a window of his

cabin and shot and killed one of the deputies. McKenzie ordered
that the occupying force be increased to nine. That night the Finn
crept up to the cabin and exploded a charge of dynamite under it
which killed two of the men and wounded two others. McKenzie,
realizing that the Finn had to be stopped or he would serve as an
example to other victims who had not as yet turned violent, offered
$500 reward for the fugitive—"dead or alive or in pieces," as he
phrased it.

A score of possemen set out to pick up the Finn's trail on the
tundra. During the pursuit he fell through the ice of a creek, lost
his rifle and was in imminent danger of freezing to death. That
night he outdistanced his pursuers, built a fire and thawed himself
out. He managed to restore circulation to his benumbed arm, but
it was obvious that his left leg was a goner. Stoically wielding his
clasp knife, he amputated the leg and staunched the flow of blood
with a handful of moss; then he lay down beside the fire he had
built and went to sleep. Next morning, using a tree limb for a
crutch, he hobbled away toward the hills where he was certain the
posse would never find him.

The possemen came across his overnight camp later than morning and found the left leg he had abandoned.

One man vomited and said, "I'll go to hell before I'll chase a man
like that."

The others agreed they'd rather chase the devil home than con-
tinue that particular man hunt: the Terrible Finn simply wasn't
human.

So the search was abandoned, with the leader of the posse bringing the leg back to Nome and claiming the reward from McKenzie.
By that time there were more serious matters to distract McKenzie
than one crazy Finn and he brushed his henchman aside with a
brisk order to take the macabre trophy elsewhere. (A happy foot-
note: The Finn stayed in the hills until the following spring, somehow nursing himself back to a semblance of health and surviving

through a supreme knowledge of how to live off the land even in the barren North Country. Williamson related that he later amassed a fortune and raised a large family of daughters and granddaughters.)

Slowly but surely, the victimized miners and mining companies who had been dispossessed by the orders issued by Judge Noyes at the instigation of Alexander McKenzie began to win back their rights. But McKenzie fought a determined delaying action. Lawyers for Lane and the Wild Goose Mining Company obtained an order from the Ninth Circuit Court of Appeals in San Francisco directing Judge Noyes to cease all proceedings in his court until further notice and for McKenzie to withhold action of suits pending and return all the property he had seized and placed under his own receivership.

McKenzie not only ignored the writs when they were served on him but refused to restore the gold and other confiscated property. Judge Noyes, his drunken Trilby, supported him by ordering the army to guard the gold they had seized and prevent its restoration to the rightful owners. All the while, of course, McKenzie was sending gold back to the States and stashing it away. Every day's delay meant several thousands of dollars.

McKenzie even stationed guards along the beaches to prevent any lawyer leaving Nome and helping press the case against him before the courts in San Francisco. Key Pittman evaded the blockade by seeking out a prospector who had once practiced law in the States but abandoned it to seek his fortune in the gold fields. Pittman furnished him with the necessary documents and authority and slipped him aboard a ship bound for San Francisco.

Now the federal government was thoroughly aroused; it could not afford to be defied even by a man whose influence reached into the highest offices in the land. The appellate court in San Francisco dispatched two deputy marshals armed with a writ calling for them to take McKenzie into personal custody and "bring the body back" to San Francisco. Another writ effectively released the gold being held in receivership in Nome. Still another ordered the seizure of certified copies of the records of Noyes's court, which were obtained only with the greatest difficulty.

Before he left Nome, McKenzie was witness to a heartrending scene: gold dust valued at $400,000 was removed from the vaults of the Alaska Banking and Safe Deposit Company and turned over to the Alaska Commercial Company for distribution to its legal owners. Not particularly crestfallen, McKenzie was returned to San Francisco to face the court whose authority he had brazenly ignored and defied. After all he was a member of the Republican National Committee, and he had been in ticklish spots before.

For all his confidence in an acquittal, McKenzie was convicted of contempt of court and sentenced to a year in prison. In May of that year, President McKinley, who had just taken office for a second term, gave his personal attention to McKenzie's pardon. He let it be known that he would not be displeased if McKenzie was returned to his ornamental place in society. "The pardon was at first refused," it was later explained by Judge Morrow of the appellate court, "but upon representation and evidence that McKenzie's health was such that he would probably not live out his imprisonment, he was pardoned—but not until he had turned over an additional quantity of gold dust he had shipped to Seattle while the proceedings were in progress." Judge Wickersham, who followed the case with great and understandable personal interest, noted sardonically that "McKenzie's health quickly recovered its normal condition" when he returned, a fully pardoned citizen, to his native North Dakota.

After the full story of the Nome scandal was revealed in the press, particularly in the Washington *Post*, the United States Senate reluctantly began an investigation. The Attorney General of the United States was forced to order Judge Noyes's dismissal. The jurist was convicted of contempt of court, but out of a respect for his black robes that he never felt himself he was let down with a thousand-dollar fine; this despite the opinion of Judge Ross of the appellate bench that Noyes had engaged in a "corrupt conspiracy with Alexander McKenzie."

Wood, the federal district attorney at Nome, was sentenced to prison for four months, although he was a lesser member of the conspiracy. He remained on the government pay roll, oddly enough, until a month after he had served out his sentence. Perhaps not so oddly.

What could have been a powder keg in more violent times turned out to be a rather damp firecracker. The villains were punished, perhaps inadequately, and the heroes for the most part were rewarded in the substance they valued above all others—raw gold.

It was time to turn the North Country over to those who sought more enduring values.

Epilogue by a Fireside

IN THE warm corner of many an American home, at the fireside or close to the stove, an old fellow nods sleepily. He probably has an ill-favored habit or two displeasing to his daughter-in-law— slyly chewing tobacco or dipping snuff, and he may take a nip too many now and then. His grandchildren find him amiable when they feel like tugging his beard, twisting his nose or begging him to tell them stories about his adventurous youth. He is an old Klondiker, and probably he has little but memory to show for his participation in the gold rush.

Something else may vex or mystify his womenfolk from time to time, when the winter winds blow and his mind drifts back a half-century or so.

He smiles inwardly, a little mysteriously, as if considering a secret he cannot share with such polite company.

The chances are that he is remembering those nights in the Yukon: the hell-raising, the bottle-tilting, the pink tights of the music-hall girls, the brazen eyes of the dance-hall women, the amiability of a bronze-cheeked Siwash maiden, the smoky uproar of a Klondike saloon when the high rollers were buying for the house. The gold he went up there to find—well, it would probably have slipped through his fingers anyway. No vain regrets.

Well might he smile, secretly.

Bibliography

Bibliography

BOOKS

Allan, A. A., *Gold, Men and Dogs*. New York: G. P. Putnam's Sons, 1931.

Bankson, Russell, *The Klondike Nugget*. Caldwell, Ida.: The Caxton Printers Ltd., 1935.

Beach, Rex, *Personal Exposures*. New York: Harper & Bros., 1940.

Becker, Ethel Anderson, *Klondike '98*. Portland: Binfords & Mort, 1949.

Beebe, Iola, *The True Life Story of Swiftwater Bill Gates*. Privately published, 1908.

Beer, Thomas, *The Mauve Decade*. New York: Alfred A. Knopf, Inc., 1926.

Chase, Will H., *The Sourdough Pot*. Kansas City: Burton Publishing Co., 1943.

Collier, William R., and Westrate, Edwin V., *The Reign of Soapy Smith*. New York: Doubleday, Doran & Co., 1935.

Davis, Mary Lee, *Sourdough Gold*. Boston: W. A. Wilde Co., 1933.

Denison, Merrill, *Klondike Mike*. New York: William Morrow & Co., 1943.

Dictionary of American Biography. New York: Charles Scribner's Sons, 1933.

Fowler, Gene, *Timber Line*. New York: Covici, 1933.

Glasscock, C. B., *Lucky Baldwin*. Indianapolis: Bobbs-Merrill Co., 1933.

Hayne and Taylor, *The Pioneers of the Klondike*. London: S. Low, Marston, 1897.

Hines, Jack, *Minstrel of the Yukon*. New York: Greenberg, 1948.

Johnson, Gerald, *Incredible Tale*. New York: Harper & Bros., 1950.

Johnston, Alva, *The Legendary Mizners*. New York: Farrar, Straus and Young, 1953.

Lake, Stuart, *Wyatt Earp*. Boston: Houghton Mifflin Co., 1931.

London, Charmian, *The Book of Jack London*. New York: The Century Co., 1921.

London, Jack, MSS. of his Klondike diary in the Huntington Library, San Marino, Calif.

London, Jack, *Burning Daylight*. New York: The Macmillan Co., 1910.

London, Jack, *Call of the Wild*. New York: The Macmillan Co., 1903.

MacDonald, Malcom, *Down North*. New York: Farrar & Rinehart, 1943.

McKeown, Martha, *The Trail Led North*. New York: The Macmillan Co., 1948.

Medill, Robert B., *Klondike Diary*. Portland: Beattie & Co., 1949.

Millis, Walter, *The Martial Spirit*. New York: Houghton Mifflin Co., 1931.

Mizner, Addison, *The Many Mizners*. New York: Sears Publishing Co., 1932.

Morgan, Edward, in collaboration with Henry F. Woods, *God's Loaded Dice*. Caldwell, Ida.: The Caxton Printers Ltd., 1935.

Morgan, Murray, *Skid Road*. New York: The Viking Press, 1951.

Ogilvie, William, *Early Days on the Yukon*. London: John Lane Co., 1913.

Palmer, Frederick, *In the Klondike*. New York: Charles Scribner's Co., 1899.

Quiett, Glenn Chesney, *Pay Dirt*. New York: D. Appleton-Century Co., 1936.

Rickard, Thomas A., *Through the Yukon and Alaska*. San Francisco: 1909.

Service, Robert W., *Ploughman of the Moon*. New York: Dodd, Mead & Co., 1945.

Stanley, William M., *A Mile of Gold*. Chicago: Laird & Lee, 1898.

Steele, S. B., *Forty Years in Canada*. London: H. Jenkins Ltd., 1915.

Stone, Irving, *Sailor on Horseback*. Boston: Houghton Mifflin Co., 1938.

Stuck, Hudson, *Voyages on the Yukon*. New York: Charles Scribner's Sons, 1917.

Sullivan, Edward Dean, *The Fabulous Wilson Mizner*. New York: The Henkle Co., 1935.

Sullivan, Mark, *Our Times,* Vol. I, New York: Charles Scribner's Sons, 1926.

Tollemache, Stratford, *Reminiscences of the Yukon*. London: E. Arnold, 1912.

Tompkins, Stuart R., *Alaska*. Norman: University of Oklahoma Press, 1945.

Walden, Arthur T., *A Dog-Puncher on the Yukon*. Boston: Houghton Mifflin Co., 1928.

Wickersham, James, *Old Yukon, Tales—Trails—and Trials*. Washington: Washington Law Book Co., 1938.

Wiedemann, Thomas, *Cheechako into Sourdough*. Portland: Binfords & Mort, 1942.

Williamson, Thomas, *Far North Country*. New York: Duell, Sloan & Pearce, Inc., 1944.

Winslow, Kathryn, *Big Pan-Out*. New York: W. W. Norton & Co., 1951.

NEWSPAPERS AND PERIODICALS

Appleton's Booklovers Magazine, "The Looting of Alaska," by Rex Beach, January through May, 1906.

California Law Review, "History of the Nome Case," by Judge Morrow, January, 1916.

Dawson *Nugget*.

Denver *Post*.

Los Angeles *Herald-Express*.

Los Angeles *Times*.

New York *Times*.

San Francisco *Examiner*.

Seattle *Post-Intelligencer*.

```
        34 500
        20 000
         3 600
        ───────
         60 100

165  6 0 1 0 0            $ 60,000
  ÷0
 3 3   70                    $ 4200
       60                      7140
      ────                   ──────
       0 0                   11340
      420
      4 2 00               $ 11340
      ─────                ────────
      4 2 00
       42
       63
      330
      140
     ──────
     5 9 5  1
        12
     ──────
       9 0
      11 9
     5 9 5  0
      5 9 5 
         7 1 4
      ────────
         7
```

$ 2100

Index

INDEX

Alger, Russell, 66
Allan, Scotty, 64
Allen, Eugene, 107, 178, 193-194, 203
Amur, steamship, 71-72
Anderson, Charlie, 226-228
Andree Salomon, 26
Anvil Creek, 261, 263

Baggs, Doc, 42, 45
Baldwin, E. J. (Lucky), 15, 256
Barbary Coast, 20
Beach, Rex, 88, 100, 116, 117-121; described, 148-149; quoted 120-121, 242, 243, 249, 250
Beebe, Iola, 110-115
Beer, Thomas, quoted, 12, 14
"Belle of Skagway," 35
Berry, Clarence J., 73
Berry, Ethel (Mrs. Clarence J.), 73
"Bertha the Adder," 83
Black, Mrs. George, 77-78
"Blue Parka Man," 162
Bonanza Creek, 15, 73, 79, 97, 197, 226, 228
Bowers, "The Reverend," 41, 45, 46-47
Boxhouses, 20, 29, 30, 143
Brandon, Kitty, 112, 114
Bruce, Jimmy, 42
Bryan, William Jennings, 16
Buckley, John, 13
Burns, Big Ed, 42
Burns, Tommy, 254-255

Cahill, Edward F., 65-66
Calamity Jane, 15, 86
Carboneau, Count, 81
Carboneau, Countess (Kate Mulrooney), 15, 78-82
Carmack, George, 80, 95-98, 228
Cashman, Nellie, 86, 89-90
Chilkoot Pass, 39, 72, 77
Chipps, Robert, 260, 263
Christy, Howard Chandler, 14
Circle City, 94, 105, 133
City of Topeka, steamship, 79
Clancy, John, 54, 68
Considine, John, 29, 141
Corey, Frank, 26
Corvee, Buck, 163-164
Coxey, Jacob S., 16, 25
Crater, Edith (Mrs. Rex Beach), 243-244
Crawford, Jack, 25
Creede, town of, 47, 48, 49, 53, 58, 223

Dalton, Aggie, 75-76
Dawson, city of, 11, 28, 77, 106, 107, 127, 140, 144, 176, 192; fires, 204-205; 241
Dexter, Molly, 101, 102
"Diamond Lil," 15, 70
"Diamond-Tooth Gertie," 15, 70, 147
Diaz, Porfirio, 52
Dixon, Syd, 40, 41
"Dog-Tooth Harry," 85-86

Dunham, Sam, quoted, 146

Dyea, town of, 33, 35, 39, 55, 69, 72

Eagle City, 28, 171

Earp, Wyatt, 15, 234, 237, 256, 257

Edwards, Henry (Yank Few Clothes), 41

Eldorado Creek, 22, 73, 79, 97, 105, 226

Excelsior, steamship, 20, 71

Fargo, Rena, 209-213, 216, 217

Fay, John E., 53-54

Fife, Duke of, 24

"Flora the Ton," 147

Ford, Bob, 48, 49, 53

Fort Cudahy, 28

Forty Mile, town of, 28, 87, 105, 166, 231

Foster, Slim Jim, 40

"Frisco Sal," 236

Gates, William F. (Swiftwater Bill), 15, 104-115, 215

Gibbs, Red, 40

Gibson, Charles Dana, 14

"Glass-Eyed Nellie," 147

Golovin Bay, 87, 101, 174

Gordon, Abraham, 75

Gould, Dr. Hannah, 76

Grauman, Sid, 141, 151-154

Green, Fatty, 42-43

"Grizzly Bear," 15, 84

Harris, Frisco Red, 42

Haskell, William B., quoted, 40

Henderson, Robert, 15, 96, 228

Hines, Jack, 87, 101, 148-149, 257

Hoar, George F., 13

Hootch, 99, 185-187

Hoven, Nettie, 77

Irish Hill, 150

Itcheruk, 174-175

Johnston, Alva, 84, 117

Juneau, town of, 26

Kane, Anna (The Nightingale of the North), 143

Kearns, Jack, 15, 219, 255-256

Kornstadt, Jake, 164

Ladue, Joe, 176

Lake Bennett, 35, 143

Lamore Sisters, 108-110

Lemmon, Lillian, 76

Lippy, T. S., 22, 105

"Little Egypt," 144

London, Jack, mentioned, 15, 224; Klondike career of, 121-129; quoted, 126, 127, 128, 129

Lousetown (Klondike City), 15, 28, 191, 202

Lynch, Jeremiah, quoted, 194-195, 205-206

McCook, James M., 178-179

MacDonald, Alexander, 80

McGillis, Frank, 75-76

McKay, John J., quoted, 71

McKenzie, Alexander, 261-269

McKinley, President William, 261, 269

McQuestion, Jack, 219

MacTavish, Angus, 229-233

Mahoney, Mike, 26, 27, 81-82, 149-150, 197, 229-233, 254-255

Meadows, "Arizona Charlie," 146, 200-201

Miller, Joaquin, 15; in the Klondike, 129-135; quoted, 131, 132, 135

Mitchell, Belle, 203-204

Mizner, Addison, 15, 209, 212, 216, 220; quoted, 210, 212, 221

Mizner, Edgar, 209, 217

Mizner, William, 209, 212, 213

Mizner, Wilson, 15, 56, 71, 82, 101, 121, 152-153, 164, 201, 233, 234-239; in Klondike and Nome, 207-223; quoted, 208-209, 251, 259-260

Moore, William, 39

Morgan, Edward, 83-84, 89

Muir, John, 18

"Nellie the Pig," 147, 236

Nome, city of, 99, 112, 140, 159, 174, 233, 241, 265

Northwest Mounted Police, 21, 29, 33, 143, 156, 170, 203, 242

Noyes, Arthur H., 263, 264, 265, 268-270

Nugget, Dawson newspaper, 74, 86, 107, 135, 142, 178, 179, 190, 193

Oatley Sisters, 142

Ogilvie, William, 159, 166, 168; quoted, 160, 165, 176-178, 183

O'Kelly, Ed, 49

"Oregon Mare," 15, 84

Page, Nelly, 87, 88

Palmer, Frederick, 23; quoted, 27-28; 79, 80, 81

Palmer, Joe, 42

Pantages, Alexander, 15, 141, 154-157, 217

Paradise Alley, 15, 191, 202

Phiscator, Frank, 22

Pickering Sisters, 83

Pittman, Key, 234, 265

Portland, steamship, 20, 21, 223

Pullen, Harriet, 69, 155

Quartz Creek, 112

Quiett, Glenn Chesney, quoted, 55

Reid, Frank H., 67, 69

Reilly, Pegleg, 231

Rickard, Tex, 15, 149, 150, 219, 234, 237, 240, 252, 253-254, 257

Rockwell, "Klondike Kate," 156

Rowe, Bishop, 161

Service, Robert W., 15; quoted, 19, 116, 137, 138; in the Klondike, 135-139, 207

"Siwash George," 92

Skagway, town of, 31, 38, 39, 41, 57, 72, 77, 140, 158, 242, 253

Smith, Jack, 106

Smith, Jefferson R. (Soapy), 15, 31; career of, 37-69; death of, 69; mentioned, 158, 218, 223, 242, 253

Stanley, William, 22

Stevens, Don Charles, 26

"Susie Bluenose," 15, 86-88

Sutro, Ikey, 144-145

Tagish Charlie, 95-98

Tanana River, 92, 113, 114, 232

Thompson, Dr. Alfred, quoted, 167-168

Tollemache, Stratford, 11, 12, 199-200

Twain, Mark, 38

Ullman, Julius, 200-201

Van Horn, Judge, 42, 45

Wag Boys, 242-244
Waite, Davis H., 51
Walden, Arthur T., 92-93, 145, 189
Warren, Sol, 257
White Horse Rapids, 78

White Pass, 39, 56, 64
Wickersham, James, 56, 162, 171-173, 240; quoted, 163, 246, 262
Wilder, George, 41
Wilkerson, John, 22
Williamson, Thames, 129, 266, 268
Wilson, Diamond Jim, 234-239
Wise, Charles L., 25
"Wise Mike," 147, 148
Wood, Joseph K., 263, 270
Wood, Thomas J., 252
Woods, Henry F., 82, 194, 198, 199, 228

Yukon stove, described, 22-23

4276

Date Due

JUL 23 '78			
JUN 0 1 1984			
FORM 109			